Ana Russell-Omaljev

Divided We Stand: Discourses on Identity in 'First' and 'Other' Serbia

Social Construction of the Self and the Other

Ana Russell-Omaljev

Divided We Stand: Discourses on Identity in 'First' and 'Other' Serbia

Social Construction of the Self and the Other

ibidem-Verlag
Stuttgart

Bibliografische Information der Deutschen Nationalbibliothek
Die Deutsche Nationalbibliothek verzeichnet diese Publikation in der Deutschen Nationalbibliografie; detaillierte bibliografische Daten sind im Internet über http://dnb.d-nb.de abrufbar.

Bibliographic information published by the Deutsche Nationalbibliothek
Die Deutsche Nationalbibliothek lists this publication in the Deutsche Nationalbibliografie; detailed bibliographic data are available in the Internet at http://dnb.d-nb.de.

Cover pictures (from left to right):
"Super Wall" graffiti from Pop-Lukina Street, Belgrade. © Ana Russell-Omaljev.
"Milošević's death: commemoration", Nikola Pašić Square, March 2006 © Aleksandar Veljković.
"Princip je da se stalno prekoračuju granice, Žarana Papić" ["Their guiding principle is to always cross the boundaries, Žarana Papić"]. Graffiti from Kosančićev Venac street. © Ana Russell-Omaljev
"Kosovo is Serbia – evening demonstrations", Resavska Street, February 2008. © White Writer, Wikipedia. Licensed under CC BY-SA 3.0 (s. https://creativecommons.org/licenses/by-sa/3.0/deed.en).

∞

Gedruckt auf alterungsbeständigem, säurefreien Papier
Printed on acid-free paper

ISBN: 978-3-8382-0881-5

© *ibidem*-Verlag
Stuttgart 2016

Alle Rechte vorbehalten

Das Werk einschließlich aller seiner Teile ist urheberrechtlich geschützt. Jede Verwertung außerhalb der engen Grenzen des Urheberrechtsgesetzes ist ohne Zustimmung des Verlages unzulässig und strafbar. Dies gilt insbesondere für Vervielfältigungen, Übersetzungen, Mikroverfilmungen und elektronische Speicherformen sowie die Einspeicherung und Verarbeitung in elektronischen Systemen.

All rights reserved. No part of this publication may be reproduced, stored in or introduced into a retrieval system, or transmitted, in any form, or by any means (electronic, mechanical, photocopying, recording or otherwise) without the prior written permission of the publisher. Any person who does any unauthorized act in relation to this publication may be liable to criminal prosecution and civil claims for damages.

Printed in the EU

What shall now become of us, without any barbarians? Those people were a kind of a solution.

> Constantine Kavafi (1904)
> *Waiting for the Barbarians*

Integration and exclusion are two sides of the same coin, so the issue here is not *that* exclusion takes place but *how* it takes place.

> Iver B. Neumann (1999)
> *The Uses of the Other*

'Basic social conflict...has spread through all areas of politics, society, culture and agriculture. Conflict is taking place between the 'European' and 'an (old) Balkan civilisation' that has resulted in division between 'Westerners and 'anti-Westerners'.

> Holm Zundhausen (2008)
> *History of Serbia*

To the lost generations

Contents

Contents vii

List of abbreviations ix

Preface and Acknowledgements xi

Introduction:
Serbia, Europe and National Identity 1

Chapter 1:
Theory and Method 29

Chapter 2:
Brief Historical Context (1987–2012) 59

Chapter 3:
Best of Enemies: "First" and "Other" Serbia 85

Chapter 4:
The Construction of "Europe" 131

Chapter 5:
Mapping the Debates: "Point of Departure" and
"Missionary Intelligentsia" 177

Chapter 6:
Serbian "Auto-chauvinism" or
"Identification with the Aggressor" 209

Conclusion 221

Bibliography 241

List of abbreviations

BIH	Bosnia and Herzegovina
CDA	Critical Discourse Analysis
DS	Democratic Party
DOS	Democratic Opposition of Serbia
DSS	Democratic Party of Serbia
EU	European Union
ICTY	The International Criminal Tribunal for the former Yugoslavia
LDP	Liberal Democratic Party
LGBT	Lesbian, Gay, Bisexual and Transgender Community
JUL	Jugoslavian Leftists
KLA	Kosovo Liberation Army
NAM	Non-Aligned Movement
NATO	North Atlantic Treaty Organization
NDH	Nezavisna Drzava Hrvatska/Independent State of Croatia
NSPM	New Serbian Political Thought
OSCE	Organization for Security and Cooperation in Europe
RTS	Radio and Television of Serbia
SAA	Stabilisation and Association Agreement
SANU	Serbian Academy of Sciences and Arts
SFRY	Socialist Federal Republic of Yugoslavia
SNS	Serbian Progressive Party/Srpska Napredna Stranka
SOC	Serbian Orthodox Church
SPO	Serbian Renewal Movement/Srpski Pokret Otpora
SPP	Serbian Progressive Party
SRS	Serbian Radical Party/Srpska Radikalna Stranka

Preface and Acknowledgements

So many books have been written about the dissolution of Yugoslavia. This is not one of them. This book is about the hearts and minds of the people who need to fathom what has happened and why and who need to take responsibility for their part. Since Yugoslavism failed as a project, new national identities needed to be formed. I understand that many years have passed since the Milošević regime was ruling Serbia, and the horrors of war were visited upon the people. First, however, that is a matter of modern history, and until the Serbian people willingly make sense of what happened in the 1990s the ghosts of that time will haunt us forever. Not to mention that certain elements of his apparatus are still in power. Second, the traumatic experience of the Yugoslav conflicts is still incomprehensible to most Serbs and needs to be examined and understood, before it can be resolved. A survey conducted in 2001 revealed that most of the Serbian citizens who participated in the survey blamed the US and the West for the dissolution of Yugoslavia. Today, more than 20 years after the Dayton agreement, the situation is not that much different. Interest in the Yugoslav break up and its consequences may never end. In order to progress toward a resolution, the role of the elites and social groups in these traumatic events, and their aftermath, needs to be examined in a narrative way. Such academic examinations must lead to understanding, rather than perpetuate confusion and antagonism. The question of the Serbian national identity still needs to be answered. This book reveals a society that has been formed during times of war, conflict and authoritarianism and has, as a result, indeed struggled to leave the past behind, as its internal structure still is largely founded on pro-war and anti-war positions. Once the past is examined, and the roles of Milošević and his cronies are determined, I am hopeful that Serbia will be able to move into the future free from the damaged perception of its own identity which it currently holds. It is important to emphasize that I do not intend to present the one true characterization of Serbian national identity. And I do not argue that 'the Serbs' are basically not horrid but delightful people, nor do I seek to add to the on-going debates as to whether 'the Serbs' should be proud or ashamed to be Serbs, or just be allowed to be a normal nation. Rather, the purpose of this book is to examine the peculiar 'First' and 'Other' Serbia as fractured constructions of national identity which have been developed to different effects during, and in the aftermath of, the dissolution of Yugoslavia.

I also seek to illustrate a range of facets of the problem of dealing with the past in Serbia, including extensive quotations translated from a variety of primary sources, for the purpose of informed debate among English-speaking readers to whom all the original Serbian sources may not be entirely accessible. More importantly, this book tries to do this from a vantage point of relatively objective insider. Although I do hold views on the topics explored in this book, I believe I have stayed impartial, to the extent possible, and I sought to neither construct nor denounce an 'acceptable' Serbian identity, which is a constant characteristic of so much literature on this subject. Finally, the starting point for this book was my doctoral thesis entitled, "'Constructing the Other/s: "First" and "Other" Serbia discourses on identity and Europe". While the majority of my research findings were retained, much of the theory, literature review and methodology was omitted in the interests of brevity. Instead, I follow Fulbrook who argues that what is most needed is analysis of the factual. Since finishing the research for this manuscript, the political situation in Serbia has changed somewhat, with Aleksandar Vučić leaning towards Western Europe and the EU, nevertheless many "First" Serbia actors do not support it. In doing this, Vučić employs somewhat authoritarian methods, which could be seen as traditionally Eastern European, and which are opposed by the pro-Western elite of 'Other' Serbia. When I started to write my doctoral thesis I could scarcely have dreamt that the recurring game of the Serbian intellectual classes, "Who is more Serbian and what it means to be a Serb today" would enter a new phase, as EU accession comes ever-closer to becoming a reality. Finally, this project was inspired by the phenomenon of "dying from otherness", as one prominent scholar put it,[1] and as is so present in the discourses on identity in the Balkans. The eternal pursuit of enemies

---

[1] Iver B. Neumann, *Russia and the Idea of Europe: A Study in Identity and International Relations.* (London: Routledge, 1996), p. 168.

within 'First' and 'Other' Serbia discourses raises the question of whether living in diversity is possible without difference deteriorating into hostility, animosity and hatred. To summarize, the Serbian "we-feeling" with Europe is likely to always be claimed by governments, yet Serbs and Serbian elites continue to be reluctant Europeans.

This book was envisaged during my doctoral work at the School of Politics and International Relations at Reading University (SPIRS). I am grateful to SPIRS for the support which they gave me in the form of necessary funding for my doctorate. I would like to take this opportunity to thanks my supervisor, Dominik Zaum and my external supervisor, Jelena Obradović-Wochnik, who provided me with expert guidance and insightful comments - our regular meetings were a great source of motivation. I also owe a debt of gratitude to numerous individuals who offered their intellectual support and expertise at critical moments. My work benefitted greatly from the insight of my professors at Reading University, Alan Cromartie and Beatrice Heuser. I would also like to give special thanks to Jasna Dragović-Soso who provided me with exemplary inspiration, and whose ideas shaped my thinking at a critical juncture. Special thanks are also due to colleagues in various institutions across Europe whom I consulted and who kindly agreed to talk to me about my topic, share their passion about these ideas, and suggest reading material that was of great use.

I offer sincere thanks to some dear people who understood the headaches that writing a book on Serbia can bring. Some deserve particular recognition for their willingness to spend hours discussing the subject of 'First' and 'Other' Serbia. I am further indebted to Matthew White for his contribution in making this work comprehensible. In this respect, I would also like to give honest thanks to Daniel Russell, Mladen Ostojić and Marko Luković. Sincere gratitude goes to some dear people around me, such as Bojan Marković, Nadya Herrera Catalan, and Birte Gippert for their endless support and hospitality. I am also indebted to the Centre for Empirical Cultural Studies of South-East Europe and the Institute for Philosophy and Social Theory of the University of Belgrade, who published a chapter of my doctoral thesis in their volume "Us and Them – Symbolic Divisions in Western Balkan Societies." Crucially, I have been fortunate enough to have a supremely supportive family. I wholeheartedly thank them: my parents Žiža and Milan Omaljev, and my brother Dejan, for having always been there for me. While my greatest debts are to my family, the dedication of this book goes to that Yugoslav generation born in the 1950s and 1960s, who created one world and then destroyed it, and "did not see its downfall coming."

Ana Russell-Omaljev, London, 2015

Introduction:
Serbia, Europe and National Identity

How has Serbia, its people and its place in the world, been seen in recent decades by its respective public figures and political leaders? There is a vast literature in the fields of sociology, political science and anthropology written on the subject of Serbia being in between two worlds, between East and the West, between Austro-Hungarian and Ottoman Empires and between Western level-headedness and Eastern irrationality. This book is a much-needed effort to understand how such an "in-between" narrative is played out in contemporary Serbian politics and society. The friction between the two most common conceptions of Serbian national identity in response to this question, which have come to be known as "First" and "Other" Serbia, is by now a familiar topic. It can be said that these two camps are conceptualized as two responses to the idea of the modern political community and offer two different narratives of Serbian collective identity. More specifically, after the fall of Slobodan Milošević in October 2000, the groups self-identifying as the First and Other Serbia opened an ongoing dialogue in the public sphere about many topics, including the dissolution of Yugoslavia, Serbia's obligations to the Hague Tribunal, and the future of Kosovo. This book takes First and Other Serbia public discourses[2] and their construction of "Europe" as two case studies. I have been concerned for some time now with discourses that explore Serbia's identity, mission and place in the world, as well as that of Europe. So far, such empirical scrutiny of Serbian national identity as has been conducted would appear to largely confirm Ole Wæver's comment that a nation or a state's vision of Europe

---

[2] For the political contexts of the development of narratives on the "two Serbias" in the early nineties, as well as a representative collection of critical narratives on the First Serbia produced by the Other Serbia, see: *Druga Srbija deset godina posle 1992–2002* (The Other Serbia Ten Years After), (Beograd: Helsinški odbor za ljudska prava u Srbiji, 2002).

has to be compatible with its vision of itself.[3] Do First and Other Serbia[4] political approaches to Europe differ significantly? When did Serbia become a democracy and establish its first government? Do its culture, sport and music possess any significant weight of soft power in terms of Europe? In simple terms, does the vicinity of Europe bring Serbia more harm than good? This book will consider these questions.

Since the wars of the 1990s Serbia has attempted to regenerate itself as the antithesis of the hostility, bloodshed and loss of war. But has that been the experience of Serbians? In fact, was Serbia officially even involved in the war? How, then, does a country deal with the legacy of a war that it was not officially involved with? The hasty exercise of democracy just after 2000 generated a sense of Self among Serbians, and particularly a Self that desires democracy, but it also resulted in social relations being reorganized in a dichotomized way, reducing the relationship between pro-European and anti-European groups to one of enmity. In recent years, with the changes of the very framework of international politics wrought by the economic recession in 2008 and the rise of the Middle and Far East, it has become increasingly clear that the world stage is again shaped by international superpowers. Serbia, as a successor to Yugoslavia, wishes to be taken seriously again on the world stage, yet realistically will only achieve that aim through attachment to one or more powerful states or blocs. This book considers that Serbia's best hope for such an alliance lies with Europe. Serbia might also take into account certain other options, especially given that it had, at one

---

[3] Ole Wæver, Identity, Communities and Foreign Policy. Discourse Analysis as Foreign Policy Theory, in L. Hansen and O. Wæver, eds., *European Integration and National Identity: The Challenge of the Nordic States*, (London and New York: Routledge, 2002), p. 25.

[4] In simple terms, the terms "First" and "Other" Serbia appear to have been coined in *Druga Srbija* (Beogradski Krug, Beograd, 1992) edited by Aljoša Mimica. Other Serbia was proposed to describe a grouping of public and political figures in Serbia distinct from the establishment, one that is anti-war, critical and civilized. The expression First Serbia was intended to be understood as the exact opposite: bellicose, pro-Milošević and nationalist. After 2000, the meaning of such epithets for these elite groups (consisting of professors, writers, media figures as well as politicians) polarized along pro- and anti-Atlanticist, or pro- and anti-West/Europe, lines generally. Additionally, in the Serbian language, the term *drugi/o/a* means both *other* and *second*. This play on meaning is significant as it implies the superiority of the First Serbia.

point, four pillars of foreign policy: the EU, Russia, the US and China. By way of illustration, the current US Ambassador to Serbia Michael Kirby notes that "Alexander Vučić is trying to lead [Serbia] onward toward the European Union but the Serbs are slightly schizophrenic—their heart pulls them toward the East, while at the same time their head pushes them toward the West."[5] A certain representation of Serbian national identity in terms of being truly part of neither the East nor the West but, rather, being considered by the West as being part of the East and being considered by the East as being part of the West ("East for the West, West for the East"), is not difficult to find as these images and ideas are commonly employed both in diplomatic and common speech. Also, perspectives on Serbia's belonging either to the East or the West differ significantly whether they come from First or Other Serbia. First Serbia wishes Serbia to be a particular type of entity: turbulent but with a clear desire to be economically and politically stable; defeated in the last wars but still dignified and proud; tolerant but only toward those we see as "ours". It wishes Serbia to be rather isolationist and neutral, not global enough in its outlook to integrate with the modern globalized economy nor European enough in the modern sense to meet the expectations demanded of an aspiring future EU member state. It sees Serbia as part of Old Europe, and implores Serbs not to let themselves lose their identity. Nonetheless, First Serbia recognizes Serbia as dominant in the Balkan region, with such dominance exerted principally through soft power in Serbian-populated parts of Bosnia and Croatia, the so-called our lands.

In contrast, Other Serbia understands Serbia to be a defeated country: still too hesitant and apprehensive to repent for its recent sins; bellicose toward its closest neighbors. For Other Serbia, the answers to Serbia's woes lie in winning over allies outside Serbia, for fear that by itself Serbia might not succeed in fully democratizing itself, facing corruption, improving its bureaucratic apparatus and conducting other necessary reforms. Other Serbia argues that, because the whole Balkan region is so

---

[5] "U.S. ambassador says Serbs are 'a bit schizophrenic'," *B-92 online* (April 6, 2015). http://www.b92.net/eng/news/politics.php?yyyy=2015&mm=04&dd=06&nav_id=937 06

turbulent and explosive, joining Europe is the only hope for redemption through positive change.

Additionally, it is important to recognize that these disparate political visions are each a product of the manner in which other states and political actors recognize Serbia. Does the European perception of Serbs differ or overlap with their own self-understanding? Malksoo maintains that Eastern Europe has often been seen by the Western states of the continent as being in many ways different and inferior, and that this has in part constituted the image that elites in Eastern European states have of themselves and their position in the modern European polity.[6] The principal focus of this book is the examination of one such dominant perception: how Serbs see and understand Europe. As a result of such "politics of becoming European"[7], one needs to ask if Serbia wants to be part of the EU? If Serbia considers itself as already part of Old Europe? Do Serbs desire to be "proper" Europeans? This book will explore the various practices of differentiation employed by First and Other Serbian actors with regard to the nation, Europe[8] and the EU, and analyze the inter-relationships between these groups of actors. I will explore the practices of differentiation implicated in the confrontation between Self (Serbian Subject/State) and Other (Europe), and reveal the representational paradigms used by both the First and Other Serbia groups which, in Hamilton's view, represent the whole repertoire of imaginary effects through which difference toward Europe is represented at any historical

---

[6] Maria Malksoo, *The Politics of Becoming European: A Study of Polish and Baltic post-Cold War Security Imaginaries*, (Routledge, 2013), p. xiii.

[7] Malksoo maintains that to cross the threshold from candidate country to fully-fledged member of the EU would entail giving up the dearly-held and enduring self-conceptualization of being at the same time "Europe but not quite Europe." The related paradox that new Europeans' sense of "liminal Europeanness" seems to linger on for a time also cries out for proper investigation. Ibid., p. 2–3.

[8] The terms Europe, East, and West are used here as classifications of symbolic and politico-geographical spaces, which are never fixed and evolve over time. In particular, when these terms are used in this book, their intended meanings are those that "First" and "Other" Serbia actors attach to these classifications. See Mikael af Malmborg and Bo Stråth, eds., *The Meaning of Europe: Variety and Contention Within and Among Nations*, (Oxford: Berg, 2002).

moment.⁹ The operation of exclusionary practices by both First and Other Serbia groups, which will be analyzed in Chapters 3, 4 and 5, are fundamentally at odds with the declared motivation for positive and enduring European integration professed by both major political groupings in Serbia: the Progressives and the Democrats. These arguments about Europe, and Serbia's place in it, are not only arguments about the Serbian nation, its national self-reflection and its territorial integrity, but also about the value of the form of governance that the EU tends to promote as the ideal, and about the value that is placed upon European ideals by Serbians.

The object of study

As Obradović notes, much public dialogue in Serbia is dominated by actors representing directly opposing sides of an issue (e.g. pro- and anti-International Criminal Tribunal for the former Yugoslavia (ICTY), pro- and anti-EU, rural/urban dichotomies) with the effect that the debate appears both polarized and polarizing.¹⁰ Scholarly works on Serbia have described it as a society divided between liberal and illiberal, or civic and uncivic values.¹¹ The polarization between "First" and "Other" Serbia, as Ramet noted back in 2011, has frequently been cited as an illustration of the lack of agreement in Serbia on issues such as EU integration, attitudes toward the ICTY, apportioning responsibility for war crimes, and other issues arising from Serbia's wartime past.¹² However, as this manuscript is going to print, the situation is quite the reverse: the Progressives, who are former Radicals, openly support Serbia's path to EU accession and the left-leaning intellectuals, influenced by the Greek financial crisis, oppose EU accession on anti-imperialist grounds. This

---

9   Peter Hamilton, "Heroes or Villains," in Stuart Hall, ed., *Representation: Cultural Representations and Signifying Practices* (Thousand Oaks, CA: Sage, 1997), p. 223.
10 Jelena Obradović-Wochnik, "Revisionism, Denial and anti-ICTY Discourse in Serbia's Public Sphere: Beyond the 'Divided Society' Debate," in James Gow, Rachel Kerr, and Zoran Pajić, eds., *Prosecuting War Crimes, Lessons and Legacies of the International Criminal Tribunal for the Former Yugoslavia* (2013), p. 3.
11 Sabrina Ramet et al., eds., *Civic and Uncivic Values: Serbia in the Post-Milošević Era* (Budapest: Central University Press, 2011), p. 3/4.
12 Ibid., p. 3/4.

post-2012 polarization will be further addressed in the conclusion. Still, although often couched in social and cultural terms, the driving force behind these "cognitive divisions", as they have been described by Edward Said,[13] was and is remarkably political. Suggestions have often been made, after 2000, that as much as the civil society activists and other liberals are working hard to expose Serbia's complicity in the war crimes of the 1990s on the one hand, the revisionists are working equally hard to deny Serbian responsibility for war crimes and genocide on the other.[14] I propose to transcend this, at first glance, seemingly complex choice by deconstructing the dualist logic employed by First and Other Serbia and exposing the manner in which these positions toward Europe have forged, and are even now forging, Serbian national, political and cultural identities.

Public debates among Serbia's elites after 2000 persistently refer, either implicitly or explicitly, to rearticulating the notion of the Serbian nation and its place in Europe and history in order to legitimize the government's political decisions and foreign policy choices. The issue of Serbia belonging to Europe or not remains highly contentious in elite discourses, regardless of the actual state of Serbia's relations with particular EU member states at any given moment. First and Other Serbia elites and political leaders have constructed a conception of the European Union, and a much broader concept of Europe, in a plethora of ways. What can be characterized as the anti-European position, in its many forms, has formulated Europe as a definitive threat to Serbian national interests, as an attack on national sovereignty in respect of Kosovo, and lastly, in cultural sense, as an attempt to supplant the traditional values associated with the Serbian Orthodox Church with a European foreign-imposed secular identity. Such reluctance to embrace the European project, it has been argued, stems from a variety of sources including the legacy of Serbian's proud history as a dominant force in the region, the

---

[13] See Michael Sprinker, ed., *Edward Said: A Critical Reader* (Oxford: Blackwell, 1993), p. 12.

[14] Jelena Obradović-Wochnik, "Revisionism, Denial and anti-ICTY Discourse in Serbia's Public Sphere: Beyond the 'Divided Society' Debate," in James Gow, Rachel Kerr, and Zoran Pajić, eds., *Prosecuting War Crimes, Lessons and Legacies of the International Criminal Tribunal for the Former Yugoslavia* (2013), p. 3.

distinctive character of the Serbian collective experience, and the relationship between the Serbian and the Yugoslav identities.[15] The ever-present theme is that Serbia has a difficult geopolitical position in the mental map of Europe: that it is neither here nor there, that it is East for the West, and West for the East. This resulted in a specific in-between historical narrative and strong national myths. The constant state of transition in recent decades contributed to a strong sense of what Malksoo calls liminality, which she describes as "the twentieth-century political predicament of Eastern Europe." The problems associated with displacement, and resulting uncertainty, resentment and general longing are all features of this "liminal character."[16] Additionally, during the course of the last two decades, First Serbia's intelligentsia has continuously questioned whether Serbia belongs to Europe, and consequently has questioned Serbia's EU candidacy on essentialist grounds. Even so, throughout the period since October 5, 2000 and the change of regime, the question of whether Serbia is European and "who Serbs ought to be" has been at the heart of debates among public figures, intellectuals, journalists, writers and distinguished scholars. If Serbia is to gain closer ties with Europe there is a fear, that comes both from the radical left and right, that this would bring economic slavery, political repression and hardship. In contrast, certain figures over the years have stressed the economic importance of the EU, and of Serbia being part of the European trading bloc, and have advocated the vision of Serbia in Europe far beyond the narrow interests of the inward-looking elite. For instance, former head of the Office for EU integration, Milica Delević, has repeatedly stressed that Serbia needs to make an assessment of Serbian national interests which recognizes that the EU is its biggest economic partner and its largest source of foreign investment[17]. Delević has said that, "we are in Europe, we are surrounded with those countries that wish to be

---

[15] Veljko Vujačić, "Re-examining the 'Serbian Exceptionalism' thesis" in *Filozofija i Društvo*, (January, 2003), p. 12.

[16] Maria Malksoo, *The Politics of Becoming European: A study of Polish and Baltic post-Cold War Security Imaginaries*, (Routledge, 2013), p. 43.

[17] "Delević: Početak pregovora u skorije vreme," *Blic online*, (May 9, 2013). http://www.blic.rs/Vesti/Politika/381653/Delevic-Pocetak-pregovora-u-skorije-vreme

there, and Europe is our destiny."[18] Also, current Prime Minister Aleksandar Vučić recently emphasized that Serbia will not abandon the European path, because, in his view, EU membership represents the best type of society: "I think that is the best possible kind of society that we could aspire to. We already feel as a part of the European family."[19] This ongoing identity debate about the character of Serbian society takes center stage domestically, but is also aimed at foreign audiences and Serbian diaspora.

Although the content of the debates has changed following moments of crisis and to take account of unfolding historical events including the assassination of Prime Minister Zoran Djindjić[20] in 2003, Kosovo's declaration of independence in 2008, and Serbia's full EU membership candidate status in early 2012, the issue of how the domestic intelligentsia first perceives and second represents Serbia's Europeanness remains extremely complex. The subject of my close consideration in this book is this contestation of Europe that results in the extreme contestation of national identity. In general, national identity can be found in policies, laws, culture, film, national myths, and collective historic remembrance. Yet, more importantly, national identity is this psychological "we" feeling, of connectedness and belonging, that binds the nation together. This study highlights the ways in which both past and current politics in Serbia reflect the uneasy relationship between history, nation, Europe and identity. All four concepts remain politically contested because Serbian elites have yet to reach agreement on an accepted model of political community. Since the fall of Milošević and the democratic elections in 2001, the normative goal of the governmental apparatus has been to promote EU accession. At the beginning of the decade there was almost universal agreement as to the necessity of joining the EU, but by

---

[18] "Delević: Rešenje za krizu samo u EU," *Blic online*, (April 25, 2012). http://www.blic.rs/Vesti/Politika/319039/Delevic-Resenje-za-krizu-samo-u-EU

[19] "Aleksandar Vučić: Mi se već osećamo kao deo evropske porodice," *Srbija Danas online*, (May 24, 2015). http://www.srbijadanas.com/clanak/vucic-imam-puno-poverenje-u-platformu-predsednika-nikolica-24-05-2015

[20] Zoran Djindjić studied in West Germany thanks to the intervention of former German Chancellor Willy Brandt, under professor Jürgen Habermas in Frankfurt. He obtained a PhD in philosophy from the University of Konstanz in 1979.

the end of 2005 there was no longer such a consensus among democratic circles and political parties. Yet the current Serbian Prime Minister Aleksandar Vučić, previously a vehement anti-European, has since had a change of political course and since 2008 has fully supported Serbia's European path. Vučić said, "EU accession is the only possible path for our country—this is what I said to President Vladimir Putin and what I have said in Brussels, Belgrade, Paris, everywhere."[21] I will reveal this process of fluidity and change as I analyze the perceptions of Europe which have, at various times, been held by actors of First and Other Serbia. These public debates create a nation's conception of itself that largely determines what that nation can achieve in wider international politics.

A focus on Serbia is relevant to the broader debate on EU expansion and ever closer union precisely because Serbia is not a major political power or primary shaper of the EU integration process but, quite the contrary, it is a country on the margins, an outsider whose own post-conflict affairs are intrinsically linked to Europe's perception of it. In the aftermath of the Milošević regime, the democratic ethos was not entirely fostered and encouraged by the newly-elected democratic government. Consequently, Serbia has struggled to reconcile its relations with Europe in light of its war-torn past. In this respect, Serbia shares certain similarities with parts of Eastern Europe that are seen as lacking a broadly shared narrative of post-authoritarian identity, as there is "a lack of symbolic closure of the state socialist period and the negotiation-based transition."[22] Furthermore, the issue of Kosovo, which has been described as "the most expensive Serbian word,"[23] has been at the forefront

---

[21] "Aleksandar Vučić:'L'objectif de la Serbie est d'adhérer à l'UE," *Le Figaro*, (July 4, 2014).

[22] Jan Kubik and Amy Linch, "The Original Sin of Poland's Third Republic: Discounting 'Solidarity' and its Consequences for Political Reconciliation," in *Polish Sociological Review*, 153, no. 1 (2006), p. 12. I have found that Serbia similarly lacks a broadly accepted narrative of post-authoritarian democratic identity.

[23] This quote, which is attributed to Matija Bećković, became a prominent catch-phrase of "First" Serbia, but has also been widely used, ironically, by "Other-Serbians." For the rest of the quote see Matija Bećković, "Kosovo je najskuplja srpska reč" in *Glas Crkve: časopis za hrišćansku kulturu I crkveni život* (1989), 19–28. The quote is taken from

of political debate since 2007 and also features centrally in the debate on Europe. Whether Serbia would choose Kosovo over Europe was one of the burning issues in the aftermath of Kosovo's unilateral declaration of independence in 2008, and ever since. As a result, the lack of a widely shared narrative of post-authoritarian democratic identity, coupled with the loss of Kosovo, have buttressed the foundation of the illiberal public sphere such that it is stronger than even before. Yet, not only has Other Serbia failed to provide a set of instrumental post-conflict narratives and national symbols to effectively supplant authoritarian ones, but also the rhetorical device of politically correct speech has been misappropriated by the associates of the nationalists of First Serbia. In this light, following Dragović-Soso, this book will argue that the 2002 and 2003 *Vreme* debates confirmed the existence of two alternative narratives of the Serb experience of the wars of the 1990s, and two deeply opposed visions of the roles played by the West and by Europe in Serbia's democratic transition.[24] Yet, I add that the legitimacy of liberal or nationalist discourse is dependent on the extent to which elites succeed in shaping their strategies and goals to correspond with the prior construction of collective identity. Rather than simply identifying First and Other Serbia as two monolithic constructions of identity, this book investigates the extent to which the two constructions can be seen to be changing over time and how this difference is located in spatial and temporal constructions of identity. Hansen notes, in the light of Europeanization in Central and Eastern Europe, the frequent construction of the Other as temporally progressing, toward the (Western) Self.[25] This is a central theme of these Central and Eastern European development discourses as well as in discourses of democratization and human rights.[26] Is the Serbian Self

---

Marko Živković, *Serbian Dreambook: National Imaginary in the Time of Milošević* (Bloomington: Indiana University Press, 2011), p. 176.

[24] Jasna Dragović-Soso, "Collective Responsibility, International Justice and Public Reckoning with the Recent Past: Reflections on a Debate in Serbia," in Timothy Waters, ed., *The Milošević Trial—An Autopsy*, (Oxford: Oxford University Press, 2013), p. 2.

[25] Lene Hansen, *Security as Practice: Discourse Analysis and the Bosnian War* (Routledge, 2006), p. 48.

[26] This topic gained significance, especially in recent years. See Ricard Zapata-Barrero and Anna Triandafyllidou. eds., *Addressing Tolerance and Diversity Discourses in Europe:*

being constructed as progressing toward the European Other or away from it, as Europe and the West are increasingly portrayed as villains? This issue raises a series of new questions which this book will attempt to answer.

Europe and national identity

In the vast scholarship on European identity, it is a fundamental precept that Europe as a whole has been fused from many different identities, brought together as a consequence of a diverse range of countries trying to shape their common history throughout many centuries. Yet, it is clear that each of these countries mirrors and personifies its own national anxieties within the resulting image of Europe. As Gibbins points out, "Europe functions as a symbolical space where one's own ideas are reflected, where no single interpretation of Europe is correct,"[27] and where the Serbian view of that image just mirrors its own national anxieties and self-image. It is clear that the "First" and "Other" Serbia construction of Serbian national identity is projected onto European identity, and this projection has an ideological underpinning since, as Strath argues, no projection is ever non-interested/non-ideological.[28] With this in mind, how should one tackle the question of why Serbia aspires to be part of the EU in the first place?

Each year in March, the commemoration of the 1999 NATO intervention repeatedly triggers an intense and frequently contradictory debate regarding the understanding of who were victims and who were perpetrators in recent conflicts and the relevance this has for understanding the Serbian identity. Former Prime Minister Ivica Dačić[29] said,

---

A Comparative Overview of 16 European Countries, (Barcelona Centre for International Affairs, 2012); and David R. Howarth and Jacob Torfing, eds., *Discourse Theory in European Politics: Identity, Policy and Governance* (Basingstoke: Palgrave Macmillan, 2005).

[27] Justin Gibbins, *Britain, Europe and National Identity: Self and Other in International Relations*, (Palgrave Macmillan, October 2014), p. 12.

[28] Bo Strath, ed., *Europe and the Other and Europe as the Other* (Brussels: Peter Lang, 2000), p. 3.

[29] Ivica Dačić is the former Minister of Police, former Prime Minister of the Republic of Serbia, and the current Minister of Foreign Affairs. During the Milošević era he was the main spokesman for the Socialist Party of Serbia (SPS) and Milošević's right hand man.

emphasizing the importance of innocent victims who have been forgotten, "we cannot forget nor accept the notion that their victims are more important than ours[30].... Today, after surviving genocide in two world wars because we were on the right side of the international community, Serbia and Serbian national interests do not deserve such unjust treatment as Serbia has always supported the side that fought against fascism."[31] Dačić and many others frequently put forward the view that, because Serbia took part in the fight against fascism in the First and Second World Wars and suffered the ensuing sacrifices, it deserves a place in the European Union today.[32] A study of how Serbian national identity is being constructed vis-à-vis Europe and the analysis of the dominant discourses reveals both the fluidity and stability of the Serbian subject positions. One thing is certain: the ongoing public construction of pro- or anti-Europe positions by politicians, intellectuals, and academics—in other words, the main constructors of First and Other Serbia—not only interact with projections of the national-self, but, as Milutinović notes, these projections were created in order to re-define and reinvent the Serbian nation via the discursive image of Europe.[33] As an example of an anti-Europe position I cite Koštunica[34] who, in the DSS party interview, advances the idea that "Serbia is an old European state, and she has never been outside of Europe in her entire history."[35] Following this reasoning, Serbia's symbolic positioning is already inside Europe, and the narrative of the "path to Europe" and ensuing acceptance of change are undesirable and obsolete. In the First Serbia discourse, the main argument against the choice of Europe is based on Serbia's military neu-

---

[30] The Serbian Prime Minister Ivica Dačić asserted this during a visit to the village of Draginac where he took part in the commemoration of the execution of three thousand inhabitants of the Mačva region in 1941 by German occupying forces. See "The Serbian Prime Minister Commemorates," in *TANJUG*, October 14, 2012. All translations are by the author, unless otherwise stated.

[31] Ibid.

[32] Ibid.

[33] Zoran Milutinović, *Getting Over Europe: The Construction of Europe in Serbian Culture* (Amsterdam, New York: Rodopi, 2011). p. 16.

[34] Vojislav Koštunica was the last President of the Federal Republic of Yugoslavia, succeeding Slobodan Milošević and serving from 2000 to 2003. He also served two terms as Prime Minister of Serbia, from 2004 to 2007 and from 2007 to 2008.

[35] Vojislav Koštunica, *Speeches and Analysis* (DSS). http://dss.rs/category/govori-i-analize/

trality, or saying a "historical no" to NATO military affiliation. Second, what makes Russia much closer than Europe to Serbia is explained primarily on the grounds of security, religion and culture. In these comparisons, the closeness of Russia to Serbia is usually supported by making overt references to the religious heritage that Serbia and Russia share. This observation supports my findings that Orthodox Christianity appears to be a major constitutive element of Serbian identity as seen in the First Serbia discourse. In this respect, it is evident that the perceived religious differences between Eastern and Western Christianity, contribute greatly to the Otherness of "Europe."

One can see how national identity, and indeed any kind of collective identity, is built through interaction. Triandafyllidou finds that national identity is formed through contrast with, and differentiation from, Others hence helping to clarify the boundaries of the in-group.[36] A vast amount of research has been done in the field of representations of Europe and the nation in current and prospective EU member states. For instance, in the case of the membership of the Czech Republic, Vaclav Havel noted that the aspiration to membership was a goal belonging to the democratic consolidation of the entire Central European region, based on the belief that shared principles of mutual cooperation, civil society and equal rights would be the best guarantee "against nationalist hatred."[37] On the other hand, research on representations of Europe indicates that Britain's relationship with the EU can best be described as "half-detachment," i.e. not characterized by clear hostility but rather by widespread indifference.[38] Ichijo points out that Europe is a significant other for the contemporary British, yet without being the source of fear or inspiration.[39] Regarding Greece, there is an apparent tension between tradition and modernity as a result of the process of belated moderniza-

---

[36] Anna Triandafyllidou, "The Political Discourse on Immigration in Southern Europe: A Critical Analysis," *Journal of Community and Applied Social Psychology*, 10, no. 5 (2000), p. 373–390 at 374.

[37] Josette Baer, "Imagining Membership: The Conception of Europe in the Political Thought of T.G. Masaryk and Vaclav Havel," in *Studies in East European Thought*, 52, no. 3 (2000), p. 208.

[38] Atsuko Ichijo, *The Balancing Act: National Identity and Sovereignty for Britain in Europe* (Exeter Imprint Academic, 2008).

[39] Ibid.

tion. In this respect, Kokosalakis and Psimmenos note that Greek culture understands itself as a bridge between East and West.[40] In contrast, Italy has been and still is tormented by the "Southern question," the social and economic divide between North and South, and Triandafyllidou points out that Italy's significant other par excellence since national unification has been its fragmented national Self, and more specifically "the South."[41] Indeed, in Italy, (Western) Europe is framed in inspirational terms, because Europe has been perceived as a model of civic community which is sadly absent from national politics. Triandafyllidou rightly points out that in Italy, identifying with Europe was seen as providing the common civic basis necessary to consolidate national unity.[42] These examples highlight cases where "Europe" and the "European project" are reinforced either by the public or by the state, and operate with the structural tenets of democracy, as illiberal values are generally dismissed. While the literature deals with the exploration of the Self and the Other, much analysis has been undertaken in countries where belonging to Europe is not frequently questioned on essentialist grounds but is almost universally accepted. The unique contribution of this book lies in its investigation of the identity debate on Europe in a country outside the EU and in the marginal geopolitical space of Europe. This study is relevant and new exactly because Serbia is not a major political power but at the European periphery,[43] and because its post-conflict

---

[40] Nikos Kokosalakis and Iordanis Psimmenos, "Modern Greece: A Profile of Identity and Nationalism", *in Representations of Europe and the Nation in Current and Prospective Member-states: Media, Elites and Civil Society: The Collective State of the Art and Historical Reports,* Bo Strath and Anna Triandafyllidou (eds), (Luxembourg: Office for the Official Publications of the European Communities, 2003), p. 154.

[41] Anna Triandafyllidou, "Popular Perceptions of Europe and the Nation: The Case of Italy," in *Nations and Nationalism*, 14, no 2 (2008), p. 26–282 at 271.

[42] Ibid.

[43] Most of the studies conducted on South Eastern Europe are very insightful but frequently omit the complexities of the relations between the core and the periphery in Europe. This work does not ignore the Western Balkans place in this polar relationship, whereby Balkan countries can not transition from the periphery to the core without assistance from core countries, such as Germany, France or Britain. See Borut Roncević, "Path from the (Semi)Periphery to the Core: On the Role of Socio-Cultural Factors," in *IES Proceedings 1.1* (November 2002). http://www.ies.ee/iesp/roncevic.pdf

identity is in direct connection with its efforts toward European integration.

Moreover, in light of the literature on Europeanization, recent scholarly debates have been concerned with the meaning, uses and power of the promise of Europe—a power increasingly seen as being able to change mentalities. Europe is considered as a structuring discourse in as much as Europe cannot be reduced to an idea, an identity or a reality since it is itself a structuring force.[44] As Delanty notes, what is real is the discourse in which ideas and identities are formed and historical realities constituted.[45] This notion of Europe is brought into focus as a political and cultural construction and I suggest, following Delanty, that "it cannot be regarded as a self-evident entity: it is an idea as much as reality."[46] The First and Other Serbia construction of Serbian national identity is "projected" onto European identity. It is thus not a question of "deconstructing Europe,"[47] but instead one of analyzing those discourses about Europe which would claim or simply assume some relationship between the discourse itself and Europe, i.e. between speaking about Europe, and speaking about Serbia. From the Serbian perspective, Europe is not only Europe as the Other, but also Europe as an element of "Us." This means that "Europe is a category of both inclusion and exclusion",[48] which can provoke tension in communities constructed around the concept of the nation such as Serbia. Still, the Serbian self-image is also reflected in examples of the usage of the term *Europe* and its derivatives. The core strategy in the First and Other Serbia discourses on Europe is the creation of inclusion and exclusion through the construction of in- and out-groups. These demarcations are not static but in perpetual transformation. Through these constructions, Serbian discursive actors are involved in an ongoing process of identity formation: creating de-

---

[44] Gerald Delanty, *Inventing Europe: Idea, Identity, Reality* (Palgrave Macmillan, 1995), p. 1.
[45] Ibid.
[46] Ibid.
[47] For deconstruction of Europe itself, see Jacques Derrida, *The Other Heading: Reflections on Today's Europe* (Bloomington, Indiana University Press, 1992), p. 45.
[48] Gerald Delanty, *Inventing Europe: Idea, Identity, Reality* (Palgrave Macmillan, 1995), p. 5.

grees of difference from Europe and Europeans. Europeanization in this sense[49] indicates a clear awareness of "Us" and "Them," and of an Other that possesses certain European features which "We" want to acquire. In general, Malksoo notes, Eastern Europeans' relation to this hierarchy has been a mixture of acceptance and resistance.[50] On the one hand, Western Europe is the idealized Other whose recognition Serbs crave and desire but, as all other Eastern Europeans, they see themselves as being truer to the idea of Europe than Western Europeans.[51] One can be sure that, in First and Other Serbia contested dialogues where two different historical and political visions of Serbian society meet, *Europe* is understood, as Milutinović notes, as a set of values, a concept, a principle, an idea, and a place where structural ideas of Europeanization are taken seriously.[52]

Aims of this book

A number of important questions frame this project. How have "First" and "Other" Serbia elites constructed and reconstructed identity discourses in post-Milošević Serbia? Why does one discourse become more dominant on certain issues? What images were utilized and why were these images used and not others? The central enquiry of this study is the question of how Serbian national identity has been forged and constructed by divergent, competing visions of First and Other Serbia. My analysis is directly concerned with First Serbia's attempts to construct the Other Serbia as an enemy within, especially in connection with their construction of Europe as a foreign, distant, and threateningly alien place. In this way, First Serbia creates a new Euroskeptic, anti-West political identity for itself through the rearticulation of certain elements of

---

[49] The term *Europeizzare* in Italian appears for the first time in 1908, meaning to "render comfortable with European usage or taste, to give a European imprint to the civilization and habits of a country outside Europe." Ibid., "The Dual appeal of 'Europe' in Italy" in Bo Strath and Mikael af Malmborg, eds., *The Meaning of Europe: Variety and Contestation Within and Among the Nations* (Oxford and New York: Berg, 2002), p. 42.

[50] Maria Malksoo, "The Politics of Becoming European: A Study of Polish and Baltic post-Cold War Security Imaginaries," (Routledge, 2013), p. 62.

[51] Ibid., p. 63.

[52] Zoran Milutinović, *Getting Over Europe: The Construction of Europe in Serbian Culture* (Amsterdam/New York: Rodopi, 2011), p. 12.

old discourses about the nation, identity and Europe which derive from the Milošević era. This book will examine this practice of othering of Europe, and of each other, in the First and Other Serbia discourses, and the role such othering plays as a strategy in the discursive construction of collective Serbian identity. Which traits, characteristics, qualities and features are attributed to "Europe," and which to Serbia, in First and Other Serbia texts? From what perspective or point of view are these referential or nomination strategies, positive or negative predications of the Self and the Other, and arguments for or against Europe, expressed? I hold that First Serbia texts construct the Serbian nation, identity and Europe, as each having essential qualities, while representing Serbia as rigid, motionless and static, and resistant to the idea of change. This is in sharp contrast to Other Serbia's representation of the Serbian nation and identity as substandard, lesser and inferior to Europe, also essentialized, still backward and undeveloped, and deprived of the opportunity for positive change. Neither version can be any more true than the other, of course, as both "Serbia" and "Europe" function on the level of perceptual constructs. Any study dealing with the re-constitution of political discourses is thus confronted with ambiguity, temporality and friction. It is my hope, however, that this will produce a more nuanced view of how best to approach the research questions.

Methodological approach

Discourse theory, as Howarth and Stavrakasis note, investigates the way in which social practices articulate and contest the discourses that constitute social reality.[53] By using critical discourse analysis (CDA),[54] this

---

[53] David Howarth and Yannis Stavrakakis, "Introducing Discourse Theory and Political Analysis" in David Howarth, Aletta J. Norval and Yannis Stavrakakis, (eds.), *Discourse Theory and Political Analysis: Identities, Hegemonies and Social Change*, (Manchester and New York: Manchester University Press, 2000).

[54] Critical discourse analysis has various branches: the Dutch school of discourse analysis, as exemplified by the work of Teun van Dijk, develops a cognitive-oriented approach which emphasizes the mediating role of personal and social cognition between social structures and discourse structures. The research group at the University of Vienna, exemplified by the work of Ruth Wodak, describes its research agenda as a discourse-historical approach; the British school of critical discourse analysis, as exemplified by the work of Norman Fairclough, builds primarily on Michel Foucault's con-

study investigates how themes, discursive strategies and linguistic devices are used to construct the idea of "Europe" within the "First" and "Other" Serbia discourses. This work reflects a constructivist perspective in which different actors, at different times, relying on and interpreting history and each other's role in it, may come to view belonging in different ways. I argue that a combined model of constructivist and discourse theories can aid one's understanding of how values, beliefs and ideas are conditioned by the dominant discourse, and thus allow one to reach more definite conclusions. Additionally, by identifying the framework of competing political narratives, discourse theory tools can explain how identity is constructed in the public sphere. By placing emphasis on the contested image of Europe, this study comes to a better understanding of how the First and Other Serbia discourses utilize and embrace the liberal or illiberal value system. In this way, the range of theoretical bases applied permits the identification of the alternative political culture beneath the political surface. It will be clear from my analysis that the First and Other Serbia discourses serve both to include and to exclude, they define the "in-groups" as well as the "out-groups"; the "Us" as well as the "Other," which is most commonly Europe or other regional countries within South-Eastern Europe. More specifically, Chapters 3, 4 and 5 focus on how First and Other Serbia actors participate in dialogue. Meaning, noted Bakhtin,[55] does not belong to any of the speakers because it arises from the mutual correspondence between them. In the Bakhtinian sense, I will analyze how these actors construct in- and out-groups, and predicate certain values to the Serbian Self and the European Other.

As a result of employing these methods, there will be no real "Serbia" or "Europe"[56] to be discovered, as national identity is an constant invention.[57] Reicher and Hopkins suggested that "when one researches

---

cept of discourse and its linguistic dimension. See Ruth Wodak, et al., *The Discursive Construction of National Identity* (Edinburgh: EUP; 2nd revised edition; 2009), p. 7.

[55] Michael Holquist, *Dialogism: Bakhtin and His World* (Routledge, 2002), p. 44.

[56] At this point, it is important to stress that the use of quotation marks is intended to qualify the collective identity of an ethic group and marks my departure from any concept of the nation as an essential and historically stable concept.

[57] Stephen Reicher and Nick Hopkins, *Self and the Nation* (Sage, 2001), p. 8.

the national identity, one needs to ask not whether these identities are true or false, but what is their function in society, and whose reactions they are, and whose interests these identities serve."[58] Following Hansen, I believe that the adoption of discursive epistemology makes an intrinsic identity an impossibility.[59] To this end, social representations are not merely reproductions of reality, they are also prescriptive and serve as regulative ideas for the formation of collective identities.[60] Constructivists associate identity with studies of discourses, and have challenged pre-existing assumptions that culture and politics, and thus also national identity, are monolithic phenomena which are apparent to all members of the community despite any internal turmoil. I submit that the constructivists' parameters of Self and Other provide a useful approach for both identifying and interpreting First and Other Serbia discourses. I use these parameters in order to reveal, in some detail, the ways in which the First and Other Serbia's versions of history serve to underpin different ways of imagining the Serbian nation. First Serbia's attempt to essentialize Serbian identity as special, antique and unique, as well as Other Serbia's perception of Serbian identity as inferior and backward in relation to Europe, echoes notions of "belonging or not belonging to civilization" or "being or not being civilized." I put forward that any meaningful analysis of top-down elite constructions of Europe and of official representations of the nation state, can only be achieved through a non-essentialist approach. This study therefore aims to deconstruct various essentializations of identity, Serbia and Europe. It is pertinent to note that this book does not understand the process of differentiation as a closed process. The labels analyzed, such as *Europe, European, traitor, missionary intelligentsia*,[61] *Serbs* etc., play off one another, across a

---

[58] Ibid., p. 10.
[59] Lene Hansen, *Security as Practice: Discourse Analysis and the Bosnian War* (Routledge, 2006), p. 23.
[60] Gerald Delanty, *Inventing Europe: Idea, Identity, Reality* (Palgrave Macmillan, 1995), p. 5.
[61] The article "Missionary Intelligentsia" was published in February 2003 in *Vreme* by Slobodan Antonić. The author expressed his intention to start a discussion about the Serbian elites. An acerbic exchange immediately ensued and highlighted the main lines of the debate which lasted for the next three months: First, the question of whether there is such a thing as "missionaries" in Serbia (those who support the "At-

variety of texts and media. Thus, one observes the representation of "difference" and "otherness" across a broad swathe of Serbian public space, and the frequent repetition of similar representational practices.

"First" and "Other" Serbia discourses on Europe and identity

Here I intend to show in more detail the ways in which "First" and "Other" Serbia act as the "constitutive outside" for each other. The Serbian public sphere is dominated by debates between these groups standing at opposite ends of the ideological and political spectrum. These debates indeed demonstrate how the notion of a divided society is continually being constructed. I put forward that First and Other Serbia, as different conceptions of political community—ranging from the nationalist, Euroskeptic right, to the liberal and extremely pro-Western left—produce fields of discourse on Europe in which competing claims are worked out in the public sphere. In simple terms, the First Serbia discourse is identified as being dominated by themes of tradition, religion and a highly victim-centered understanding of history, with a nationalistic orientation which frequently puts emphasis on an illiberal value system.[62] In Ramet's descriptions in 2011, this was embodied by both ultra nationalists and soft nationalists, such as the politicians Aleksandar Vučić and Tomislav Nikolić, and academics grouped around the Serbian Academy of Sciences and Arts (SANU) such as Dobrica Ćosić and Mateja Bećković.[63] This discourse gained support from remnants of the Radical Party when in November 2014 Vojislav Šešelj returned to Serbia after 11 years spent on trial at the ICTY. Moreover, significant players outside the government include ultra-right NGOs and movements such as *Srpski sabor Dveri*—their manifesto is analyzed in Chapter 3—and

---

lanticist community") and second, what is the acceptable degree of patriotism, both issues building on themes discussed previously in the "Point of Departure" debate. The participants also sought to sustain the "Eastern" or "Western" leanings of Serbia.

[62] See Filip Ejdus, "Security, Strategic Culture and Identity in Serbia," in *Western Balkans Security Observer*, No. 7, (Belgrade, October–December 2008).

[63] Sabrina Ramet, eds., *Civic and Uncivic Values: Serbia in the Post-Milošević Era* (Budapest: Central University Press, 2011), p. 5.

Obraz, a "clerico-fascist" organization outlawed by the Serbian constitutional court in June 2012.[64]

The First Serbia discourse is a nationalist, right-wing, Euroskeptic discourse which is "turned inward." The in-group bias in predication is remarkable; First Serbia actors in general mention only what they consider to be the positive aspects of Serbian history and culture, while denying, obfuscating or simply ignoring the negative aspects of the past and present. As argued by Van Dijk, such in-group bias represents a very common ideologically-based strategy of positive self-presentation and negative presentation of the other.[65] In this discourse Serbs are constructed as victims and there is no or little reference to regional enmities of the recent past or responsibility for war crimes. The in-group bias in this particular sub-type of predication, as Wodak points out, often leads to an assertion of the superiority of one's own culture and civilization.[66] In this type of in-group favoritism, Serbia is constructed as the home of noble values and high culture.

On the opposite side of political spectrum, the work *Other Serbia* and *Intellectuals and War*, published in 1992, is the product of public gatherings, and is a representation of the core of the political and cultural life of the so-called Other (in this sense different, non-nationalistic) Serbia. This Serbia was first envisioned as opposition to the militaristic nationalism of the Milošević regime, to its xenophobia and populism, which, in the view of many, had overtaken Serbian society in the early 1990s.[67] In post-2000 Serbia, most attempts at opening a public debate have come from a relatively small group of local activists and human rights NGOs, such as *Women in Black, the Youth Initiative for Human Rights, the Belgrade Centre for Human Rights, the Humanitarian Law Centre*

---

[64] Jelena Obradović-Wochnik, "Revisionism, Denial and anti-ICTY Discourse in Serbia's Public Sphere: Beyond the 'Divided Society' Debate," in James Gow, Rachel Kerr, and Zoran Pajić, eds., *Prosecuting War Crimes, Lessons and Legacies of the International Criminal Tribunal for the Former Yugoslavia*, 2013.

[65] Ruth Wodak and Teun A. van Dijk, eds., *Racism at the Top: Parliamentary Discourses on Ethnic Issues in Six European States* (Klagenfurt: Drava Verlag, 2000), p. 45.

[66] Ruth Wodak, et al., *The Discourse of Politics in Action: Politics as Usual* (Basingstoke: Palgrave, 2009), p. 28.

[67] Ivan Čolović, *Belgrade Circle Journal Online*. http://web1.uct.usm.maine.edu/~bcj/

and *the Helsinki Committee for Human Rights* from Belgrade.[68] Within Other Serbia groupings, Ramet has identified two groups, the first being the "hard liberals" who subscribed to civic values and in many cases also advocate gender equality and tolerance of sexual minorities.[69] Adherents of the second group, the "soft liberals" (or flexible realists), avoid dogmatism, although the politicians in this group, such as former president Boris Tadić and certain Democratic Party members have been known to give a nationalistic account of the history of Kosovo's independence.[70] This split, between the soft and hard liberal groupings within Other Serbia which occurred from 2002 is analyzed further in Chapters 3 and 5. Ramet considers soft liberals to be moderate nationalists, closer to the hard liberals than to the ultranationalists; however, I approach Ramet's division critically, arguing that soft liberals to an extent take both sides within their discourse. Other Serbia discourse is in general identified as being dominated by themes including human rights, war crimes, the Srebrenica genocide, the Kosovo question, the siege of Sarajevo, and activism in support of Gay Pride, with the emphasis on Serbs being not the main victims but the main perpetrators in the post-Yugoslav conflicts. I argue that the Other Serbia discourse is hard-line and anti-nationalist, yet cosmopolitan, not turned inward, and largely secular in nature. The response of the First Serbia actors is to label members of this group as foreign mercenaries. I suggest that the Missionary Intelligentsia[71] debate from 2003 and the Point of Departure[72] debate in

---

[68] Jelena Obradović-Wochnik, "Revisionism, Denial and anti-ICTY Discourse in Serbia's Public Sphere: Beyond the 'Divided Society' Debate," in James Gow, Rachel Kerr, and Zoran Pajić, eds., *Prosecuting War Crimes, Lessons and Legacies of the International Criminal Tribunal for the Former Yugoslavia* (2013).

[69] Among non-governmental groups, so-called hard liberals include the Belgrade Circle, the Anti-trafficking Centre, the Civil Initiative, the Centre for Cultural Decontamination, among others. The most important liberal newspapers are *Republika*, the daily newspaper *Borba* and the online publication and radio show *Peščanik*. The leading hard liberal politician is Čedomir Jovanović. See Sarbina Ramet et al., eds., *Civic and Uncivic Values: Serbia in the Post-Milošević Era* (Budapest: Central University Press, 2011), p. 4.

[70] Ibid., p. 5.

[71] "Missionary intelligentsia" is a term coined by Slobodan Antonić, as stated. By missionary intelligentsia, he means a group of people who consider themselves "mission-

2002 have rearticulated the basic identity narratives and the anti-liberal discourse which had been proclaimed by the Milošević era elite, and set them in a new context. Antonić's text on the Missionary Intelligentsia[73] continued the ideological and interpretative repertoires that had dominated the public sphere in the 1990s, yet at the same time Antonić and other public actors tried to differentiate themselves from the authoritarian nationalism. I propose that the examination of similarities with, and differentiations from, Milošević era elite discourses is crucial to any investigation of the political contestation of Europe and the narrativization of the national Self in post-Milošević public space.

Chapter 3 puts forward that the charges of crimes against humanity created a key point of disagreement between the First and Other Serbia political elites during the 2000s. It is clear, thus, that the political and cultural elites behind the First and Other Serbia frameworks have constituted the subjectivity of post-Milošević Serbia in ways that are favorable to their own ideology and interests. Other Serbia groupings have developed their own ideal types of European norm and Serbian anomaly, yet these voices, similar to those of First Serbia, do not form a homogenous or coherent discourse. These different discourses foster different interpretations of the past and present or, in other words, different historical, political and cultural narratives. Narratives tend to help "establish apparently logical connections between what are otherwise unconnected, contradictory and ambivalent political events, ideas and figures."[74] Following on from this, the ambivalence of the terms First and Other Serbia further accentuates the fluidity of the attitudes they describe which are

---

aries of the Atlanticist community and its values in Serbia." The term has a pejorative meaning, and implies servitude to "foreign forces."

[72] 'Tačka Razlaza' (The Point of Departure) was a debate that unfolded in the magazine *Vreme* in 2002 between the actors of "Other" Serbia, in which the groups divided into groups of hardliners and soft liberals.

[73] In 2008, Antonić defined this phenomenon with the concept of cultural war: "It is a war led by a segment of the cultural elite against certain values and the content of such a war is denial or slighting of certain cultural values, its main form is humiliation, ridicule and cynicism directed against the principal symbols and their bearers." Slobodan Antonić, *The Cultural War in Serbia: Essays on Culture of 'Other' Serbia—from Marko Vidojković to Radomir Konstantinović* (Zavod za udžbenike, Belgrade, 2008).

[74] Ivan Čolović, *The Politics of Symbol in Serbia: Essays in Political Anthropology* (London: Hurst, 1997), p. 5.

not fixed and can, in fact, vary greatly over time. It is important to note that certain writers, politicians and public intellectuals have identified themselves in different discourses at different times, prime examples of this being Vuk Drašković[75] and Slobodan Antonić.[76] Furthermore, as Mudde pointed out, the boundaries that are set to distinguish civic society from uncivic society are problematic, both theoretically and empirically.[77] From Mudde and Kopecký's analysis it is apparent that one criterion for distinguishing civil and uncivil society is the ideology of organizations.[78] However, the academic perception that "uncivil" ideologies (most notably nationalism) are "bad," while civil society is "good" creates a weak and relative argument that reveals normative expectations.[79] This book reveals that in discourses on identity in both First and Other Serbia, identity is constructed in essentialist terms, and that actual analysis of the existing societal dialogue should not be and is not unbalanced by academic expectations of civil society. Additionally, this study does not suggest that these constitutive aspects are an all-encompassing list, nor does it claim that this list captures all possible variations of the Self/Other relationship.

Conclusion

To conclude, this book seeks to make an original contribution to the field of Southeast European studies. The contribution of this work is threefold. First, it applies a novel discursive approach to map out "First" and "Other Serbia" national identities that use Europe as their focus. Starting

---

[75] The famous writer Vuk Drašković was one of the first opposition leaders during the early 1990s. His Serbian Defence Movement (SPO) party was on the far right of the political spectrum. However, during his long political career he served as Minister of Foreign Affairs, and even agreed to run for the 2012 elections in coalition with the Liberal Democrats.

[76] Slobodan Antonić, sociology professor at the University of Belgrade's Faculty of Philosophy and a distinguished media personality.

[77] Petr Kopecky and Cas Mudde, eds., *Uncivil Society? Contentious politics in post-communist Europe* (Routledge, 2003), p. 23.

[78] Ibid.

[79] Cas Mudde, "Civil Society in Post-communist Europe: Lessons from the 'Dark Side'," in Petr Kopecký and Cas Mudde, *Uncivil Society? Contentious Politics in Post-communist Europe* (Routledge, 2003).

with a simplified pro-Europe versus anti-Europe dichotomy the analysis of the Serbian identity is then dissolved to produce a range of Serbian Selves, until now largely neglected in the literature. Likewise, too little attention has until now been paid to the interplay between the different constructs of "Europe" on the one hand, and the political and cultural identity of the two main political factions on the other. The Self/Other nexus is employed with a view to identifying the essence of national identities. In contrast to much of the existing literature, this book emphasizes the antagonistic role of radical othering, but also the potential role of friendly othering. Second, this study fills an important gap in the existing literature on post-Milošević Serbia by exploring and theorizing in a systematic way the neglected relationship between the inner workings of domestic politics and its relation to the pace of European integration. Selective empirical evidence from research on Serbia has also figured prominently in efforts to downplay the role of difference in Serbian identity construction. Thus, this book acts as the missing link by investigating domestic political elites' representation of terms such as *nation*, *patriotism, Serbia*, and *Europe* in public discourses. The relationship between political interests in the domestic political sphere gains particular relevance in the light of the process of EU integration, but especially in the light of the EU's insistence on Serbia conducting "historic dialogue" with Kosovo. Third, instead of being preoccupied with the overall weakness or strength of civic society alone, this research concentrates on the overall character of the political community, both civic and uncivic, and thus it portrays the public sphere from which civic and uncivic society arise. This research offers certain theoretical advances because it applies the conceptual vocabulary of constructivist and discourse studies to a context in which those methods have not previously been extensively used. Nevertheless, the objective of this work is primarily empirical in nature.

This project does not consider the following. First, it does not closely examine the consequences of the wars in Yugoslavia or Kosovo, or the origins of Serbian nationalism. Second, neither does it consider how the Serbian population overall understands Europe. As this book deals with the public sphere, a critical theory needs to take a closer look at "private" discourses. The analysis of bottom-up and grass roots constructions of Europe and its identity is a highly interesting and unavoidable topic. Both of these subjects require research per se and would represent interesting accounts of Serbia's historic relations with Europe. Furthermore, the intertextual reconstruction of narratives of the Self, the Other and the West during the Yugoslav socialist era would be of great interest for investigation. However, these subjects lie largely outside the scope of this book and are only briefly touched upon.

The structure of the book will be outlined in this way. Chapter 1 sets out the framework for the theoretical analysis and the conceptual vocabulary of the thesis, concentrating on the contextualization of First and Other Serbia postulates. Chapter 2 outlines the historical and political context behind First and Other Serbia, which is a prerequisite to understanding the impact of such societal and cultural classifications. Chapters 3, 4, 5 and 6 draw an empirical analysis of the Serbian public sphere from the beginning of 1992 until the end of 2012. In this respect, the structure of the book is intrinsic to the research design. It helps to elucidate the differences between pre- and post-2000 discourses and their key actors. More specifically, Chapter 3 draws on the context outlined in the previous chapter, in which I show from where the identity discourse of First and Other Serbia originated during the Milošević years, with a detailed exploration of the role of academics, politicians, writers and public intellectuals. Chapter 4 outlines the prominent identity narratives in connection with the construction of "Europe." This chapter puts forward that, in contrast with EU countries where Europe might be perceived as a choice, in the Serbian case, the West in general and Europe in particular is seen as a necessity. This resulted in the inability of Other Serbia civil actors after 2000 to appropriate a feasible model of political community that would link Serbian identity to the values of Europe, which has impeded the achievement of democratic maturity and European integration. Chapter 5 is a detailed study of the 2002 Point of Departure and 2003 Missionary Intelligentsia debates. The 2002 Point of Departure debate touched upon themes of Serbian guilt and responsibility, as well as those of victims and perpetrators. I suggest that the Point of Departure debate formed the contextual base for subsequent debates. Following on from this, Chapter 6 explores the manner in which the subject of "Serbian auto-chauvinism" developed after the fall of Milošević in 2000. This chapter summarizes the basic identity narratives of First and Other Serbia, focusing primarily on their reproduction in the post-Milošević era by key discursive actors.

Chapter 1:
Theory and Method

Introduction

National identity is a complex construct. It is the crossing point of several theories and concepts that together constitute a specific self-image of a nation and its place in world affairs. This project is committed to an approach which combines a plurality of methods. It attempts to show that interdisciplinary approaches, which unite critical discourse analysis devices with the concept of the Self and Other nexus from the critical constructivist vocabulary, are suitable for an analysis of Serbian national identity. There is a realm of civil society which is unregulated by state institutions, that which Habermas refers to as the *Lebenswelt* or the "public sphere."[80] What is missing is to address the issue of what constitutes the political sphere. One of the primary weaknesses of the conventional approach to political rhetoric, as Wodak and Krzyzanowski note, is that it sees the political sphere as referring exclusively to the practices of politicians.[81] One can argue that this understanding neglects the facts that politics both penetrates the cultural and private spheres and consequently daily intrudes upon the activities of non-politicians, and that other elites and intellectuals produce political rhetoric on various levels and in various contexts. In the light of such arguments, this book considers politics to be a collection of processes of "articulation of political interests and positions of dissent or consent."[82] The reason for the adoption of a discursive methodology for this book is, accordingly, to access the broader understanding of the political which it offers.

---

[80] According to Habermas, the social world and the objective world together constitute the public sphere, and the subjective world constitutes the private sphere. See Axel Honneth and Hans Joas, eds., *Communicative Action: Essays on Jürgen Habermas's The Theory of Communicative Action* (Cambridge: Polity, 1991), p. 57.

[81] Ruth Wodak and Michael Krzyzanowski, "Analyzing Political Rhetoric," in *Qualitative Discourse Analysis in the Social Sciences* (Palgrave Macmillan, 2008), p. 97.

[82] Ibid., p. 98.

The first layer: discourse analysis

Both the approaches of constructivism and discourse analysis are used, not only due to the fact that they address identity, but also because they emphasize the role of language and discourse in constructing reality. Constructivism is defined by its emphasis on the socially constructed character of the interests and identities of actors, and by its faith in society's susceptibility to change.[83] Thus, the central thesis of constructivism built upon in this analysis is the assertion that, in social reality, nothing is either constant or immutable but rather, as Delanty notes, everything is a product of a continuous process of becoming.[84] That position suggests a discursive dimension to the constructivist process meaning that social reality is negotiated in discursive contexts rather than existing independently of the relevant discourses. Hence, importantly, deconstruction is not a tabula rasa; Badredine suggests that it cannot destroy existing (linguistic, conceptual, or theoretical) structures from the outside.[85] Instead, post-positivist political thought is influenced by Foucault's "archaeology of knowledge," which notes that actually discourse is about the production of knowledge through language.[86] Discourse, as defined by Foucault, refers to "ways of constituting knowledge, together with the social practices, forms of subjectivity and power relations which inhere in such knowledge and relations between them. Discourses are more than ways of thinking and producing meaning. They consti-

---

[83] Martin Griffiths (ed.) *International Relations Theory for the Twenty-First Century* (Routledge, 2012), p. 60.

[84] Gerard Delanty and Chris Rumford, *Rethinking Europe: Social Theory and the Implications of Europeanization.* (London: Routledge, 2005), p. 12.

[85] Arfi Badredine, *Re-thinking International Relations Theory via Deconstruction* (London: Routledge 2012), p. 17.

[86] Foucault is seen as personally contributing to the confusion around discourse by admitting that he uses the term in a number of different ways: as the grand domain of all statements, as just groups of statements, and sometimes as a *regulated practice* that accounts for a certain number of statements. See *Michael Foucault, The Archaeology of Knowledge (Routledge, 1969), p.* 80. This project will attempt to transcend that confusion, but unfortunately the nature of these definitions makes this difficult.

tute the nature of the body, unconscious and conscious mind and emotional life of the subjects they seek to govern."[87]

It is important to note that the concept of discourse, when used in this way, is not purely a linguistic concept. It is about both language *and* practice.[88] Discourse, Foucault argues, constructs the topic, and thus it constructs the social reality around us.[89] And indeed, by taking an interest in the discursive one directs one's attention toward the *constitutive* nature of discourse that gives shape and form to different categories of experience and identity. In the methodological sense, discourse analysis refers to the practice of analyzing empirical raw materials and information as discursive forms.[90] Consequently, I treat a wide range of linguistic and non-linguistic data—including speeches, reports, manifestos, historical events, interviews, policies, ideas, and even organizations and institutions—as "texts" or "writing." I employ discourse analysis to denaturalize a number of categories, such as Europe, nationalism and national identity, by exposing them as the product of particular discourses (e.g. the "First" and "Other" Serbia discourses). In turn, these categories permit that our understanding of reality depends on social, political and historical contexts. Thus, when questioning what is implied in the notions of identity and difference, it is necessary for scholars of identity politics to fully understand the correspondence between language and identity in post-positivist terms, as a relation between knowledge and power.[91] This is the principal reason that the essence of

---

[87] Cited from Chris Weedon, *Feminist Practice and Poststructuralist Theory* (Oxford: Blackwell, 1997), p. 108.

[88] Foucault's understanding of discourse is highly materialist, as it is formed and operates at the intersection of language and the material world, and thus is not limited to language and representation. See Pushkala Prasad, *Crafting Qualitative Research: Working in the Post-positivist Traditions* (Armonk, NY: Sharpe, 2005), p. 24.

[89] See Michael Foucault, *The Archaeology of Knowledge* (Routledge, 1969).

[90] David Howarth and Yannis Stavrakakis, "Introducing discourse theory and political analysis," in David Howarth, Aletta J. Norval and Yannis Stavrakakis, eds., *Discourse Theory and Political Analysis: Identities, Hegemonies and Social Change*, (Manchester and New York: Manchester University Press, 2000), p. 7.

[91] Power and knowledge have an interdependent nature, and must not be thought of as separate or as distinct phenomena. Knowledge and power are mutually dependent and constitute one another. See David Macey, *Dictionary of Critical Theory* (Penguin Books, 2000), p. 145.

discourse theory is rooted in the study of both spoken and written language; the language the actors use when defining reality gives that reality its meaning. However, this begs the question of whether language can reveal discourses that are sufficiently structurally fixed as to be meaningful if one assumes that language is inherently unstable? This postpositivist epistemological stance on discursive causality, and the ontological mutual constitutiveness of the identity/language relation, provide this research with its ontological and epistemological bases. Discourse analysis as a methodology is perhaps not readily associated with claims of substantive causality, however at the same time the study of discourses is very much the study of conceptions of causal relations between a set of agents.[92] Discourse analysis puts forward an epistemological stance known as "discursive causality." As Hansen suggests, "discursive epistemology implies the analytical focus to be on the discursive construction of the identity as both constitutive of and a product of certain policies; it is consistent with the ontological emphasis on language but the practical epistemological focus should be on how identities and policies are articulated."[93] I draw my conception from such argumentation as to what characterizes political discourses and the assertion that politicians will often present the adoption of a practice as the result of a particular representation of identity.[94] This interconnectedness of subjects and objects can be revealed empirically using the conceptual tools of linking, differentiation and subject positioning. It is using these same three processes that the practice of identity formation can be established.

Why discourse analysis?

Discourse analysis is first and foremost an empirical tool and it helps us illuminate the power structures which lie behind what is written and

---

[92] Claudio M. Radaelli and Theofanis Exadaktylos, *Research Design in European Studies: Establishing Causality in Europeanization*, (Basingstoke: Palgrave Macmillan, 2012).
[93] Lene Hansen, *Security as Practice: Discourse Analysis and the Bosnian War* (London and New York: Routledge, 2006), p. 36, and Ruth Wodak, et al., *The Discursive Construction of National Identity* (Edinburgh: Edinburgh University Press, 2009), p. 23.
[94] Ibid., p. 14.

communicated. Actually, it is, for a number of reasons, the only appropriate tool for studying the manner in which the liberal and national intelligentsia within the Serbian public sphere reproduces so-called facts about Europe. The first of such reasons is that discourse analysis, together with the constructivist approaches, focus on the multidimensionality of identity. If this is compared with the rationalist approaches, which often posit that values and identities tend to have a static and fixed nature, the analysis of the discourse can be seen to offer a broader perspective and to explain how identities change and evolve over time. Furthermore, discourse analysis is a socio-political[95] method. Accordingly, it is explicitly concerned with the relationship of language to other elements of social processes and power.[96] In Fairclough's words, it intends to reveal the "non-obvious ways in which language is involved in social relations of power and domination, and in ideology."[97] Power, in this context, involves control, namely by members of one group over members of other groups. Such control mostly pertains to cognition, that is, a powerful group may use persuasion, dissimulation or manipulation, among other strategic ways, to change the minds of others in its own interests.[98] Therefore, instead of considering power to be a given, I have adopted an approach that suggests that interests are constructed though the medium of language and discourses. Hence, discourse analysis helps to illuminate power structures, and to expose and critique the "commonsense" of the social and political world. As such, this approach brings to light new and fresh perspectives on structures which were previously often somehow accepted as being reflective of the natural order of things. One must first explore the context of meaning-production in order to grasp the web of meaning that the Serbian intelligentsia attach to Europe and to Serbian national identity. This book will reveal the structures of the dominant "First" Serbia discourse, which is, as Hansen notes, both constraining and enabling for political ac

---

[95] Teun A. van Dijk, "Principles of Critical Discourse Analysis," in *Discourse and Society* 4, no. 2 (1993), p. 249–283.
[96] Norman Fairclough, *Critical Discourse Analysis* (Boston: Addison Wesley, 1995), p. 6.
[97] Norman Fairclough, *Language and Power* (London: Longman, 2001), p. 229.
[98] Teun A. van Dijk, "Principles of Critical Discourse Analysis," in *Discourse and Society* 4, no. 2 (1993), p. 249–283.

tors/discursive agents;[99] my intention being to clearly identify the basic discourse upon which the subordinate discourse of "Other" Serbia identity is built. Indeed, the effort of this book is not to examine the monolithic formulation of a single identity but, instead, to analyze what Wæver calls the "confluctual nature of competing identities."[100] Rather than focus on the mere description of context, the analysis of these conflicting discourses can provide a deeper understanding of how, for instance, the First Serbia elites have re-formulated some elements of their old ideological and political repertories in the new post-Milošević context. The final reason for using a discursive approach is that it enables one to draw an intertextual analysis by drawing on various textual sources, as well as institutional and media sites. The concept of intertextuality emphasizes the dialogical properties of texts and, as Hall argues, the text is explicitly or implicitly "in dialogue with" other texts and gains its meaning in relation to them.[101] Intertextual analysis also facilitates the exploration of the ways in which a particular idea draws upon older discourses and these discourses are re-articulated in a new context.[102] As such, this book provides a theoretical framework capable of elucidating politics and international relations.

How to find meaning in discourse

The linguistic devices of linking and differentiation are utilized to explain the creation of meaning in language. Hansen has ably employed these techniques in her study of discourse of the Bosnian war, and I draw on her work, as well as the work of others. I adopt Hansen's understanding of identity as the product of the processes of linking and differentiation as this provides an empirical account of how the creation and recreation of discourses should be approached.[103] Similarly, my

---

[99] Lene Hansen, *Security as Practice: Discourse Analysis and the Bosnian War* p. 12.
[100] Ole Wæver, "Identity, Communities and Foreign Policy. Discourse Analysis as Foreign Policy Theory," in L. Hansen and O. Wæver, eds., *European Integration and National Identity: The Challenge of the Nordic States*, (London and New York: Routledge, 2002), p. 25.
[101] Stuart Hall, The Spectacle of the 'Other' in *Representation: Cultural Representations and Signifying Practices* (Thousand Oaks, CA: Sage. 1997), p. 223.
[102] Ibid.p, 223,
[103] Lene Hansen, *Security as Practice: Discourse Analysis and the Bosnian War* p. 42.

interpretation of the discursive strategy is heavily indebted to Wodak's concepts of "presupposition of sameness" (strategies of assimilation) and "presupposition of difference" (strategies of dissimilation).[104] I will briefly explain these concepts individually for the purposes of clarification and convenience. From a methodological perspective, one should begin by identifying those terms which indicate a clear construction of the Other, such as *evil, traitor, pest, spy* and *decadent*; or of the Self, such as *good, moral, civilized, exclusive* or *unique*. Identity construction, however, is not accomplished solely through the designation of one particular sign for the Other or the Self, but rather through the *location* of these signs within a larger system.[105] For instance, to construct "Serbia" as being different from "Europe" does not create much meaning unless this construction is situated within a discourse which links and differentiates these signs, that is, which places it at a point in the web of meaning of the "First" and "Other" Serbia. One habitual discursive possibility, as in the Other Serbia discourse, is to link Serbia to the terms *undeveloped, irrational, backward, primitive, retrograde* and *violent*, and then differentiate it from a *controlled, developed, civilized, rational, orderly, peaceful* and *responsible* Europe. Analytically, the empirical construction of identity should therefore coincide with a careful investigation of which signs for the Self and Other are articulated by a particular discourse or text. But, how can these linguistic concepts be practically employed? Hansen notes that spatial and temporal constructions of identity are analytical lenses through which important political subjectivities can be brought into focus by the analysis of linking and differentiation.[106] Hansen understands identity as being *spatially constructed.* Understanding political identity through spatial constructions implies the existence of space delineation. This view holds that identity is relational and always involves the construction of boundaries and the delineation of space.[107] Such territorially bounded identities are typically given political content and political subjectivities as happened in Western debates in the 1990s

---

[104] Ruth Wodak et al., *The Discursive Construction of National Identity* (Edinburgh: Edinburgh University Press, 2009), p. 33.
[105] Lene Hansen, *Security as Practice: Discourse Analysis and the Bosnian War* , p. 42-44.
[106] Ibid., p. 62.
[107] Ibid., p. 47.

with the linking of the Balkans to being *violent, irrational, backward* and *barbarian*.

Similarly, reading political identity through *temporal constructions* implies the existence of progress and change over time. I contend that articulations of temporal identity such as development, change, transformation and continuity are crucial to the analysis of constructions of identity within the First and Other Serbia debate on EU candidacy and membership. Wæver notes that, in the light of Europeanization in Central and Eastern Europe, a frequent occurrence is the construction of the Other (the country in question) as temporally progressing toward the (Western) Self.[108] This is a central theme in development discourses as well as in discourses on democratization and human rights.[109] In general, the temporal construction of identity locates the possibility of *progress* within the discourse: thus, the object can be less temporally developed or even temporally superior. This technique of subject positioning refers to the fact that subjects and objects are always produced in respect of other subjects and objects. Does the Serbian Self want to transform and even transcend its radical Otherness to become more like the desired Self? Or is this Self not able to break with its "backward" identity as constructed within the Other Serbia discourse? Hansen and Wæver note that European temporal construction of identity is precisely the reason why the EU is in general constructed not against an external Other but rather against the temporal Other of its own violent past.[110] Thus, "the past" plays a significant role in the construction of the EU's discourse on European identity. Finally, I pose a query in respect of Todorov's three questions.[111] What is the framework of knowledge within which the Other is seen? What moral judgment is made of the Other? What relationship is proposed between Serbia and the European Other? I ask

---

[108] Ole Wæver, "Identity, Communities and Foreign Policy: Discourse Analysis as Foreign Policy Theory," in Lene Hansen and Ole Wæver, eds., *European Integration and National Identity: The Challenges of the Nordic States* (London and New York: Routledge, 2001), p. 20–47.

[109] Ibid., p. 47.

[110] Ibid., p. 49.

[111] Tzvetan Todorov, *The Conquest of America: the Question of the Other* (New York: Harper Perennial, 1992).

similar questions to each text in order to extrapolate meaning and to ascertain how subject positioning exposes the relation between various subjects and objects. As such, we do not start from an empty page with our perceptions, be they perceptions of Europe or any other political entity. Rather, we hold pre-existing notions about the attributes a phenomenon has and expectations of what it will do. Discourse analysis, therefore, helps to uncover our assumptions and to reveal how Serbia, Europe and other subjects and objects are formulated according to preconceptions, especially in relation to the dissolution of Yugoslavia and the 1999 NATO intervention. A discourse, therefore, should not be understood as a solitary sign of meaning but as a set of relations, linkages and differentiations, which are often hierarchical in nature.

The second layer: Self/Other analysis

My research addresses a particular international relations issue which involves a significant identity dimension. Some notable scholars maintain that research into this area requires a theoretical framework which surpasses the predominantly essentialist approaches of the neo-realist and neo-liberal perspectives.[112] I follow Wæver in suggesting that issues such as identity, nationalism, religion, gender and many more are absent from this "neo-neo synthesis".[113] The social constructivist and postmodern approaches to international relations provide such an alternative. The case of Serbia, given the fierce identity friction between "First" and "Other" Serbia, provides a good example through which to explore relations between culture, nation, state, religion, identity and politics — themes which have been extensively covered in the critical constructivist literature. Undertaking the constructivist theory perspective thus entails exploring how identity is understood and interpreted in post-Milošević Serbia, asking what knowledge is available and what is invoked by First and Other Serbia actors to construct the nation and Europe, and asking

---

[112] Bo Strath, ed., *Europe and the Other and Europe as the Other* (Brussels: Peter Lang, 2000), p. 9.

[113] Ole Wæver, "The Rise and Fall of the Inter-paradigm Debate," in Steve Smith et al., *International Theory: Positivism and Beyond* (Cambridge: Cambridge University Press, 1996), p. 163.

how the tension and contradictions between these factors has led to the identity politics which are prevalent today.

The assumptions of Self/Other analysis and theories of alterity

The classical description of the relationship between the Self and the Other is to be found in Sartre's phenomenological account[114] in which the relationship with the Other is always conflict-ridden and antagonistic because it is based on the dialectic in which the only possibilities are either being dominated or being dominant.[115] Contracting this is the thought of Lévinas, who notes that the encounter with the Other is positive, as the identity of the subject is dependent upon an Otherness that is always and already present before the subject is constituted, and is founded by the ethical demand to take responsibility for the Other.[116] As mentioned, one of the first applications of the Self-Other relationship to enter political theory was made by Todorov who argued that one may "locate the problematics of alterity" along at least three axes: value judgment about the Other, rapprochement toward the Other and knowledge about the Other.[117] Der Derian and Shapiro[118] remark that foreign policy is generally about making (creating) an Other, and later David Campbell applied this insight to the US Self which he understood as a narrative structure.[119] In respect of Europe, Rumelili proposes a non-adversarial and more positively identified Otherness that also has a

---

[114] The 1944 play *No Exit*, in which Sartre famously writes, "L'enfer, c'est les autres" ("Hell is other people").

[115] David Macey, *Dictionary of Critical Theory* (Penguin Books, 2000), p. 286.

[116] Ibid., p. 286.

[117] See Tzvetan Todorov, *The Conquest of America: the Question of the Other* (New York: Harper Perennial, 1992).

[118] See James Der Derian and Michael J. Shapiro, eds., *International/Intertextual Relations Postmodern Readings of World Politics* (Lexington, MS: Lexington Books, 1989).

[119] David Campbell, *Writing Security: United States Foreign Policy and the Politics of Identity*, (Minneapolis, MN and Manchester: University of Minnesota Press/Manchester University Press, 1998), p. 87.

constitutive role in the constructions of collective identities.[120] In the EU context, Lévinas finds that the degree of difference of the Other from the Self may also vary, as more than one Other can exist, differing in their ontological distance from the Self, but the same in their Otherness.[121] Concerning the extent of identification with the Other, Wendt argues that there is a "continuum from negative to positive, that is, from conceiving the Other as anathema to the Self to conceiving it as an extension of the Self.[122] Thus, the images of the Other might be perceived as a continuum, and a long-abominated enemy could conceivably turn into an ally, an extension of the Self, over time."[123] This is particularly true, for example, of Germany, France and Britain, in the context of European Union.

On the other hand, Neumann notes that it is the absolute or radical difference toward the Other that accomplishes its constitutive role in the formation of collective identities.[124] Difference, however, need not be entirely radicalized in order to guarantee the delineation of one's own identity. The tendency to demonize the Other, to perceive the Other as an entirely radically negative entity, Connolly argues, "is a temptation rather than a necessity."[125] Other possible configurations of alterity of the Other also exist, especially in the phenomenological tradition and postcolonial theory,[126] but an examination of such matters lies outside the scope of this book.

---

[120] In relations to Europe/EU, see Bahar Rumelili, "Constructing Identity and Relating to Difference: Understanding the EU's mode of Differentiation" in *Review of International Studies*, 30, no. 1, (January 2004) p. 27–47.

[121] David Macey, *Dictionary of Critical Theory* (Penguin Books, 2000), p. 286.

[122] Alexander Wendt, quoted from Iver B. Neumann and Jennifer M. Welsh, "The Other in European Self-Definition: An Addendum to the Literature on International Society" in *Review of International Studies*, 17, no. 4 (October 1991).

[123] Ibid.

[124] Iver B. Neumann, *Uses of the other: "The East" in European Identity Formation* (Manchester: Manchester University Press, 1999), p.12.

[125] William Connolly, *Identity/Difference: Democratic Negotiations of Political Paradox* (University of Minnesota Press, 2002), p. 8.

[126] See Rabah Aissaoui, *Immigration and National Identity: North African Political Movements in Colonial and Postcolonial France* (London: Tauris Academic Studies, 2009); and Madina Tlostanova, *Gender Epistemologies and Eurasian Borderlands* (New York: Palgrave Macmillan, 2010); and Taric Modood, "Multicultural Citizenship and Muslim Identity Politics," in *Interventions: International Journal of Postcolonial studies*, 12, no. 2, (2010),

Friendly, non-radical and radical Others

Identity can only exist in relation to what one is not. To claim that somebody is not European, for instance, makes only sense if one is able to comprehend the vast range of non-European identities, such as Latin American, Asian, African. While accepting these assumptions, I would also add another important dimension to the concept that the Self is configured solely through difference. Can a similar Other function as a shaper of the Self's identity? Of course, as not only enemies, but friendly states can outline national identities. Much literature has been concerned with debating the nature of identity formation,[127] but there is also the question of whether it is necessary to theorize similarity before difference. As Connolly points out, identity exists only in a relational context, it "requires difference in order to be, and it converts difference into otherness in order to secure its own self-certainty."[128] Delanty makes this clear by using the term *non-self*—acknowledging that all identities are based on some kind of exclusion, as the identity of the self can be defined only by reference to a non-self.[129] The set identity/difference has in fact become a mark of social and political theory and most discussions about identity politics end up developed around these binary oppositions. Thus, a similar Other can function as shaper of the Self's identity, as in the case of countries with special relationships such as America and Great Britain, but identity is not truly *unitary*, as identity in fact perpetually alters *otherness* into *difference*. In truth, identity is established in relation to a series of differences or similarities that have become so-

---

p. 157–170; Frederic Regard, *British Narratives of Exploration: Case Studies on the Self and Other* (London : Pickering and Chatto, 2009).

[127] See Michael Kenny, *The Politics of Identity: Liberal Political Theory and the Dilemmas of Difference*. (Cambridge: Polity Press, 2004); B. Greenhill, "Recognition and Collective Identity Formation in International Politics," in *European Journal of International Relations,* 14, no. 2, (2008) and R. Sakwa, "The Problem of 'the International' in Russian Identity Formation', in *International Politics,* 49, no. 4 (2012); M. Friedner, "Identity Formation and Transnational Discourses: Thinking Beyond Identity Politics," in *Indian Journal of Gender Studies,* 15, no. 2 (2008).

[128] William Connolly, *Identity/Difference: Democratic Negotiations of Political Paradox* (University of Minnesota Press, 2002), p. 144.

[129] Gerard Delanty, *Modernity and Postmodernity: Knowledge, Power, the Self* (London: Sage, 2000), p. 4-5.

cially recognized.[130] Nonetheless, the differences are essential to the creation and continued existence of that identity. If the differences did not coexist, the identity would not persist in its distinctness and solidity.

Others can be categorized as friendly or unfriendly, and as radical or non-radical. The empirical analysis concerns itself with the interrelatedness of those actors in the public sphere whose discourse is governed by radical Others. Antagonistic and conflictual identities can have many shades of meaning and degrees of extremism. A polar differentiation between hostility and friendliness therefore fails to fully capture the breadth of opinion which actors may hold in their definitions and perceptions of one another. Even while conducting an analysis of the processes of radical Otherness, one should ensure that the Other is not perceived as a farcical villain. A tendency to such over-simplification may stem from the overriding judgments of binary politics— East against West, Christians against Muslims, global South against global North, just to name a few illustrations. The nexus of Self and Other poses a more multifaceted spectrum of possibilities because the national Self can be shown to have a multiplicity of possible positions, as in the Serbian case. In short, the theoretical bases suggest examples of each category: Others can be internal or external to the Self, imagined or symbolic, or even radical at one point in time and friendly at another, Germany being a good example. As a consequence of this difference being inconstant, one can trace the ever-evolving narrative of the construction of the identity and capture the configuration of Others at different points in time. This is particularly relevant to the highly changeable subject-object relations in the region of former Yugoslavia.

Debates and historical events

The historical events on which I have focused are gathered around certain moments of crisis such as the assassination of Prime Minister Zoran Djindjić[131] in 2003, Kosovo's declaration of independence in 2008 and

---

[130] William Connolly, *Identity/Difference: Democratic Negotiations of Political Paradox* (University of Minnesota Press, 2002), p. 144.
[131] Zoran Djindjić studied in West Germany thanks to the intervention of former German Chancellor Willy Brandt, under the professor Jürgen Habermas in Frankfurt.

Serbia's EU membership bid in 2011, and certain public debates that followed those events, including the 2002 Point of Departure debates, the 2003 Missionary Intelligentsia debates and the 2008 Anti-chauvinism debates. There are two main reasons why I have chosen these events and these debates. First, within the general time frame I have chosen two specific periods, namely the periods from 2002 to 2003 and from 2008 to 2012. My analysis focuses particularly on these periods because they represent moments of social dislocation, when the identity discourses of the state and the elites were de-stabilized. These periods were critical junctures when crises challenged the Serbian political elites to redefine themselves, and to do so in terms of the meaning that Europe had for them. The period after the change of regime which culminated in the assassination of the first democratic Prime Minister Zoran Djindjić functions as an acute illustration of the extent to which divisions over Europe and identity are fundamental to Serbian politics—so much so that these divisions can enrapture social movements, political parties and even political assassins. The period following Kosovo's declaration of independence from Serbia highlights radically changing attitudes toward Europe and acts as the high point in the battle over national sovereignty. Kosovan independence can be regarded as the most important recent episode in terms of galvanizing Serbian elites to debate the nature of Europe. Kosovo remains at the forefront of the Serbian political debate on Europe and never fails to evoke familiar identity-related themes. Second, the events and debates chosen add a comparative aspect to the research design of this book, as they allow us to track the changes in the identity discourses that happen over time. Thus, the events and debates are grouped according to temporality and discourse. For example, I focus on differences in how Europe was perceived before and after the fall of Milošević, and especially after Kosovo's declaration of independence. This research considers not only the manner in which identity has been constructed in the 1990s, and the historical events which have shaped it, but also how certain linkages have formed and served to create new identities that are still relevant today, and perhaps can provide some insight into the reformulations of identity which will occur in future.

Official discourses and textual material

The discourses of "First" and "Other" Serbia, being the political and cultural elites which I have selected for study, focus primarily on what heads of state, scholars, artists, historians, film directors, writers and journalists have said or written. The term *political and cultural elites* is not unproblematic. It is not always clear whose voice is recorded, and some political protagonists have more media space than others. However, within the 2002 Point of Departure, the 2003 Missionary Intelligentsia and 2008 Anti-chauvinism debates, I have taken political elites to include actors and texts which were in some way connected to shaping popular opinion on Europe. The methodological contribution of this research is threefold. First, I introduce various new texts which have not so far been used in the context of academic studies of Serbia. A wide range of such sources are drawn on, including texts found in political handbooks, weekly magazines, the main political tabloids, political interviews in the press, certain official documents, religious texts, online media texts, the writings of prominent academics, publications by powerful NGOs and debates in the quality press. Second, this research points to a new reading and interpretation of the existing primary and secondary literature. This is because the research questions and the methodological tools utilized depart from previous interpretations of these texts. I have included secondary texts, which provide historical background and analysis to the events in question and help to set the scene for the elite debates, including commentary and statements. Finally, this research draws upon a close reading of most of the texts in their own original language, Serbian. Given that identity construction involves analysis of language structures, being a native speaker has helped me to detect the subtleties of First and Other Serbia actors' communications. The reason I have not made much use of official government documents and official discourses is that they often feel rather scripted, whereas the debates opened the actors up to question and challenge and allowed a more genuine examination and presentation of their positions.

The two particular political journals used for analysis, *Hourglass* and *New Serbian Political Thought*, are at different ends of the political spectrum and represent Other and First Serbia actors respectively. In addition, the conservative quality daily newspaper *Politika* is consulted on various issues, as it is still considered the daily newspaper of record in Serbia. For wider background data, all articles available on the website of *B92* (a well-known Serbian broadcaster which also publishes its articles in English) in its Euro-Atlantic Integration, Kosovo in Focus sections etc. have been scanned for relevant content. Some B92 and similar articles also form part of the selection of key texts for analysis, as they contain important statements and interviews with First and Other Serbia protagonists. I also pay particular attention to debates in *Vreme* magazine, which sparked three long months of heated discussions in 2002. I suggest that during the 2002 Point of Departure debate,[132] the 2003 Missionary Intelligentsia debate, and the 2012 Auto-chauvinist debate, the basic identity narratives and the anti-liberal discourse, as proclaimed by the Milošević elite, were each time re-articulated and set in the new context.

New Serbian Political Thought (NSPT) is a Belgrade-based quarterly magazine dealing with politics and policy studies. Founded in 1994 under the name *Srpska politička misao* (Serbian Political Thought), the magazine typically attracts conservative political scientists, philosophers, sociologists, psychologists and economists who weigh in on topical and sometimes controversial political questions. *Hourglass* is a radio program produced by a media house of the same name. It has been broadcast on radio *B92* since February 2, 2000, with Svetlana Vuković and Svetlana Lukić acting as both newscasters and editors. A collection of texts from the program was published in a book called *Hourglass FM*, while texts are published daily as an online journal on the *Hourglass* web site. According to their web page, *Hourglass* regularly attracts an audience of up to 400,000 listeners.[133] The program's motto is: "If you think everything's okay, forget it." It follows an extremely civic political line and is in favor of a complete break with Serbia's 1990s nationalist herit-

---

[132] "Tačka Razlaza" (The Point of Departure) was a debate which unfolded in *Vreme* magazine in 2002 between Other Serbia actors, in which the groups divided into hardliners and soft liberals.

[133] "About Us," Pescanik Series, Retrieved from http://pescanik.net/

age. Cooperation between *B92* and *Hourglass* ended on June 10, 2011, a good illustration of the former split between soft and hard-line liberals.

Within the dialogues analyzed in this book, I try to capture the game of finding true Serbian national identity that is played, not only by professional scholars or commentators, but also by a range of other players across the Serbian political spectrum. This is still a favorite pursuit among articulate right-wing and left-wing Serbians alike usually with the aim of some political points-scoring. One can observe the complete range of opinions, from the conservative desire for the resurrection of combative national pride, to arguments against joining the European Union increasingly coming from the far left of the political spectrum. On the political right, there are authors such as Siniša Kovačević and Vladimir Kecmanović arguing for a rejection of the culture of collective shame and for the embracing once more of the old nationalist Serbian identity. In the liberal middle, there are the LDP and various intellectuals associated with them, such as Nenad Prokić and late Jovan Ćirilov. This grouping also brings together Serbian scholars, and Anglo-American diplomats and other policy makers from the foreign embassies for measured deliberations on Serbian identity and the future. On the social democratic left, there is to be found the notorious writer Vladimir Arsenijević and *E-Novine's* journalist Petar Luković. Even among those articulate left-liberals who explicitly support European integration, there is often a diffuse sense of shame and collective unease at "being Serbian" (particularly after Srebrenica), as if to be Serbian is impliedly to be a nationalist. The specific political actors to which I pay particular attention include Djordje Vukadinović, director of NSPT, whose texts I prominently consider, and Slobodan Antonić, a sociology professor and a regular contributor to NSPT, who has published many articles and books about the Serbian elites in recent decades. His 2008 *The cultural war in Serbia: Essays on the culture of 'Other' Serbia– from Marko Vidojković to Radomir Konstantinović* is briefly touched upon in Chapters 2 and 3. Chapter 6 has a detailed analysis of a series of interviews carried out by Rade Ivković with distinguished writers and historians and published in NSPT in April 2012. Interviewees included young aspiring writer Vladimir Kecmanović, well-known historian Predrag Marković, the screenwriter and current presidential advisor Radoslav Pavlović, and well-known writer Siniša Kovačević. As this book emphasizes the relationship between domestic politics and discourses on Europe and identity, the "relevant actors" whose texts are systematically analyzed are those who have held both high societal positions and high positions within their political parties/groups. This means they were prominent in the media, publishing frequently on the subject of Europe and First and Other Serbia, as well as acting as advisors to the highest offices in the country, the President and Prime Minister. Such actors include Radoslav Pavlović, a screenwriter who as mentioned above is currently serving as a cultural advisor to President Tomislav Nikolić. I have also paid particular attention to texts produced by Vojislav Koštunica and *Dveri* spokesman Vladan Glišić, both of whom are prominent discursive actors of the post-Milošević period on themes of state and Church.

Koštunica was the last President of the Federal Republic of Yugoslavia, succeeding Slobodan Milošević and serving from 2000 to 2003. He also served two terms as Prime Minister of Serbia, from 2004 to 2007 and from 2007 to 2008. After the fall of Milošević in 2000, Koštunica's political orientations maintained continuity with the previous regime's rhetoric even in the transitional period: his political position can be described as that of a "moderate nationalist." Koštunica's texts have been chosen for analysis because he addresses themes including the "defense of Serbian national interests" and Europe. The first democratic government is, however, commonly identified primarily with the figure of Djindjic and, only secondly, with the figure of Koštunica. I have found the DSS's party manifesto and Koštunica's public speeches to be a rich resource of both official state discourse and the conservative DSS's discourse on identity and Europe.

Similarly, the Serbian *Dveri* Congress is a citizens' association and non-parliamentary political movement which bases its views on St Savism,[134] Serbian nationalism, Euro-skepticism and anti-globalism. Its main activities consist of publishing a magazine called *Dveri srpske*, which is the core of the movement, and organizing social and humani-

---

[134] St. Savist nationalism is a right-wing political ideology which represents a fusion of Serbian nationalism and Orthodox Christian clericalism.

tarian actions and political debates in Serbia, Republika Srpska, and Montenegro. It has been active since 2011 under the name Movement for the Life of Serbia. In 2009 *Dveri* expressed a desire to organize a "family walk" as a response to Belgrade Gay Pride. On March 24, 2009 the movement organized a commemorative gathering at Belgrade's Sava Centre dedicated to the victims of the 1999 NATO intervention. *Dveri* has also organized several round tables dedicated to topics such as agriculture, the Serbian economy and foreign policy. At a press conference held on February 10, 2011, *Dveri* announced that it was entering politics and would participate in the next parliamentary elections. I suggest that *Dveri*'s role in societal dialogue has become increasingly prominent over the last decade, and especially *Dveri*'s influence on structuring the terms of the debates on Europe. Some members are proponents of the St Sava variety of nationalism, of teaching creationism in schools, and of the "Greater Serbia" idea. Their role in the riots at the 2010 Belgrade Gay Pride Parade, and in the cancellation of the 2011 and 2012 parades, is of interest due to their vehement rejection of the rights of sexual minorities, which is seen as a European value, and of homosexuality which is seen as a foreign import.

The specific political and civil actors of Other Serbia to whom I pay special attention are those who frequently publish and are often cited. Given the emphasis of this work on the relationship between civil society groups and discourse on Europe and identity in the public sphere, the relevant actors from Other Serbia, whose texts are systematically analyzed here include those who have been prominent in the NGO sector, such as late Vojin Dimitrijević, Nataša Kandić and late Srdja Popović. Also included are those who hold high government positions, such as Vesna Pešić.[135] Other prominent Other Serbia actors in the public sphere given particular attention here include journalist Teofil Pančić as well as professors and public scholars Latinka Perović, Vesna Rakić-Vodinelić, Dubravka Stojanović, Lazar Stojanović, Nebojša Popov, late Olivera

---

[135] Pešić is a distinguished professor at Faculty of Philology in Belgrade and was a democracy activist during the 1990s. After 2000, she became an MP and Serbian ambassador to Mexico. She is one of the prominent names of 'Other' Serbia as she writes and speaks regularly in *Peščanik*.

Milosavljević, Vladimir Gligorov and late Ljubiša Rajić. As many people would identify Other Serbia with these prominent public figures, I consider their texts to be the principal subject matter in respect of which to carry out my exploration of the Other Serbia discourse on Europe and identity. My methods for data gathering follow Wodak's prescribed restrictions: first, the corpus gathered must be manageable; and, second, the main criteria must be the typicality[136] of the texts, the focus therefore being on content rather than quantity. I am interested most in those texts in which Europe or identity are the prevailing themes.

A final consideration concerning the texts is the manner in which they are organized. The First and Other Serbia division is invoked for several reasons. First, the state of public affairs in Serbia points quite clearly to this demarcation. The evidence suggests that agnostic or sitting-on-the-fence attitudes are rare, and that Europe and its policies have been fundamental to the way Serbia sees itself. However, here, a particular warning is required. The adoption of a pro- or anti-EU categorization has the danger of equating that categorization with a broad range of related positions precisely because what is meant by pro- or anti-EU is dangerously clouded. An anti-EU position, for instance, might indicate an anti-capitalist or anti-human rights stance or could perhaps indicate a more fundamental opposition to an ideological viewpoint dominant among European nation-states. As a result, it is quite common within the debates for actors to adopt a pro-Europe position when Europe is seen to represent structure, organization and financial stability, while being anti-Europe where Europe is considered in its historical and cultural sense. Also, the pro/anti dichotomy is an ideal type, which synthesizes many viewpoints into a coherent whole. Finally, the categorizations First and Other Serbia are undeniably simplifications. As such, this conceptual divide might require to eventually become softer in order to produce a less rigid formulation of how identity becomes configured.

---

[136] Typicality refers to the representative meaning of the text. The texts chosen have all the main attributes which other texts coming later also had, just in a summarized form.

Serbian national identities

In order to assess how Serbian national identity has been configured in the aftermath of the dissolution of Yugoslavia, it is worth briefly recapitulating some of the major themes that arise in the debates. Suffice it to say, the list is by no means exhaustive. My research is mainly concerned with the nature of perceptions and how the elite imagine their country. Is Serbia seen as being humiliated after four lost wars or dignified in loss? Do ordinary members of the Serbian population understand themselves as belonging to a Serbian nation? What is Yugoslavia to the Serbs? And, finally, who are "the Others" in opposition to which the Serbian nation defines the Self? There follows, coupled with these themes, a particular investigation of Yugoslav cultural and political heritage. Two points are worth making at this juncture. First, while historical discourse on Serbia and Europe, whether arising from Chetnik or communist quarters or otherwise, are deeply enmeshed within the national psyche, the images of Serbianness produced have not always remained static. Although the ideas of "First" and "Other" Serbia recur frequently, and consequently are historically dominant, they have infrequently been molded into other configurations including "Third"[137] Serbia. Second, this book highlights the viewpoint from which Serbian elites draw their ideas and the manner in which they construct their arguments. I support the view that spokespeople should, to the extent possible, articulate the broader societal and historical meaning within their arguments in order for their message to resonate more with the wider public. These contested views of Serbian identity do not, therefore, exist in a political vacuum, but in an active dialogue between the various actors and their audience.

---

[137] "Third Serbia" was an initiative that sought to bridge the existing identity conflict in the 1990s. However, after 2000, it became a synonym for those segments of First Serbia which embraced the "good" nationalism. In 2012, a "Third Serbia" political party was established by exiled members of Dveri.

Interpreting history

How far does the past identity of the Serbs determine who Serbs are now? Political and cultural elites do not devise their arguments from scratch but instead make references to already deeply entrenched and historically rich imagery, myths, prejudices and stories. This is particularly so in the case of Serbia. The near-obsession with defining a Serbian national identity is by no means a new fashion. Since the Serbian Kingdom of the Middle Ages, a variety of Serbian literati have been deeply engaged with the mission of identifying what it is to be Serbian. This pursuit has continued, more or less unabated, throughout the Ottoman invasion, the "First" and "Second" Serbian uprisings and independence from the Turks, the Balkan wars, the creation of Yugoslavia, the communist revolution and the Second World War, socialism, Tito, the Yugoslav wars, the refugee crises, the resurgence of Orthodox Christianity, Milošević's semi-authoritarianism, the democratic revolution, and Aleksandar Vučić's democracy. A relatively wide range of answers has been offered in response to this enquiry from "Načertanije" in 1844 to the SANU Memorandum in 1986 and beyond. Serbian nationalist ideology, and its version of Serbian national identity, provokes intensely problematic questions about Serbian national identity after Milošević. As we shall see, both the question of how Serbia should deal with its past and the process of defining national identity became almost an obsession in Serbia at two distinct times, the first being immediately prior to the dissolution of Yugoslavia in the 1980s and the second being after the regime change in 2000 and Milošević's flight to the Hague, at which time the old obsession recurred with renewed intensity. In this book I place a narrowly focused analysis of these debates into broader perspective, locating the unique case of the fractured Serbian identities within the context of general theoretical interpretations of national identity construction. When Serbian nationalism was on the rise in the late 1980s, Koča Popović, the former Yugoslav minister for foreign affairs, a communist with aristocratic pedigree, surrealist poet and a military officer, shared his opinion about Milošević in his *Diaries*:

> When he spoke about Milošević he called him a 'Chetnik in new guise,' although he was neither a Chetnik nor a Bolshevik. Koča said: "Rabble, scum, and waste of humanity stood up to rebuild Dusan's empire. The Serbs only turn against those that try to help them smarten up, but they support ecstatically anyone who downgrades them and makes them stupider and unhappier. It is a sad fact that in terms of culture and civilizational values the Serbs have stayed at the level they were at a hundred years ago. It is wrong to think that the Serbs are in conflict with the rest of the world. They are in conflict with themselves as they return to wearing peasant's sajkaca and opanak that their fathers and grandfathers barely got out of. I was and I remain a Serb, but I am not a sick and shallow bigger-than-thou Serb. People like that have betrayed and dishonored the Serbian people and have made a mockery out if its glorious history."[138]

One thing is sure - the nationalist-oriented parties turned their attention to the less-educated, more rural segments of the population, and indeed it has been noted that the wars of the 1990s were as much between the country and the city as they were between different ethnic and national groups.[139] In the complex game of identity politics during the dissolution of Yugoslavia, all sides used historical and class divisions for their political ends, and yet history itself came to play a key political role in the conflicts of the 1990s. After the unexpected and violent conflict during the collapse of Yugoslavia, came the rapid creation of new states, and an experimental transition from socialist dictatorship to capitalist democracy. Enduring feelings of fraternity, nostalgia and sadness at lost unity, in respect of former Yugoslavia, posed serious problems to identity construction in Serbia, and in other former Yugoslav republics such as Macedonia and Montenegro. On the extremist fringes, in the aftermath of the Milošević regime, there was a resurgent of right-wing racism and ethnic hatred expressed in violence against human rights activist, gay activists, Roma and other ethnic minorities, and other groups who at the relevant time were labelled as "Others."

This study must, of course, consider the question of how Serbian national pride or patriotism can endure, and do so in an acceptable form, in light of Srebrenica and the massacres of the Yugoslav war. The definition of Serbian national identity is central to much of Serbian for-

---

[138] Dušan Čkrebić, "The Secret of Koča Popović," in *Vreme* (No. 1117, May 31, 2012).

[139] See Andrew Baruch Wachtel, *Making a Nation, Breaking a Nation: Literature and Cultural Politics in Yugoslavia*, Stanford, (CA: Stanford University Press, 1998), p. 112. Also see Bogdan Bogdanović, "Murder of the City" *The New York Review of Books*, (May 27, 1993).

eign policy and public debate over at least the last two decades. In a broader context, Serbia can be said to have, since 1945, been a divided nation in which partisans and nationalists have been continuously locked in debates over its history and identity. Another significant factor is the constant presence of the two world superpowers, the US and the Russian Federation, and their unfinished Cold War, within the Serbian mind-set. The legacy of Yugoslav identity is also poignant. The rest of Europe has always seen Yugoslavia as part of the Eastern bloc, but urban Yugoslavs never understood themselves in that way.[140] We will see how the political definitions of identity were never in line with personal subjective definitions; but yet, these political identities created some sense of a common national identity, a sense of belonging together in Yugoslavia.

Upon his departure, Milošević definitely left two behind distinct conceptions of Serbia. Both of these conceptions of Serbia sought to define new partial identities—with pro-left or pro-right inclinations—in different reinterpretations of designated aspects of the common past. The constant reinterpretation of the Yugoslav times and the so-called red crimes (including some topics on which there is little available research) has become an essential and often hotly contested element of the present. For instance, the first exhibition about the victims of the communist regime in the aftermath of the Second World War, "In the Name of the People," which opened in 2014, tackled the usual taboo themes: the surveillance of suspected "enemies of the people," the execution of political prisoners, the Naked Island and other camps, nationalization of agricultural land, and so on. The exhibition was staged in the Museum of Yugoslav History and prompted a long discussion about the so-called red crimes.

---

[140] One of my interviewees, shocked at my suggestion that Serbia be placed in the East, argued "Belgrade was never Eastern Europe."

Yugoslavia and Serbia

In Yugoslavia,[141] by contrast, after accepting a modern version of communism, a new notion of national identity defined in *class* terms was propagated: the SFRY became officially the state of workers and peasants, and sought to develop a specifically Yugoslav national identity which was premised on there being numerous Yugoslav nations and therefore premised on *brotherhood and unity*. Also, the SFRY officially propagated a sense of pride in being truly a land of the partisans and an anti-fascist state. The new occupying power, the communists, and its political allies, brought a clear political message which was imposed on the populace, willing or unwilling. Partisan heroes were celebrated in street names and displayed in statues. The Fascists, the Germans, and the partisan's heroic struggle against them, were to be portrayed in cinema, and the sites of historic battles, for instance the Battle of Sutjeska in 1943, became places of pilgrimage. There are some twists and turns in this otherwise fairly simple story. Some heroes fell from grace, as was the case with Stalin in 1948. The 1948 split with Stalin pushed Yugoslavia out of the Soviet orbit and, as Baruch Wachtel notes, the new overarching themes of Serbian identity which were formed, including the idea of Yugoslavia as a mediator between East and West, provided an even better model for a unique, supranational and unified Yugoslav culture.[142] Still, in the years which followed, many from among the old partisan leadership adopted this new model, for instance, Koča Popović and Milovan Djilas. Former concentration camps, such as Staro Sajmište, were often not turned into historic monuments but instead into blocks of flats. Baruch Wachtel argues that Yugoslav supranational culture did form some kind of communal identification, but in his view, the breakup of Yugoslavia sprang from the gradual destruction of the concept of a Yugoslav nation.[143] The history of Yugoslavia was told in the beginning

---

[141] To pursue this question further would require a separate chapter, or even a whole book. As this might not be of interest to those readers eager to resume their pursuit of the collective Serbian identity after Milošević, I will make do with the summary set out in this section.

[142] See Andrew Baruch Wachtel, *Making a Nation, Breaking a Nation: Literature and Cultural Politics in Yugoslavia*, (Stanford, CA: Stanford University Press, 1998), p. 123.

[143] Ibid. p. 11.

in terms of an idealized story of modernization, growth and betterment, but then naturally there were also ever-present simplified themes of villains and heroes. During the rise of nationalism in the 1980s, a gradual, but complete, change in the symbolism and meaning attached to particular villains and heroes in Yugoslavia took place over time, coinciding with changing pro-nationalist political interests. Those that were considered to be heroes during Yugoslav times, including the nationalist ones, were castigated as the nobodies of history. The street signs were changed once more. Currently, new heroes are unexpectedly resurrected, recently examples of which include the Roman Emperor Constantine, who was born on the territory of Serbia, and Prince Petar Karadjordjević.

I see the processes of Americanization and Sovietization of Yugoslav culture, and current Serbian culture, as worthy of study but consider that these have not to date been the subject of sufficient research, with the exception of Vučetić's research.[144] Some fervent reactions against the politics of the US can be observed yet, undeniably, the further Americanization of Serbian culture continues. The cultural and political disdain[145] of the US come from most diverse quarters: on the one hand, as might be expected, groups from the far left of the political spectrum to the more lenient center-left protectors of "our freedoms," such as *Anonymous* which is quite strong in Serbia; on the other, those of older generations who espouse a relatively traditional nationalistic stance. Yet, the former Yugoslav republic was, in many respects, a thoroughly Americanized society, reflected in the cosmopolitan spirit of its world-traveling red bourgeois professional elites, and their good command of English language. The Yugoslav state constituted a paradox in that it was thoroughly Americanized in terms of culture while at the same time its anti-Americanism was reflected in protests against US government policy, as was seen in 1968, when massive students protests were hap-

---

[144] See Radina Vučetić, *Coca-Cola Socialism: The Americanization of Yugoslav Popular Culture in the 1960s*, Belgrade: Sluzbeni Glasnik (2012).

[145] Serbia and Pakistan share first place as countries have the most negative opinion of the US, according to a 2009 Medium Gallup poll. Some 53 percent of those polled had a positive opinion of Russia, while 61 percent thought negatively of the US. See "Strongest anti-American Sentiment in Serbia, Pakistan," in *B92 News* (July 7, 2009).

pening in Belgrade as well as in Berlin and Berkeley. However, there was more to this resistance to the influence of American culture than just a protest against government policy.

The importance of Western culture, principally through music, film and television in Yugoslavia should be carefully qualified. According to Vučetić, the Yugoslav "imagined community" which was sustained by the influences of Western music, film and culture was very much Western orientated, in comparison to other Central and Eastern European socialist countries.[146] People enjoyed dubbed Hollywood movies in great numbers, preferring these to French and Italian cinema, the Yugoslav rock music scene of the 1970s and 1980s was influenced by broader Western cultural development and, in general, people had little interest in the happenings in the East. It is clear from this perspective, that Yugoslav culture was rather more Americanized than Sovietized. Although it might sound a little paradoxical, the Americanization of Yugoslav culture from the early 1960s onwards was, in truth, a continuation of a pre-existing, and more radical, albeit gradual, break with the Eastern European political project which could be said to have begun in the 1950s. Also, in terms of popular culture, from the films of the 1950s and 1960s, to 1988 when the first McDonalds restaurant in the whole of Central and Eastern Europe opened in Belgrade, and beyond, the pervasive impact of American culture cannot be overlooked. There was a much lesser degree of genuine Sovietization of the Yugoslav or Serbian culture than that which was evident in Bulgaria or Poland for example. There has, however, for a long time been significant interaction between Serbian and Soviet culture in the arts and Serbian pupils learn Russian as their second language in schools. Yet, Serbia's location in South-Eastern Europe has always placed it geographically far from the epicenter of Russian cultural influence. It may be surprising, therefore, that Russia is positioned as the first friendly Other in the anti-European debates. Currently, the Russian Federation is recognized as having historical ties with Serbia based on economic and energy collaboration, as well as certain cultural and religious commonalities and a similar language. This

---

[146] See Radina Vučetić, *Coca-Cola Socialism: The Americanization of Yugoslav Popular Culture in the 1960s*, Belgrade: Sluzbeni Glasnik (2012).

articulation also features against the background of Russia as a rising power. That is, Russia is seen not as a peripheral economy but as being in the process of reaffirming itself globally. The Serbian Self, in contrast to the Yugoslav Self, can therefore be seen as part of the pan-Slavic network that seeks to build strong relations with the Russian Other. Such relations, as already mentioned, build on historically defined notions of mutual cooperation and kinship. In this sense, Serbian national identity can be configured as extra-European and Eurasian because these special relations exemplify a symbolic status, not based on geography. One overriding formulation of identity effectively locates Serbia as the bridge between Europe and Russia, owing largely to the fact that it retains elements of both. The anti-European groups frequently perceive pro-Europeans as being stuck within a restricted mentality due to their refusal to recognize that Russia remains a significant political, cultural and economic force in the wider Non-Aligned world: a world that Yugoslavia helped to shape. Current narratives proposing a third way build upon the Yugoslav Cold War years, when the Yugoslav republic was one of the co-founders of the Non-Aligned Movement, and position the future of Serbia to be "in-between" East and West, ideologically aligned to neither.

In terms of the everyday lives of ordinary people in Serbia, the echoes of life in socialist Yugoslavia are still visible, predominantly in social contexts. Life in socialist Yugoslavia was organized on the basis of collectivity which fostered, purposively of course, the sense of collective identity. This started almost at birth, as mothers in SFRY could go straight back to work due to the comprehensive childcare system. Also, in primary and secondary schools, pupils were encouraged to repeat lessons by heart, rather than to question, which encouraged conformity. There were many youth organizations, and military service was obligatory and highly regarded. This collectivity, coupled with guaranteed jobs without fear of unemployment, resulted in an absence of individual competitiveness in the transitional period. The Yugoslav regime could perhaps rightly be said to have been a repressive regime, but that cannot be said of Yugoslav society. The myth of the "repressed society" is difficult to prove where the texture of the social experience was more multifaceted. Within the middle classes, individualistic lifestyles became the prevailing norm. University diplomas and social mobility were seen as important signs of achievement. Comparing this with the situation in contemporary Serbia, one can notice widespread disappointment that this is not the case any more, as university diplomas no longer have the meaning and value which they once had and the more successful and wealthy strata of society are seen as having got there "by other means." It would be ridiculous to overgeneralize, of course, but it is significant to make the general point that, in Yugoslav times, the roles which people played, and their aspirations, were deeply affected by the character of Yugoslav society, and that influence continues to be felt today, albeit to a lesser extent.

When does the past change into history and endure only in the history schoolbooks? Fulbrook suggests, by way of an answer, when "it is no longer imbued with innumerable contemporary sensitivities, pieties, taboos—when it is no longer of vital contemporary significance."[147] In Serbia, regarding both its recent and distant past, this has not yet come about. Fulbrook explains that "if the nation is unable to tell a collectively acceptable story about its own past, that nation has serious problems with developing a stable collective identity in the present that does not demand constant soul-searching and repeated attempts at redefinition."[148] It is clear that there never was just one single "collective memory," one generally accepted dialogue about the past, within the Serbian public sphere. Differences, grounded in part in differences of class, generation and gender, but particularly in differences of political ideology, proliferate and flourish. Such differences are often grounded in experience, and are almost invariably more striking than the similarities. Former anti-nationalist activists, victims of the regime and their relatives, or young liberals, on the one hand, and their former political enemies, the vigorous nationalists, on the other, find it hard to inhabit the same mental terrain. There is a dramatic generational contrast between those who were adults during the dissolution of Yugoslavia and

---

[147] Mary Fulbrook, *German National Identity after the Holocaust*, Cambridge: Polity Press (2007), p. 141.
[148] Ibid.

those who were born or came into maturity in the very different political climate of the 2000s. At first, the young people appeared to have little or no sense or knowledge about the facts concerning the Yugoslav conflicts. There is a sense of detachment and of distance, plus the Yugoslav past is frequently presented through a nostalgic lens, with the result that it seems to have nothing to do with them, particularly if they were not alive at the time. Such emotional detachment represents a significant failure of personal engagement, of any desire to know and understand what actually happened. Additionally, the young people's knowledge about the conflicts appears to be more deeply influenced by the stories which they were told in their families than by the official picture presented by historical textbooks or media reporting. Obradović-Wochnik's book tackles this storytelling side of the Yugoslav conflicts, and characterizes these personal reflections and interpersonal interactions in everyday life as acts of resistance to the dominant Western narrative.[149] She also points out the fact that history is not over yet, at least not for most Serbs, who continue to speak of the past as if it were still occurring.[150] It has been suggested numerous times that in order to grow a real historical awareness, beyond that which can be mended together from textbooks and from family stories, one must travel. Sadly, many Serbs do not take the opportunity to travel, whether within the former Yugoslavia or to Kosovo or to other sites relevant to the Yugoslav conflicts, or further afield, with the exception of a majority of Serbs who holiday in Greece.[151] In fact, around 75 percent of Serbs never visited Kosovo. One can imagine the extent to which this absence of any physical encounter with the places that are so relevant to the events which shaped the nation's recent past could obstruct the processing the past in both the individual and popular perceptions.

---

[149] Jelena Obradović Wochnik, *Ethnic Conflict and War Crimes in the Balkans: The Narratives of Denial in Post-conflict Serbia*, London: International library of war studies, IB Tauris (2013), p. 9.

[150] Ibid., p. 224.

[151] Only 15 percent of Serbs hold passports.

Chapter 2:
Brief Historical Context (1987–2012)

Serbia in the 1990s is a particularly good example of the uneasy dynamics between national identity and authoritarianism, and before moving on to detailed empirical analysis, it is necessary to develop an understanding of contemporary Serbian political space and outline a chronology of the crucial events.[152] First, there is an overview of authoritarian rule in Serbia during the nineties including the protests of 1996–97. This is followed by an examination of the factors which brought about the "democratic revolution," including the civic youth movement *Otpor* and the creation of civil society foundations after 2000. Finally, this section provides a brief analysis of post-Milošević politics, focusing on the principal challenges to further democratization taking place in Serbian society. Consequently, the overall inquiry sets up the conceptual framework for understanding the notions of "First" and "Other Serbia" and their evolution over the last two decades. Here, I outline the main organizations, events and social actors involved, and the consequent rifts dividing First and Other Serbia into four or more different factions. Such context is a prerequisite for grasping the impact of First and Other Serbia societal and cultural divisions and classifications.

The 1990s: the nationalist-authoritarian regime

Serbia exhibits many characteristics, which distinguish it from the other countries of Southeast Europe and the Western Balkans. The two distinct characteristics relevant to our analysis are the identity friction between "First" and "Other" Serbia actors and the specificity of the nationalist

---

[152] The necessary historical chronology of the event that lead to the Yugoslav conflicts are recognizable to many, and I would suggest that any readers familiar with the Yugoslav dissolution is advized to omit this part. Others can easily refer to it while progressing through the manuscript if necessary.

ideology of the Milošević regime. This section is fully dedicated to understanding how this identity friction and nationalism are reproduced in the discourses of the liberal and nationalistic intelligentsia. It is important to emphasize that the main discursive strategy within the countries of the Eastern block after the fall of the Berlin wall was that of the "return to Europe."[153] However, I find that this famous phrase coined by Havel cannot be applied to the Serbian case, as its pre-Second World War democratic practices were never too definite.[154] In other words, the political progression which unfolded in Serbia had little similarity to other Eastern European states as these processes departed from the easy route from communism to democratization. Thomas notes that although the Yugoslav socialist regime was replaced with a semi-authoritarian system during the Milošević regime, this shift away from one-party totalitarianism to pluralism was not fully realized during the 1990s.[155] The term coined by Eric Gordy fully describes the Milošević regime: *nationalist-authoritarian,* where he refers to a set of circumstances in which an authoritarian regime seeks to justify its continuation in power by means of nationalism.[156] The reason for using this explanation is that this term is more precise than any others (including *nationalist*) and it describes all different modalities of post-communism in Serbia.

In fact, political processes in Serbia under Milošević deserve a reasonable amount of attention, as the social milieu created during the 1990s influenced the segmentation of deeper societal divisions. Having

---

[153] Václav Havel, Czech playwright and President, coined the phrase *Return to Europe* which gained common currency among the majority of politicians in Central European States.

[154] According to some figures, in the course of the 200 years from 1800 to 2000 Serbia has spent only about thirty years, or 15 percent of the time, as a democracy. The Parliamentary Monarchy lasted a total of twenty-six years and eight months (January 1889–April 1893; June 1903–October 1915; December 1918–January 1929). The Parliamentary democratic republic has lasted since October 2000. Altogether, Serbia had had forty years of democracy by 2014. See Timothy Edmunds, "Adapting to Democracy: Reflections on 'transition' in Serbia and the Western Balkans" in *Western Balkan Security Observer*, No 7/8. (October 2007).

[155] Robert Thomas, *Serbia under Milošević: The Politics of Serbia in the 1990s* (London: Hurst, 1999), p. 3.

[156] See Eric Gordy, *The Culture of Power in Serbia: Nationalism and the Destruction of Alternatives* (Park, PA: The Pennsylvania University Press, 1999), p. 8.

said this, the principal difficulty which arises when dealing with Milošević is the fact that his regime was a semi-authoritarian dictatorship, as Ostojić notes, that still left certain segments of society unrestrained and gave an impression of democratic accountability as elections were regularly held.[157] Peculiarly, Milošević frequently used nationalist discourse to strengthen his position, while on the other hand his absolute power consistently derived its legitimacy from the electoral process.[158] Elections throughout the 1990s had a degree of legitimacy sufficient to allow pro-democratic forces some room for maneuver and therefore provide just an impression of democracy. This impression consisted of a real presence of civil initiatives, and also the existence of independent media, such as B92 and Studio B, but while different pro-democratic political parties competed at the elections, yet real space for democratic competition was non-existent.

Serbia's road to war: misuse of political symbolism

Milošević rose to power in 1987 by taking control of the Serbian Communist Party. From the mid-1980s in former Yugoslavia, as Dragović-Soso notes, Serbia's intellectual opposition, including some critical intellectuals, transferred the focus of its political activism from the struggle for freedom of expression to the so-called Kosovo question.[159] Milošević's discourses constantly drew on Serbian national grievances, and by 1990 Serbia experienced a transition away from communism and toward nationalist authoritarianism. Milošević abolished the independence given to the autonomous provinces by the 1974 constitution and shifted the focus to the Serbs in Bosnia and Croatia by promoting their right to self-determination.[160] The 1981 riots in Kosovo set the foundation

---

[157] Mladen Ostojić, *Between Justice and Stability: The Politics of War Crimes Prosecutions in Post-Milošević Serbia* (Farnham, UK and Burlington, VT: Ashgate, 2014) p. 58.

[158] Eric Gordy, *The Culture of Power in Serbia: Nationalism and the Destruction of Alternatives* (University Park, PA: The Pennsylvania University Press, 1999), p. 26.

[159] Jasna Dragović-Soso, *"Saviours of the Nation": Serbia's Intellectual Opposition and the Revival of Nationalism* (London: Hurst and Montreal, McGill-Queen's University Press, 2002), p. 115.

[160] Lenard J. Cohen, *Serpent in the Bosom: The Rise and Fall of Slobodan Milošević* (Boulder, CO: Westview Press, 2001), p. 123.

for the province to represent a cause which allowed the ruling regime to adopt the role of guardian of both universal and national values.

However, Dragović-Soso suggests that the way the intellectual opposition came to define the Kosovo question turned it away from its liberal, universalist aspirations toward a more narrow nationalist agenda.[161] The constitutional reform of the 1970s provoked considerable resentment in the subsequent decades, especially on the Serbian side, as Kosovo[162] was generally perceived as the "cradle" of Serbian culture. In other words, Milošević relied heavily on the already established nationalistic tendencies within the elites and the population in general.[163] Structurally, the populations were mobilized and homogenized by nationalism into a pre-political movement, especially during the anti-bureaucratic revolution.[164] Milošević frequently used nationalism, initially for his political campaign in order to get elected, but more importantly this practice of "nationalist mobilization" continued throughout the 1990s as a way of keeping Serbian society in a state of permanent crisis.[165]

Milošević's solution to the "national question" revealed itself as essentially undemocratic and repressive and clearly went against the

---

[161] Jasna Dragović-Soso, *"Saviours of the Nation": Serbia's Intellectual Opposition and the Revival of Nationalism* (London: Hurst and Montreal, McGill-Queen's University Press, 2002), p. 115.

[162] Kosovo province has hundreds of sites which Serbs consider to be so culturally or historically important that they lie at the heart of their national identity. These include the battlefield of Kosovo Polje—the site of their 1389 defeat at the hands of the advancing Ottoman Turks—and religious sites in Peć, Gračanica and Dečani, the location of Serbia's largest monastic church. In general, the Serb populations are concentrated to the north and on the eastern border. See Robert Marquand, "Why Kosovo is Central to Serb National Epic," in *The Christian Science Monitor* (October 12, 2007).

[163] Eric Gordy, *The Culture of Power in Serbia: Nationalism and the Destruction of Alternatives* (University Park, PA: The Pennsylvania University Press, 1999), p. 34.

[164] The term anti-bureaucratic revolution relates to a series of rallies, called "Rallies of Truth," in which Milošević's supporters successfully overthrew the local governments of the autonomous provinces of Vojvodina and Kosovo, as well as the republic of Montenegro, and replaced them with allies of Milošević. For further developments in the social movements organized by Milošević, see Nebojša Vladisavljević, *Serbia's Anti-bureaucratic Revolution: Milošević, the Fall of Communism and Nationalist Mobilization* (Basingstoke; New York: Palgrave Macmillan, 2008).

[165] Robert Thomas, *Serbia under Milošević: The Politics of Serbia in the 1990s* (London: Hurst, 1999), p. 5.

democratic orientation proclaimed by the critical intelligentsia in 1990.[166] However, after 1991 longstanding opponents of the regime started to regard him as a historic leader because he had deliberately and forcefully returned to the Serbs their national dignity. An important part of his new agenda was the reconstitution of the dominant state discourses of the previous forty-seven years of "Yugoslav nationality," in which the main ideological repertoire was cooperation and consanguinity between the peoples of the Balkans. The overwhelming importance given to political symbols in daily politics made it impossible for any true democratic reforms to take hold in Serbia, and enabled Milošević to appeal to the Serbian populace through symbols and myths which were already heavily ingrained in society.[167] As Thomas argues, the "dominance of symbolism over politics" was a major factor in the failure to create a legitimate democratic system in Serbia after the transition from communist rule.[168] In a similar key, Bowman finds that following this course Milošević, the regime-prone elite and even his opponents such as the Serbian Renewal Movement (SPO) brought into existence the discursive project of transforming the other nations into enemies and created new discourses on ethnic antagonism.[169]

In fact, since the early 1990s, as Pešić notes, a particular form of *ressentiment* nationalism emerged in the shape of primordial identity, and was seen across former Yugoslavia presenting a factor of aggression.[170] She further argues that a policy based on such an identity can be seen as psychological preparation for war.[171] According to Bowman, this discur-

---

[166] Jasna Dragović-Soso, *"Saviours of the Nation": Serbia's Intellectual Opposition and the Revival of Nationalism* (London: Hurst and Montreal, McGill-Queen's University Press, 2002), p. 115. p. 1/2.

[167] For the influence of political symbolism in Serbia see Ivan Čolović, *Bordel ratnika: folklor, politika i rat (The Bordello of the Warriors: Folklore, Politics and War)* (Belgrade: Slovograf, 2000); Ivan Čolović, *The Politics of Identity in Serbia* (NYU Press, 2002).

[168] Thomas Robert, *Serbia under Milošević: The Politics of Serbia in the 1990s* (London: Hurst, 1999), p. 22.

[169] Glen Bowman, "Xenophobia, Fantasy and the Nation: The Logic of Ethnic Violence in Former Yugoslavia," in Victoria A. Goddard, Josep R. Llobera and Cris Shore, eds., *Anthropology of Europe: Identity and Boundaries in Conflict,* (London: Berg, 2004), p. 152.

[170] Vesna Pešić, "Serbian Nationalism and the Origins of the Yugoslav Crisis," Peaceworks No. 8. (United States Institute for Peace, 1996). p. 36.

[171] Ibid., p. 36.

sive shift was effectively allowing muted memories of the Second World War, such as the concentration camp at Jasenovac, to become the central points of new definitions of identities.[172] Others point out that the central element of Milošević's use of political symbols was his own role as a strong leader of a "national crusade."[173] More importantly, the rhetoric he utilized during his ascent to power was widely propagated by the state media, which was fully in Milošević's control by the end of 1990. The further exploration of this First Serbia rhetoric follows in the next chapter. Both Milošević's rise to power and the path to war were made easier by the takeover of the daily newspaper *Politika*,[174] the weekly magazine *NIN*, and the national broadcasting service *Radio Television of Serbia (RTS)*. Various newspapers were the key arenas for public sphere participation and helped create and maintain the First Serbia vocabulary. Although independent newspapers, television and radio stations connected to Other Serbia emerged following a brief wave of pluralism in 1990, most were rarely available outside Belgrade. Maintaining restraint over sources of information was a key element of the regime's plan of action for staying in power.

The full process of Yugoslavia's disintegration started with Slovenia's declaration of independence in June 1991, followed by Croatia. Macedonia voted for independence the same September, Bosnia did so on March 3, 1992, and the dissolution culminated with the foundation by

---

[172] Glen Bowman, "Xenophobia, Fantasy and the Nation: The Logic of Ethnic Violence in Former Yugoslavia," in Victoria A. Goddard, Josep R. Llobera and Cris Shore, eds., *Anthropology of Europe: Identity and Boundaries in Conflict*, (London: Berg, 2004), p. 152.

[173] In this sense, Milošević was tapping into a long Balkan tradition of strong, patriarchal leaders, which accorded both with communist "power relations" and South Slav folk traditions. For further examination of this see, Nebojša Popov, ed., *The Road to War in Serbia* (Central European University Press, 2000); and Vesna Pešić, "Serbian Nationalism and the Origins of the Yugoslav Crisis," Peaceworks No. 8. (United States Institute for Peace, 1996), p. 36.

[174] *Politika* (Politics) the government-controlled daily, is the oldest and most respected newspaper in Belgrade. As the "respectable" regime paper, its content is usually light on propaganda. On the other hand, the paper did take on a more openly propagandistic character during the period of war and the time leading up to it. For detailed analysis of the newspapers in Serbia please see Eric Gordy, *The Culture of Power in Serbia: Nationalism and the Destruction of Alternatives* (University Park, PA: The Pennsylvania University Press, 1999); and Pål Kolstø (ed.), *Media Discourse* and the Yugoslav Conflicts: Representation of the Self and Other (Farnham, UK: Ashgate, 2009).

Serbia and Montenegro of the Federal Republic of Yugoslavia in April 1992. Different causes for dissolution of Yugoslavia have been well documented in existing research.[175] Although the army under Serbian command and staffed by Serbian volunteers took part in the conflict in Bosnia and Croatia, official institutions and the regime continually denied any official involvement. Still, Milošević's role in the 1995 Dayton peace agreement, in which he played the role of "factor of stability" in the Balkans, did not come as a surprise. This epithet was coined by Western observers and significantly contributed to the Socialist Party of Serbia's (SPS) peacekeeping discourse after the agreement. Bieber suggests that, at that point Western diplomats genuinely saw Milošević as the only legitimate factor of peace, as the pro-democratic opposition remained deeply fragmented and was unable to unite.[176]

The distinct characteristic, which is relevant to the analysis here, is the fact that two different public discourses started to emerge: the dominant "First" Serbia and the subordinate, "Other" Serbia. Observers took notice of the fact that the ethnic Serbian population was increasingly divided in terms of their views toward Serbian involvement in the war in Croatia and Bosnia, mostly along the lines of whether they were supporters or opponents of the regime.[177] However, the political and ideological differences between those taking nationalist and anti-nationalist positions are not necessarily only connected with the pursuit of different policies. They also arise from different political traditions or cultures. One needs to understand these differences as consequences of the fact that the Milošević regime was constituted as both a continuation of, and a departure from, the old communist regime.[178] From Gordy's viewpoint,

---

[175] For a detailed political, economic and social analysis of the disintegration of the Yugoslav space, see Dejan Jović, *Yugoslavia: the State that Withered Away*. (Central European Press, 2008); See Lenard J. Cohen and Jasna Dragović Soso, *Collapse in South-Eastern Europe: New Perspectives on Yugoslavia's Disintegration*, (West Lafayette, IN: Purdue University Press, 2008).

[176] See Florian Bieber, "The Serbian Opposition and Civil Society: Roots of the Delayed Transition in Serbia," *International Journal of Politics, Culture and Society*, 16 (2003), 73–90, p. 75.

[177] Ibid., p. 76.

[178] Eric Gordy, *The Culture of Power in Serbia: Nationalism and the Destruction of Alternatives* (University Park, PA: The Pennsylvania University Press, 1999), p. 8.

this is closely related to the fact that the regime succeeded, through appropriating the discourse on national unity, in briefly uniting both sides of the present cultural pro-nationalist and pro-liberal schism.[179] Yet, Milošević offered a strong, state-sponsored discourse of unity and a radically different understanding of history and vision of the nation, and in this way the First and Other Serbia were briefly eradicated. On the other hand, Naumović points out that these political divisions, like that between the pro-Milošević and anti-Milošević camps, which in his view did not overlap completely with the division between the "two Serbias" in the sense that some of those belonging to the First Serbia were also vehemently against Milošević,[180] are historically rooted in divisions like those between Serbianism and Yugoslavism, monarchism and republicanism, Chetniks and Partisans, or Orthodox culture and secularist culture.[181] Therefore, constant disagreements over some of the themes around which the initial two Serbias were constituted at times provoked the construction of other conceptions of Serbia and their inclusion into the conflictual nexus, such as the conception of a Third Serbia.[182] In the aftermath of these events, it was clear that the Serbian public sphere was made, as Naumović notes, even more complex by practices that brought about the radicalization of the public and its further fragmentation into bitterly opposed segments.[183]

---

[179] Ibid., p 14

[180] The segments of "First" Serbia Naumović mentions are those who would be against his communist background, such as the Monarchists, the anti-communist nationalists, some members of the Serbian Diaspora and the Serbian Renewal Movement and its leader Vuk Drašković. Also, certain pro-democratic nationalists such as Slobodan Antonić, whose texts are analyzed in Chapters 5 and 6. I argue that the great part of post-2000 "First" Serbia actually metamorphosed from liberal-nationalist segments of the elites.

[181] Slobodan Naumović, 'On 'Us' and 'Them': Understanding the Historical Bases and Political Uses of Popular Narratives on Serbian Disunity'. *CAS Sofia Working Paper Series*, issue: 1 (2007) 19.

[182] "Third Serbia" was an initiative that would bridge the existing identity conflict in the 1990s. However, after 2000, it became a synonym for those segments of 'First' Serbia which embraced the "good" nationalism.

[183] Slobodan Naumović, "On 'Us' and 'Them': Understanding the Historical Bases and Political Uses of Popular Narratives on Serbian Disunity." *CAS Sofia Working Paper Series*, issue 1 (2007) 19.

In this respect, by applying patriotic rhetoric the regime in fact sidelined any criticism and by applying nationalist propaganda in the media it substantially shaped public opinion. Milošević's speeches were riddled with references to external enemies plotting against the country, including the West in general, though considerable emphasis was placed on "traitors" inside the country who we would characterize as affiliates of Other Serbia. These were direct attacks against parts of the society holding anti-nationalist positions.[184] Serious attempts by the opposition to bring about liberalization of the media either through protest or in other ways were ignored or suppressed by use of force. Ramet argues that the government maintained its control over symbolic instruments of power, for instance by influencing certain nationalist intellectuals involved in the production of traditional and communist myths and the Serbian Orthodox Church, and over concrete levers of power such as the economic infrastructure, the army and the regular and secret police.[185] It can be said that Milošević established legitimacy and secured his power through "the destruction of alternatives" first through control of the state media and second by controlling elections, in order to create political inertia and apathy.[186]

The war in Bosnia and Croatia provided the regime with a guise of "national interests" and any attempt by the democratic opposition and Other Serbia affiliates to contradict its policies or criticize it could result in accusations of treason against those who spoke out. In an orchestrated effort with the ruling party, right-wing paramilitary leaders together

---

[184] An in-depth analysis of the anti-war movement and the civil society bloc in Serbia before 2000 and later, when the ideological rift became more visible, will be given further consideration in the next chapter.

[185] Sabrina P. Ramet and Vjeran Pavlaković, eds., *Serbia Since 1989: Politics and Society under Milošević and After*, Jackson School Publications in International Studies (Washington University Press, 2006), p. 18. For religious symbolism please see Mitja Velikonja, "In Hoc Signo Vinces: Religious Symbolism in the Balkan Wars 1991–1995' in *International Journal of Politics, Culture, and Society*, 17, no. 1, Studies in the Social History of Destruction: The Case of Yugoslavia (Fall, 2003), p. 25–40. For the nationalist symbolism please see Xavier Bougarel, "Yugoslav Wars: The 'Revenge of the Countryside' between Sociological Reality and Nationalist Myth," in *East European Quarterly*, 32, no. 2, June 1999, p. 157/175.

[186] Eric Gordy, *The Culture of Power in Serbia: Nationalism and the Destruction of Alternatives* (University Park, PA: The Pennsylvania University Press, 1999), p. 2.

with the Serbian Radical Party (SRS), including warlord Arkan and his Party of Serbian Unity, rapidly gained political influence and started to play major roles on the political scene. Gordy argues that these parties acted as a counter-opposition to the pro-democratic parties, creating political balance and positioning Milošević in the center, meaning that Milošević could present himself as the only moderate choice.[187] Also, the regime experienced political trouble as a result of its behavior toward the Serb leadership in Bosnia and Croatia after they refused to accept unquestioning obedience to Milošević. As a consequence Milošević imposed economic sanctions on Republika Srpska, which angered their nationalist and extreme right-wing supporters in Serbia proper. In this respect, the Milošević-controlled media in Serbia marginalized the events that followed, such as the rapid fall of Krajina in Croatia in 1995.[188]

In addition, the economic sanctions imposed by the UN, and Serbia's consequent international isolation paradoxically assisted the regime, increasing its popularity. This was because it became difficult for Serbian citizens to travel and access outside news and information, and they were left in economic chaos, with many facing bankruptcy, while the former communist elites converted their political resources into private capital.[189] The escalation of the conflict in Bosnia, and particularly the imposition of international sanctions, gave specific groups of people an opportunity to plunder the economy directly (the spoils of war) or indirectly (state generated hyperinflation) and gain control of enormous wealth.[190] The newly-formed stratum of wealthy individuals which resulted, according to Lazić, largely originated from the circles of the ruling hierarchy or had close connections with it.[191] These factors contributed to the creation of segments of First Serbia which formed a specific

---

[187] Ibid., p. 34.
[188] Robert Thomas, *Serbia under Milošević: The Politics of Serbia in the 1990s*, (London: Hurst, 1999), p. 12.
[189] Mladen Lazić, "The Adaptive Reconstruction of Elites" in John Higley and György Lengyel, eds., *Elites After State Socialism: Theories and Analysis* (Lanham, MD: Rowman & Littlefield,(2000), p. 123.
[190] See Mladen Lazić, ed, *The Winter of Discontent: Protest in Belgrade*, (Budapest: Central European University Press, 1999), p. 7/8.
[191] Ibid., p. 7/8.

coalition between the regime, pro-regime elites of First Serbia, and the nouveau riche, with a shared interest in blocking the process of post-socialist transformation of Serbian society for as long as possible. Naturally, the international blockade enabled these segments to retain power and thereby continue the transfer of social wealth into private ownership unimpeded.[192]

Political discontent: crises and the call for democratization

Soon after the Dayton agreement, under the terms of which the hostilities in Bosnia formally ceased and a new constitution of the Federation of Bosnia-Herzegovina and Republika Srpska was put in place, the regime started working to increase its legitimacy in economic terms as the unbearable circumstances within Serbia were increasingly becoming more important to the regime than the alleged external culprit.[193] The regime's transition from a "peacemaking" discourse toward the defense of national interests, in relation to Kosovo, in fact brought and mobilized strong support from the previously-indifferent silent majority who had been focused on the economy and private life. As the war in Bosnia ended, the domestic political situation was ripe for the opposition to unite and attempt to seriously challenge the regime. In the wake of the pro-democratic protests of 1996–97, official propaganda tried to prove that the remnants of communism had already been discarded and democracy had already been introduced and that Serbian people needed unity rather than internal dissent.[194] The main cause for the protests, described by many as the "Happening of the Citizens," was that, despite the fact that the *Zajedno* coalition had won the local elections outright in fourteen of the most important towns and cities in the country, the official election commission refused to recognize the results. As the opposition started gathering at the Republic Square in Belgrade, its leaders, liberal politicians and intellectuals Zoran Djindjić and Vesna Pešić and (then)

---

[192] Mladen Lazić, *The Winter of Discontent: Protest in Belgrade*, (Budapest: Central European University Press, 1999), p. 7/8.
[193] Ibid., p. 12.
[194] Ibid., p. 12.

nationalist-democrat Vuk Drašković,[195] sought to present their case to the diplomatic community, holding meetings with a number of Western ambassadors, and protesting at the attempts to annul the election results.

In late November a Student Protest Committee was formed both to pursue their own demands, including removal of the unpopular chancellor, and to support the *Zajedno* coalition. The demonstrators established a regular pattern, meeting every day on Terazije before taking a walk around central Belgrade while chanting anti-government songs, carrying banners and throwing eggs (as a symbolic form of peaceful protest)[196] at the key-institutions of the Serbian state media which refused to give any coverage to the protests.[197] Thomas suggests that it was evident that these protesters expressed their "internationalism" with banners such as "Belgrade is the World," in line with the desire of *Zajedno* leaders to emphasize to the outside world their pro-western orientation. It can be added that the demonstrators held the belief that Serbia needed to "return to Europe" and were requesting the adoption of European standards and practices of government.

The tipping point was in late December when the SPS and JUL organized a counter meeting, bringing 60,000 supporters from outside the capital, but they were outnumbered by the chants and whistles of 300,000 *Zajedno* supporters.[198] The protests lasted from November until late February, and even nationalist-writer Dobrica Ćosić and thirty

---

[195] The famous writer Vuk Drašković was one of the first opposition leaders during the early 1990s.

[196] The chants and initiatives of the protestors frequently take the form of increasingly inventive jokes such as bombarding the RTS building with paper aeroplanes. Young women protestors carried bunches of flowers in order to emphasise their pacifist intent. Robert Thomas, *Serbia under Milošević: The Politics of Serbia in the 1990s*, (London: Hurst, 1999), p. 278.

[197] Events in the capital were mirrored by those taking place in the provinces. On November 27, the eighth day of protests, while 200,000 demonstrated in Belgrade, at the same time 20,000 people were on the streets of Niš, 15,000 in Kragujevac, and 5,000 in Kraljevo.

[198] On December 24 Milošević gave a speech about strong Serbia, its threatened integrity by the forces outside the country with the help of the "fifth column" from the inside whose aim is to weaken Serbian's unity. Second, the crowd chanted to Milošević that he is loved by them, at which point he replied that he loved them back.

members of SANU signed an appeal supporting the demands of the students and opposition demonstrators. The Belgrade Circle, an anti-war NGO representing a liberal perspective, issued a declaration in which they invited friends and allies from abroad to support the civic option in Serbia.[199] After a violent protest on February 2, the OSCE recommended a legal framework that would recognize the *Zajedno* victories. *Lex specialis*, a special law acknowledging the results was adopted by the Serbian government. However Ostojić argues that *Lex specialis* was merely a face-saving exit for the regime that allowed it to give the appearance of respecting the election result while maintaining largely intact many of its instruments of power.[200] In late February 1997, the *Zajedno* coalition gathered to celebrate the democrats taking power in Belgrade. Symbolically significant was the removal of the five-pointed communist star from City Hall, followed by a state media report that connected the star with the events of the Second World War, and suggesting that the removal insulted every patriot.[201] Curiously, Western governments, including that of the US and UK, largely still perceived Milošević as a guarantor of peace and did not offer direct support to the opposition or any leaders of pro-democratic movements or Other Serbia associates.

The crisis in Kosovo in 1998 saw a partial return to international isolation for Serbia and the reintroduction of sanctions that again bolstered Milošević's position and set in motion the well-established mechanisms of national mobilization against the "foreign enemy." Some notable scholars agree that the 1999 NATO intervention created a cohesive patriotic front against what was widely perceived as foreign aggression against Serbia.[202] During the bombing campaign,[203] which started in

---

[199] Robert Thomas, *Serbia under Milošević: The Politics of Serbia in the 1990s*, (London: Hurst, 1999), p. 296.

[200] Mladen Ostojić, *Between Justice and Stability: The Politics of War Crimes Prosecutions in Post-Milošević Serbia* (Farnham (UK) and Burlington (VA): Ashgate, 2014), p. 58.

[201] Robert Thomas, *Serbia under Milošević: The Politics of Serbia in the 1990s*, (London: Hurst, 1999), p. 312. The star was replaced by an eagle—a symbol of freedom.

[202] See Lenard J. Cohen, *Serpent in the Bosom: The Rise and Fall of Slobodan Milošević*, (Boulder, CO: Westview Press, 2001), and Jansen S., "Victims, Underdogs and Rebels: Discursive Practices of Resistance in Serbian Protest," *Critique of Anthropology* 20, no. 4, (2000), p. 393–420.

March 1999, the regime closed down independent media, suppressed the autonomy of the universities, and increased repression against the opposition by assassinating possible political candidates and journalists. More importantly, the 1999 NATO intervention resulted in UN resolution 1244 that established an UN peacekeeping mission and later an EU rule of law mission in Kosovo. But, more significantly, the 1999 NATO intervention severely undermined the pro-western position of the democratic forces in the Serbian political space. In fact, this effect continues to be felt to this day. The NATO air strikes proved to be a profound psychological shock to the nation which, despite ten years of nearby conflict, had not had to confront the harsh realities of war on its own soil. After the intervention, according to LeBor, many feared that Milošević, who had cemented his rule by finding enemies among Slovenes, Croats, Bosnians and Albanians, and had lost all of these territories to independence, would now turn against Montenegro.[204] In a similar vein, Naumović argues that the destructive potential in the public sphere reached its peak in 2000, when the dominant tendency of the Milošević discourse was to enforce quasi-ethnic identity splits as a means of eliminating political adversaries by hinting at their non-Serbian ethnic origins and by unveiling their "foreign mentors and financiers,"[205] and was radicalized by the certainty that the endgame was rapidly approaching.[206]

The opposition unites: Bulldozer Revolution

By 2000, the principal motivation for bringing the regime down shifted and became tied to the disastrous socio-economic situation, as half of the

---

[203] The 1999 NATO intervention came as the consequence of the regime's war with the Kosovo Liberation Army (KLA) which resulted in a UN resolution 1244 and the withdrawal of Serbian administration from Kosovo. The atrocities committed by the Serbian army and security services provoked an outburst of international condemnation.

[204] Adam LeBor, *Milošević: A Biography* (Yale University Press. 2004), p. 302

[205] Certain newspapers vilified certain "Other" Serbia actors by demonizing them as Nazis or willing members of the Hitler Youth.

[206] Slobodan, Naumović, "On 'Us' and 'Them': Understanding the Historical Bases and Political Uses of Popular Narratives on Serbian Disunity," *CAS Sofia Working Paper Series*, issue: 1 (2007), p. 20.

population were at the level of bare survival. The general political apathy and pessimism which had for some time been growing were taking their toll and hampered any desire for social and political change. In these circumstances, it was clear that the unification of the majority of the opposition parties would be a precondition for the removal of Milošević.[207] The unification of the opposition came in January 2000 with the creation of the Democratic Opposition of Serbia (DOS), on the initiative of the Serbian Renewal Movement (SPO), in which the sixteen most important leaders of opposition parties agreed on joint strategy.[208] This loose coalition put forward Vojislav Koštunica as the candidate for the presidential elections despite the fact that his opposition party, the Democratic Party of Serbia (DSS), was marginal. In fact this was his key advantage and, as a result, he had the best chance of winning of all the opponents to Milošević. Koštunica's ideological position was close to that of the moderate nationalists of the time and in his speeches he always addressed the defense of Serbian national interests.[209] I suggest that his political stance was a conservative one, and closer to the "First" than to the "Other" Serbia position, as confirmed by the course of his later political career. Koštunica was firmly critical of Western involvement in the Balkan region, which was a necessary position in order to dispel any potential accusation of being a "foreign stooge," in the way the regime often portrayed opposition leaders. According to Cohen, Koštunica was chosen because he was considered to be an uncompromising and incorruptible democrat, whose integrity and commitment to the rule of law were beyond reproach.[210] The choice of Koštunica as leader can be seen as a response to the widespread political apathy and distrust of politicians and anything political, and to the practical difficulty of converting popular support into votes.

---

[207] Lenard J. Cohen, *Serpent in the Bosom: The Rise and Fall of Slobodan Milošević*, (Boulder, CO: Westview Press, 2001), p. 428.

[208] See Obrad Kesić, "An Airplane with Eighteen Pilots: Serbia after Milošević" in Sabrina Ramet and Vjeran Pavlaković, eds., *Serbia since 1989: Politics and Society under Milošević and After* (Seattle: University of Washington Press, 2005), p. 95–121.

[209] Lenard J. Cohen, *Serpent in the Bosom: The Rise and Fall of Slobodan Milošević*, (Boulder, CO: Westview Press, 2001), p. 430

[210] Ibid., p. 412

Even so, democratic activism and the role of civil society and of student and other civic organizations continued to be crucial in taking down the regime. Milošević's final enemy was the youth civil movement *Otpor* (*Resistance*), founded at Belgrade University in the autumn of 1998. Their clenched-fist symbol soon appeared on walls across the country, often accompanied by the slogan "Gotov je!" (He is finished!).[211] The organization was dynamic in organizing protest events, innovative in its tactics and decentralized.[212] Eventually more than 70,000 young Serbs joined *Otpor* in its information war against the regime.[213] Civil society organizations in particular fomented youth mobilization as support could not be promulgated through the media, which was tightly controlled by the regime. American newspapers reported that, in total, over 70 million US dollars were paid to the Serbian opposition to support its democratic efforts.[214]

The Yugoslav presidential elections held on September 24, 2000 were followed by mass protests, the *Bulldozer Revolution* and eventually

---

[211] For further insight into the importance of Otpor in bringing down the Milošević regime, see: T. Kuzio, Civil Society, Youth and Societal Mobilization in *Democratic Revolutions, Communist and Post-communist Studies*, 39, no 3, (2006), p. 365–386.

[212] Two of *Otpor*'s most prominent members were students Srdja Popović and Ivan Marović, who both developed into globally influential intellectuals after 2000. Popović accepted his nomination as one of Foreign Policy magazine's top 100 global thinkers in 2012. After Otpor, Popović founded the *Centre for Applied Non Violent Action and Strategies,* or CANVAS, and began training activists interested in copying the Serbian model of bottom-up regime change. CANVAS has worked with people from forty-six countries, and graduates of Popović's program include organisers of the successful movements in Georgia, Lebanon, Egypt and the Maldives. The young Iranians protesting against Ahmadinejad in 2009 downloaded 17,000 copies of Popović's guide to nonviolent action. The Syrians currently standing up to Bashar al-Assad are the latest in the long line of revolutionaries who have sought Popović's advice. With little fanfare, Popović has become an architect of global political change. See "The Revolutionist," *Atlantic Magazine*, March 2012. http://www.theatlantic.com/magazine/archive/2012/03/the-revolutionist/308881/

[213] Their activists translated sections from Gene Sharp's book *From Dictatorship to Democracy: a Conceptual framework for Liberalization* and passed them from cell to cell. In his book, Sharp listed 198 methods of non-violent action, many of which could be employed in Serbia and were emulated as "color revolutions" in Ukraine, Egypt, Tunisia, Iran, Syria, etc. See Adam LeBor, *Milošević: A Biography*, (Yale University Press, 2004), p. 303.

[214] Ibid., p. 304

Milošević's defeat. The model of "electoral revolution" operated in Serbia, whereby the authoritarian rule refused to acknowledge the election result and as a consequence the opposition, together with *Otpor*, resorted to protest. The DOS coalition claimed they had won in the first round, while the regime suggested the coalition had less than 50 percent of the vote and called for a second round of voting. As a result, the democratic politicians, together with Other Serbia, launched a widespread campaign of civil disobedience and strikes, which culminated on October 5, 2000 when thousands of people gathered in front of the parliament. The assembled mass then entered the building, as well as taking control of other regime institutions such as Radio Television of Serbia (RTS) and several government buildings around Belgrade. After a bloodless revolution, Milošević was forced to step down, as he did not receive support from the army.[215]

As part of a compromise, the democratic opposition's joint strategy combined a peaceful call for democracy with an agreement that no radical lustration would take place in the transitional scenario. The fact that, with the exception of Milošević and his ministers, a large part of the existing First Serbia political elites stayed in power was seen by many as an acknowledgment of the will of the people but, on the other hand, was seen by others as missing an opportunity to address certain grievances and thereby possibly achieving a radical break with First Serbia's ideological heritage. After the democratic government took over, the cracks in DOS started to become visible, as the only thing that had united the new ruling class had been its opposition to Milošević. The new coalition immediately split into two camps: the conservative nationalist camp under Yugoslav President Vojislav Koštunica, and the pro-Western reformers under Serbian Prime Minister Zoran Djindjić. The US openly stated that future economic aid depended on Milošević's extradition to the Hague Tribunal. Koštunica, together with the DSS, was opposed to the International Criminal Tribunal of the former Yugoslavia (the ICTY),

---

[215] Birch S., "The 2000 Elections in Yugoslavia: the 'Bulldozer Revolution" in *Electoral Studies: International Journal* 21, no. 3, (2002).

but Djindjić took a more pragmatic approach toward the issue and extradited Milošević[216] on June 28, 2001: St. Vitus' Day (Vidovdan).[217]

It is unquestionable that "October 5," as it has become known, was the defining moment in Serbia's return to a democratic path. However, one of the reasons why it also brought about a "delayed transition"[218] can be found in the fact that there was institutional continuity with the previous regime. The Socialist Party of Serbia (SPS) participated in the provisional government until the next elections which left some room for the party to save its legitimacy. As the old head of the security services was kept in place throughout the interim period, they were able to arrange the destruction of crucial evidence of the regime's wrongdoings, thus limiting the possibility of bringing to justice those responsible and thereby making a clear break with the past more difficult. As indicated above, two different approaches to regime change emerged: one more cautious and one more radical.[219] This divergence threatened to cause, or at least be a principal cause of, the dissolution of the democratic coalition and further fragmentation of political options. As a result of the failure to immediately reform the security sector, the new government could not establish full control over the security apparatus for several years after the removal of Milošević.[220] It is clear that the post-Milošević dynamics, characterized by a clear delineation between the political and

---

[216] Between his overthrow and extradition, Milošević retired from public life but by no means disappeared. In an interview he said that his conscience was clear and that he could sleep well. Adam LeBor, *Milošević: A Biography*, (Yale University Press, 2004), p. 315.

[217] In terms of the calendar of political symbolism, Vidovdan is an important national date, and has a very symbolic meaning. It was the date of the Battle of Kosovo in 1389, and also when Gavrilo Princip assassinated Archduke Franz Ferdinand in Sarajevo in 1914.

[218] Florian Bieber, "The Serbian Opposition and Civil Society: Roots of the Delayed Transition in Serbia," *International Journal of Politics, Culture and Society*, 16, (2003), p. 73–90.

[219] See Mladen Ostojić, *International Judicial Intervention and Regime Change in Serbia 2000–2010*, PhD thesis, University of London, (2011).

[220] See Timothy Edmunds, *Security Sector Reform in Transforming Societies: Croatia, Serbian and Montenegro*, (Manchester: Manchester University Press, 2007); and Filip Ejdus, *Democratic Security Sector Governance in Serbia*, (Frankfurt am Main: Peace Research Institute Frankfurt, 2010).

cultural elites of First and Other Serbia, resulted to a significant extent from the manner in which regime change unfolded in Serbia.

Milošević's legacy

Gordy finds that, all things considered, the explanation for the paradox of Milošević's longevity lies partially in his mobilization of ethnic hatred, and partially in the mobilization of opinions in his favor and the elimination, sidelining and removal of alternative political options.[221] The significance of Milošević's ideological legacy cannot be ignored when one considers the curious fact that Serbia occupied the undefined zone between democracy and national-authoritarianism for such a long period and, as Ramet and Pavlaković suggest, is still a society important segments of which are in "denial of the liberal project itself."[222] Gordy suggests that the legacy of the Yugoslav wars presents the most serious obstacle to integration between political communities in the region of former Yugoslavia that have economic, cultural and developmental goals in common.[223] Not surprisingly, the process of closer integration in the Western Balkans is simultaneously part of the processes of reconciliation, democratization and transformation.

In light of these facts, it is necessary to explore further the emergence of the notions of "good" and "bad" nationalism in the Serbian public sphere through the prism of First and Other Serbia discourses. Gow suggested that the biggest impact of the war on Serbian society was on morale and morality, where hostility and misrule created conditions in which optimism was almost absent, and where there was no confidence in politics, or indeed in the future in general.[224] I argue that the

---

[221] Eric Gordy, *The Culture of Power in Serbia: Nationalism and the Destruction of Alternatives* (University Park, PA: The Pennsylvania University Press, 1999), p. 2/3.

[222] Sabrina P. Ramet and Vjeran Pavlaković, eds., *Serbia Since 1989: Politics and Society under Milošević and After*, Jackson School Publications in International Studies, (Washington University Press, 2006), p. 16.

[223] Eric Gordy, "Postwar Guilt and Responsibility in Serbia: The Effort to Confront it and the Effort to Avoid it," in Sabrina P. Ramet and Vjeran Pavlaković, eds., *Serbia Since 1989: Politics and Society under Milošević and After*, (Jackson School Publications in International Studies., Washington University Press.), p. 184/5.

[224] James Gow, "The Impact of the War on Serbia: Spoiled Appetites and Progressive Decay" in Sabrina P. Ramet and Vjeran Pavlaković, eds., *Serbia Since 1989: Politics and*

ideological tendencies toward the West of the continuing remnants of the pro-Milošević elite, which were symbolic actions in politics utilized by First Serbia ("psychological warfare," in the words of Susan Woodward[225]), remained after 2000, and impacted to a certain degree upon Serbian political and social realities. Furthermore, I will argue that the processes of "re-traditionalization" of societal values strongly supported by the First Serbia discourse lead to a rise in religiosity among the population. As Cohen notes, the "ethnification of consciousness" that took place during the 1990s had a deep impact on the reconstitution of societal values after 2000."[226] It is clear that the dominant and prevailing First Serbia discourse had the power to greatly influence the structure of all emerging discourses after 2000, including the resilient but still subordinate Other Serbia discourse.

Transitional adjustments and the perspective of EU accession

The geopolitical transformations that were taking place at the beginning of the twenty-first century in Central and Eastern Europe, with Slovenia, Romania, Bulgaria and even Croatia becoming members of NATO and the European Union, raised additional challenges for Serbia's perspective on its own political future. [227]

Initially, after the democratic change of the regime, the sense of the urgent need to move forward was evident, despite the continued use, internationally, of the phrase "post-conflict status" in describing Serbia's

---

Society under Milošević and After, (Washington University Press, 2006), p. 184/5 and p. 156.

[225] Susan L. Woodward, "Miloševic Who? Origins of the New Balkans," in *The Hellenic Observatory*, Discussion Paper No. 5; The European Institute, London School of Economics & Political Science, (2001). http://eprints.lse.ac.uk/3328/1/Milošević_Who.pdf

[226] See Lenard J. Cohen. *Serpent in the Bosom: The Rise and Fall of Slobodan Milošević,* (Boulder, CO: Westview Press, 2001), p. 422.

[227] It is clear that the Western Balkans, including Serbia, even after a such a turbulent recent history, does have the hope of a peaceful and European future or, at least, many scholars, politicians and authors argue that such a future is very likely. For further insight into this argument, please see Wolfgang Petritsch, Goran Svilanović, and Christoph Solioz, eds., *Serbia Matters: Domestic Reforms and European Integration,* (Paris, Vienna, Geneva: Nomos, 2009).

political situation. Nonetheless, for a long time the main themes in the ongoing dialogue between the European Union and Serbia were the need for stability and security as conditions of accession.[228] The beginning of transition in post-communist countries was generally marked by a social consensus in favor of joining Europe, which is absent in the Serbian case. This comes as a consequence of many compromises which the incoming opposition made with the outgoing regime, the first as early as October 6, 2000, when Koštunica secretly met with Milošević and the army Chief of Staff, Nebojša Pavković.[229] After the October 2000 overthrow of Milošević the process of real democratization and Europeanization of institutions started. However, the failure to overhaul First Serbia's existing civil service structures severely limited the scope for progress toward a modern, European style of governance. In addition, Koštunica soon afterwards defined himself ideologically as a "democratic nationalist"—a label that reflected both his adherence to legal principles and democratic governance and his commitment to the idea of Serbian national unity and statehood.[230] Zoran Djindjić, one of the most pro-

---

[228] This is clear from the Commission's annual reports about Serbia which remain preoccupied with more technical issues rather than ideational factors. This occurrence is quite normal as identity is not part of the Copenhagen criteria for membership, but nevertheless, some express the belief that the likelihood of rule adoption will increase as Serbia identifies more with the EU. Please see Florian Trauner, "From Membership Conditionality to Policy Conditionality: EU External Governance in South Eastern Europe," *Journal of European Public Policy*, 16, no. 5 (2009), p. 774–790 and Florian Trauner, Stephan Renner, "Creeping membership in Southeast Europe: the dynamics of EU rule transfer to the Western Balkans," *Journal of European Integration*, 31, no. 4 (2009) and Florian Trauner, "Deconstructing the EU's Routes of Influence in Justice and Home Affairs in the Western Balkans," *Journal of European Integration*, 31, no. 1 (2009), p. 65–82.

[229] This meeting happened on the initiative of the Russian Foreign Minister, Sergei Ivanov. Some observers suggest that the subject of this meeting remains a secret to this day although there are some signs that the Milošević family got political asylum in Russia afterwards, and that Koštunica promised Milošević he would not be sent to the ICTY. For further insight into the days after October 6 please see St. Protić, Milan, *Democratic Revolution Betrayed*, (Iznevrena revolucija), (Belgrade, Čigoja Štampa, 2006). Also, Mladen Ostojić, *International Judicial Intervention and Regime Change in Serbia 2000–2010*, PhD thesis, Queen Mary, University of London, (2011), p. 66.

[230] See Lenard J. Cohen and Jasna Dragović-Soso, *Collapse in South-Eastern Europe: New Perspectives on Yugoslavia's Disintegration*, (West Lafayette, IN: Purdue University Press, 2008), p. 205.

liberal leaders of the DOS coalition perceived himself, on the other hand, to be a political pragmatist. There were deep disagreements between the political parties in the coalition on questions of transition, the relationship with the European Union, and extraditions to the ICTY. St. Protic, formerly DOS leader himself, argues that their only common platform was to bring down the Milošević regime.[231] As mentioned above, ideological and practical differences emerged early, with some advocating a softer approach to reform and others, more in line with Other Serbia, advocating a radical break from the past. It was this disagreement which would finally bring the DOS coalition to its end.

Milošević was extradited to the ICTY in 2001 and on March 11, 2006, Serbia's former President died in his prison cell in the Netherlands. Prime Minister Djindjić was assassinated on March 12, 2003. Following Djindjić's assassination, newly-elected president Boris Tadić from the Democratic Party (DS) was said to be continuing Djindjić's political course. However, Tadić's government established a new politics of "cohabitation" and power-sharing with Koštunica as Prime Minister. This, according to many analysts, failed to put the country on an active path to reform, nor did it fully address the consequences of the past or establish a national consensus about Serbia's geopolitical orientation.[232] Cooperation with the ICTY continued during the decade or so which followed Tadić's accession to the presidency and culminated with the arrests of Radovan Karadzić in 2008 and Ratko Mladić in 2011.[233]

The disintegration of Yugoslavia continued after the removal of Milošević when first Montenegro in 2006 and later Kosovo in 2008 declared

---

[231] St. Protić, Milan, *Democratic Revolution Betrayed*, (Izneverena revolucija), (Belgrade, Čigoja Štampa, 2006), p. 45.

[232] Jelena Subotić, *Hijacked Justice: Dealing with the Past in the Balkans*, (Ithaca, NY: Cornell University Press, 2009) and Sabrina Ramet and Vjeran Pavlaković, eds, *Serbia since 1989. Politics and Society under Milošević and After*, (Seattle: University of Washington Press, 2006).

[233] The newspapers and TV provided detailed coverage of even the most unimportant details of their years in hiding, but only a few stories dealt with the subject of the Hague indictments or, even in general, the crimes they were accused of committing in Bosnia. For detailed analysis of the approach of the Serbian press to the arrests please see Vesna Perić Zimonjić, "Serbian Press Lionises the Cunning Fugitive, Not the Criminal," *Independent*, July 25, 2008 and Jelena Subotić, *Hijacked Justice: Dealing with the Past in the Balkans*, (Ithaca, NY: Cornell University Press, 2009).

independence from Serbia. Between these historic events, Serbia's voters decided in the 2008 elections to support the democratic option, to accept political realities, and to proceed toward candidacy for the European Union. President Tadić from the Democratic Party won the 2008 election in a narrow runoff with 50.5 percent of the vote, only narrowly defeating his opponent Tomislav Nikolić from the then Radical Party who received 47.9 percent. The Democrats led the coalition "For a European Serbia" on the platform "Both Kosovo and Europe." The coalition was directly supported by the US and the EU, as shown by the signing the evening before the election of the Stabilization and Association Agreement, the signing of a framework agreement between Fiat and a former Serbian car producer, and the continuation of negotiations on easing the visa regimes. However, frequent public opinion polls reveal that the population is yet again divided between those adopting "First" and "Other" Serbia positions. In response, the government is once again attempting to simultaneously pursue the seemingly irreconcilable foreign policy goals advocated by each position.[234] In line with his First Serbia orientation, having made Kosovo the central issue of domestic and foreign policy, Koštunica orchestrated the entrenchment of this policy as a central pillar of the new constitution of the Republic of Serbia in 2006. Since Kosovo's declaration of independence in 2008, Serbia has begun a vigorous diplomatic offensive to dissuade additional states from recognizing it and to dissuade international organizations, such as the UN, from admitting Kosovo as a member. I find that in post-Milošević Serbia, the perception, widespread in popular society, that a choice must be made between joining Europe and keeping Kosovo, shows the existence of a very particular *problematique* in that Serbia's

---

[234] According to Gallup Balkan Monitor, the role of the international community over the last twenty years was depicted as extremely harmful by 40.6% of surveyed participants. Moreover, half of the Serbian population thinks NATO is still extremely hostile toward Serbia and even 69% disapprove of US leadership in the region. See *Survey on Geopolitics* (Gallup Balkan Monitor, 2011). References to "four pillars of Serbian diplomacy" can be found in documents on national strategy, but also expressed in the press by president Tadić at various times: "President Boris Tadić says that Serbia has Four Pillars of Foreign Policy: EU, Russia, US and China" (RTS: 2009, August 30). This perspective on policy is also expressed in the lecture on *Serbia's Foreign Policy: Substance and Rhetoric*, given by Ljiljana Smajlović at the Harriman Institute in New York.

progress toward EU membership is constrained by very domestic political dynamics. Later in this book, I will explore, through analysis of empirical research, the discursive construction of the "Europe or Kosovo" societal dilemmas.

There can be little doubt that the prospect of EU membership has been a key motivating factor for the systemic transformation, stabilization, democratization and reform of Serbia's judiciary and security apparatus. Serbia found itself directly facing these dilemmas, coupled with the legacy of war crimes, only after 2008 when the pressure from Brussels strengthened. The new coalition after the 2008 elections was established between the Democrats (DS) and Socialists (SPS). In this way, soft liberals, with Tadić at their fore, accepted the politics of cohabitation with First Serbia political fragments of society. The coalition considered the maintenance of the territorial integrity of Serbia (including Kosovo) as a top priority, but European integration also ranked very high. Until recently, Kosovo and cooperation with the ICTY were the two major issues that threatened to seriously hamper Serbia's accession process, its economic progress and the stability of the wider region.

Today's party politics is considerably different from that of the 1990s. The fragmentation of First Serbia's right-wing, including the Radical Party (SRS) led by Vojislav Šešelj seems to continue unabated, as does that of the center-right parties. The battles taking place around the reform agenda, the issue of Kosovo, and the question of EU accession, are seen as a far cry from the ideological landscape during Milošević's time in power. The Other Serbia democratic bloc, established before the Bulldozer Revolution, had most ideological orientations in common between themselves, such as the removal of Milošević, the establishment of full democracy, and the acceptance of Serbia within the international community. The First and Other Serbia blocs did not, however, agree over attitudes toward the ICTY or on the policies of continuity/discontinuity with the previous regime. This disagreement was evident in what became known in 2002 as the Point of Departure debate in the weekly magazine *Vreme* which will be analyzed in the empirical chapters. According to Ramet, following the fragmentation of the DOS coalition there began a fragmentation of the Other Serbia bloc into *hard liberals* and *soft liberals* (or flexible realists), a political fragmentation which continues to this day.[235] This can be seen in the large numbers of SPS supporters who have switched their allegiance to the DSS, and the split in the Democratic Party in 2005 into the DS, Liberal Democrats and Tadić's Social Democratic Party. The Radical Party also split, in 2008, into the Radicals and the Progressives (who are in power at the time of publishing). Political observers now perceive deep-rooted rivalry among the new political elites. These structural developments have opened the way for the lasting polarization of the Serbian political scene, which is a major obstacle to the institutional reforms necessary for the consolidation of democracy.[236]

I will argue that the existence of mutually opposing views as to how the transformation of the Serbian state should unfold greatly affected the unity of both democratic and nationalist political blocs and promulgated their subsequent polarization. Goati argues that in the post-revolutionary period, the Serbian party system was characterized by the presence of anti-system parties, and the absence of political consensus among political and cultural elites.[237] In this context, it is important to make it clear that anti-system parties were those parties that did not see the democratic state as the only political option (the most important examples are the SRS and the SPS in the aftermath of Milošević's downfall). The revival of the Serbian Radicals (SRS) in 2003 and the Serbian Progressives (SNS) in 2008 allowed the democrats to be the counterweight to the oppositional nationalist political manifesto. In addition, in terms of EU integration, diplomatic relations with the West

---

[235] See O. Listhaug, S. P. Ramet and D. Dulić, eds., *Civic and Uncivic Values: Serbia in the Post-Milošević Era*, (Budapest: Central University Press, 2011), p. 4.

[236] See Florian Bieber, "The Serbian Opposition and Civil Society: Roots of the Delayed Transition in Serbia," *International Journal of Politics, Culture and Society*, 16, (2003). p. 73–90 and Obrad Kesić, "An Airplane with Eighteen Pilots: Serbia after Milošević" in Sabrina Ramet and Vjeran Pavlaković, eds., *Serbia since 1989. Politics and Society under Milošević and After*, (Seattle: University of Washington Press, 2005), p. 95–121 and Mladen Ostojić, *International Judicial Intervention and Regime Change in Serbia 2000–2010*, PhD thesis, Queen Mary, University of London, (2011), p. 72.

[237] Vladimir Goati, ed., *Partijska scena Srbije posle 5 Oktobra 2000* (*The Party Scene in Serbia after October 5 2000*), (Belgrade: Friedrich Ebert Stiftung and Institute of Social Sciences, 2002), p. 225.

deteriorated and the EU accession process twice came to standstill, in 2007 and 2010, as a result of the failure to arrest Hague indictees. Furthermore, in 2011 Kosovo and Serbia established diplomatic dialogue on trade, freedom of movement, registry and recognition of diplomas, because the EU had prescribed that achieving consensus on those issues is a condition for Serbia's candidacy for EU membership. In December 2011, the European Council postponed the decision on the candidacy bid, prescribing further progress in the talks between Pristina and Belgrade as a further condition for candidate status.[238] In the empirical chapters I will discuss the definition of the First and Other Serbia public actors mentioned here and further analyze their strategies of identification within their "interpretative repertories."[239] Additionally, I will further explore the ideas introduced in this chapter and further investigate the spectrum of meaning that First and Other Serbia actors have attached to Serbian identity.

---

[238] See "Serbia and Kosovo to Resume Talks Soon," *Balkan Insight* (February 17, 2012).
[239] See M. Wetherell, "Positioning and Interpretative Repertoires: Conversation Analysis and Post-structuralism in Dialogue," *Discourse and Society*, 9, no. 3, (1998), p. 387–412 at p. 388.

Chapter 3:
Best of Enemies: "First" and "Other" Serbia

Introduction

Even during the period leading up to the dissolution of Yugoslavia the uncertainty as to whether Serbia belongs to Europe, who the Serbs are, and who the Serbs ought to be, lay at the heart of debates between politicians, intellectuals, journalists, writers and scholars. It has been argued that Milošević managed to stay in power by creating the image of a Serbian nation threatened by foreign enemies and of his regime as the only possible savior of that nation.[240] Of course, in reality there were also threats to his regime posed by rival Western-orientated Other Serbia elites protesting in Belgrade, and not only by foreign adversaries. Gagnon was concerned with the Milošević elites' perceptions that they were threatened by other elites; however, Gagnon does not discuss the extent to which those threats were, when viewed objectively, credible, nor does he explore the extent to which other ethnic groups felt threatened.[241] Similarly, this book is not concerned with whether there is an actual threat to a group, or an actual enemy, rather at issue is how these perceptions, beliefs and narratives are constituted in the discourse on identity. Kolstø has analyzed the connection between violent conflict and media discourse during the Yugoslav wars, arguing that the reduction of people that one has lived alongside for many years to an "enemy" requires considerable preparatory ideological work.[242] As a result, a key feature of the analysis in this book refers to processes of predication and self identification of actors of Other Serbia. How do Other Serbia's elite

---

[240] Valère Philip Gagnon, *The Myth of Ethnic War: Serbia and Croatia in the 1990s* (Ithaca, NY and London: Cornell University Press, 2004), p. 12.
[241] Ibid., p. 23.
[242] Pål Kolstø, ed., *Media Discourse and the Yugoslav Conflicts: Representation of the Self and Other* (Farnham, UK: Ashgate, 2009), p. 9.

imagine their country and do members of this community understand themselves as belonging to a Serbian nation? Who are the Others in opposition to whom the nation defines the Self? In answering these questions, I will consider which positive and negative traits, qualities and features have been attributed to constructed Other Serbia actors by their own affiliates in their own discourse, which first arose as a reaction against the all-penetrating and dominant discourse of First Serbia. I will address the identity/difference boundary that was established in the First and Other Serbia discourses of the 1990s, and further analyze the character of this boundary as it exists today. Here, it is vital to mention a concept of the Copenhagen school of constructivism, which sees *politicizing* the issues of identity and the Self and Other as a discursive strategy.[243] The construction of the national Self, and the extent to which the Other is more or less radically different, amicable or threatening, indicates the degree to which difference and Otherness has been constructed within public discourses. More specifically, the analysis reveals the strategies employed by First and Other Serbia actors in public dialogue in order to dominate the discursive/political field by dominating the public sphere.

Rather than simply identifying First and Other Serbia as two different constructions of identity, I will investigate the extent to which the difference between them is located in spatial and temporal constructions of identity. Therefore, the repertoires of representation around *difference* and *otherness* in First and Other Serbia discourses are the central theme of this book. At the same time, the questions as to whether and, if so, in what ways those repertoires have changed since Milošević, and whether earlier repertoires from the 1990s remain intact in contemporary Serbian society, will also be considered. The terms First and Other Serbia are highly ambivalent; neither of them has a fixed meaning. Other Serbia, for instance, could, for a large part of the 1990s, be defined as including all those who opposed Milošević's policies and state-controlled media from a civic, anti-nationalist and pro-European position. There is also a significant degree of overlap between these two self-designated groups.

---

[243] Barry Buzan, Ole Wæver, and Jaap de Wilde, *Security: A New Framework for Analysis* (Boulder: Lynne Rienner, 1998), p. 25.

At this point, it is important to state that certain writers, politicians and public intellectuals have placed themselves within different discourses at different times. A good example is the writer Vuk Drašković, founder of the SPO, who in the early 1990s was part of the pro-monarchist and nationalist, but anti-Milošević, movement which was strongly supported by the diaspora. He went on to become Minister of Foreign Affairs in the post-2000 democratic government and later shifted his political and ideological position, running for the 2012 elections in coalition with the Liberal Democrats. Similarly, some of those actors supporting nationalistic beliefs, who were pro-war, were at the same time keenly against Milošević. It can be seen, therefore, that actors' political positions did not necessarily overlap entirely with the boundary between First and Other Serbia. Drašković was within that segment of First Serbia described by Naumović as those who would be against the communist legacy of the Yugoslav republic, and which included the Monarchists, the descendants of King Peter's personnel, the army, the anti-communist nationalists and members of the post-1945 Serbian political diaspora.[244] At the other end of that spectrum are certain pro-democratic nationalists, also against Milošević at the time, a good example being Slobodan Antonić, and the individuals gathered around the DSS, whose texts will be analyzed further later on. It is possible to trace the manner in which the elements of post-2000 First Serbia which show strong anti-West and Euroskeptic attitudes actually metamorphosed from these segments of the elites.

The existing instability and contestation of the main ideological themes in these discourses make such analysis fascinating. The meaning of the First and Other Serbia discourses is not fixed and, in fact, intentionally fluctuates between different ideological stances. I suggest that the reason for this is that individual actors perceive themselves differently at different times. The natural catalysts for changes in their understanding of political identity lay in the events of the periods before and after the fall of Milošević, and the key change from a semi-authoritarian

---

[244] Slobodan Naumović, "On 'Us' and 'Them': Understanding the Historical Bases and Political Uses of Popular Narratives on Serbian Disunity" (*CAS Sofia Working Paper Series*, issue 1, 2007), p. 19.

to a democratic regime. As a result, my research does not follow strict chronological order.

The Evolution of "First" and "Other" Serbia

During the process of dissolution of Yugoslavia from 1991 until 1995, "First" and "Other" Serbia actors opened an ongoing dialogue in the public sphere. First and Other Serbia emerged in opposition to each other, as two polarizing ideological forces holding different perceptions of history, of the Yugoslav war and of what it means to be Serbian.[245] It is clear that, during the 1990s, First Serbia affiliates and their activities politicized the issue of Serbian identity in order to secure popular support for the wars. These intellectuals openly utilized bellicose and pronationalist rhetoric and exploited the history of the region as justification for the wars and the dissolution of Yugoslavia.[246] The Radical Party, with Vojislav Šešelj as leader, emphasized and elaborated on the historical victimization of the Serbian population by the Germans and Croats in the Second World War in order to politicize national identity. Such nationalistic rhetoric had been used earlier, however, one example being Milošević's speech at Gazimestan in 1989 in which he stated: "We have been affected by disunity here in Kosovo 600 years ago ... and disunity and treason continued to follow the Serbian people throughout its history .... Six centuries later we are once again fighting and facing new battles. These new battles are not armed in nature, though even those could yet happen." [247] The discourse Milošević and First Serbia affiliates created in the 1990s focused almost exclusively on historical injustices perpetrated against the Serbs.[248] Thus, the Radicals together with Milošević's

---

[245] For the detailed political contexts of the "Other Serbia" in the early nineties, see: Aljoša Mimica, ed., *Druga Srbija deset godina posle 1992–2002* (*The Second Serbia Ten Years After*), (Belgrade: Helsinški odbor za ljudska prava u Srbiji, 2002).

[246] Drinka Gojković, "The Birth of Nationalism from the Spirit of Democracy: The Association of Writers of Serbia and the War," in Nebojša Popov, ed. *The Road to War in Serbia* (Budapest: Central European University Press, 2000).

[247] Taken from Milošević's Gazimestan speech at Kosovo polje in 1989. Quoted from Ivan Colovic, "Everything started in Serbia," in *Wall is Dead! Long live the Wall!* Edited by Ivan Čolovic, (Belgrade: Biblioteka XX vek, 2009), p. 40.

[248] See Valère Philip Gagnon, *The Myth of Ethnic War: Serbia and Croatia in the 1990s* (Ithaca, NY and London: Cornell University Press, 2004), p. 95.

Socialists portrayed themselves as the saviors of the Serbian people in its military struggle against the other Yugoslav nations. Gagnon provides several excellent examples of this portrayal in Milošević-inspired oratory, and finds that his media machine focused disproportionately on injustices being perpetrated against "innocent Serb women, children and old people .... The SPS portrayed those injustices as being essentially based on ethnicity, as having been inflicted on Serbs by non-Serbs ... they portrayed themselves not in terms of expressing ancient hatred, but rather as the instrument of righting those injustices."[249] In fact, First Serbia's victim-centered discourse can be traced back to the end of the 1980s, and to the publication of the SANU *Memorandum* in 1986, at which time there was a general mobilization of popular nationalism.[250] In this sense, the *Memorandum* offered a politicized version of Serbian identity which had been through processes of profound ethnification and victimization.[251] First Serbia discourse regarded resistance to Milošević's policy as treason and, as Bieber notes, these actors deliberately restrained the development and expression of non-nationalist forms of identity in an attempt to weaken the pro-democratic opposition.[252] In the aftermath of the demise of Milošević, key themes in the First Serbia patriotic discourse such as the "anti-Serb" West and Russia as Serbia's closest ally, among others, were taken on by the conservatives, including the SRS (Serbian Radical Party) and the DSS (Democratic Party of Serbia). In the post-2000 public sphere, as Subotić notes, active political actors of First Serbia re-interpreted the victim-centered identity which they had helped to create during the 1990s, while also seeking to improve the negative image which Serbia had earned, in the eyes of the international community, for its wartime activity.[253]

---

[249] Ibid.
[250] Christina Morus, "The SANU Memorandum: Intellectual Authority and the Constitution of an Exclusive Serbian 'People'," *Communication and Critical/Cultural Studies*, 4, no. 2, (June 2007), p. 142–165 at p. 146.
[251] Ibid., p. 145.
[252] Florian Bieber, "The Serbian Opposition and Civil Society: Roots of the Delayed Transition in Serbia," *International Journal of Politics, Culture and Society*, 16, (2003), p. 73–90.
[253] Jelena Subotić, "Europe is a State of Mind: Identity and Europeanization in the Balkans," *International Studies Quarterly*, 55 (2011), p. 309–330.

As the existing body of literature points out, the self-designated Other Serbia grouping has an anti-nationalist political orientation, which has its roots in anti-war civic opposition during the Yugoslav wars.[254] Other Serbia actors, as viewed by Ramet, are mostly from the circles of Serbia's liberal intelligentsia, having been united during the 1990s by their support for a proposed civic identity as an alternative to the nationalist ideology.[255] Dawson understands Other Serbia to be significant minority of the citizenry, the distinct liberal counterpublic, that prevented the formation of a complete illiberal consensus around nationalist and socially conservative values.[256] Yet, one should differentiate between anti-war attitudes and peace activism in the ranks of Other Serbia in the 1990s. Bilić suggests that anti-war attitudes can credibly be articulated from a nationalist perspective, while peace activism, on the other hand, is necessarily influenced by a set of broader values which come from a mostly left-leaning, political stance.[257] Thus Bilić, by drawing such a distinction, opens up several additional questions concerning the relation between the ideological background of the affiliates of these groups and the correlation which that bears to their anti-war attitudes or peace activism. Still, what kept Other Serbia activists and intellectuals together was their characterization of Serbia's involvement in the Yugoslav conflicts as aggressive.[258] Both anti-war and peace activist were against the political community and values advocated by the regime, the state-controlled media and the First Serbia affiliates in general.

The main disagreement mostly materialized between advocates of the rule of law, human rights and so-called European values, such as

---

[254] Jasna Dragović-Soso, "Collective Responsibility, International Justice and Public Reckoning with the Recent Past: Reflections on a Debate in Serbia," in Timothy Waters, ed., *The Milošević Trial—An Autopsy* (Oxford: Oxford University Press, 2014); and Ramet et al., ed. *Civic and Uncivic Values: Serbia in the Post-Milošević Era* (Budapest: Central University Press, 2011); and Bojan Bilić, *We Were Gasping for Air: Post-Yugoslav Anti-War Activism and Its Legacy* (Baden-Baden: Nomos, 2012).

[255] Sabrina Ramet et al., eds. *Civic and Uncivic Values: Serbia in the Post-Milošević Era* (Budapest: Central University Press, 2011), p. 6.

[256] James Dawson, *Cultures of Democracy in Serbia and Bulgaria: How Ideas Shape Public*, (London: Ashgate, 2014), p. 13.

[257] Bojan Bilić, *We Were Gasping for Air: [Post-]Yugoslav Anti-War Activism and Its Legacy* (Baden-Baden: Nomos, 2012), p. 25.

[258] Ibid., p. 27.

tolerance, equality and individual rights and duties, and supporters of bellicose values such as ethnic, religious and sexual intolerance, inequality and the notion that collective rights should outdo individual rights. Such a division started to disappear soon after the regime was toppled, at which time the democratic bloc found its voice, alongside numerous campaigns by non-governmental organizations. As a consequence, in the post-2000 period, the façade of unity against the war evaporated. When the unifying factor represented by the Milošević regime was missing, the focus of the Belgrade critical intelligentsia shifted to opposing attitudes among themselves, especially on the themes of the role of Western influence in the Yugoslav wars, Kosovo, and Serbia's future foreign policy. I find that, on the other hand, the principal dispute between the First and Other Serbia actors can be traced first to the issue of the victimization of Serbia and Serbian responsibility/guilt for the Yugoslav wars, in which Serbs are interchangeably seen both as the main "victims" and the main "perpetrators" by different parties. Second, it can be traced to the First and Other Serbia actors holding different, almost ambivalent, attitudes toward Europe and the West which is seen either as a friend, having common characteristics to the Serbian Self, or as an enemy, the radical and significant Other. Although First and Other Serbia are often presented as opposing each other, I put forward that the symbiosis of their relationship is clear: they are helping create and construct each other's political identities and justify each other's political concepts. The next section focuses solely on the themes which dominated First Serbia in the early stages of its development.

"First" Serbia's evolution in the 1980s and 1990s and the SANU Memorandum

At the end of the 1980s and the beginning of the 1990s, a shift away from the discourse of the *brotherhood and unity* of Yugoslavs to focus solely on ethnic boundary signification became increasingly evident. The themes discussed below are marked by this shift, as the new dominant First Serbia discourse emerged, constituted from conflicting collective identities in the making. The question formulated during the Yugoslav republic, even before the rise of Milošević, which later subjugated the public sphere: what kind of nation are the Serbs? Renowned Serbo-Yugoslav writer of the time, later to become known as a father of First Serbia, Dobrica Ćosić's,[259] inaugural speech to the Serbian Academy of Sciences and Arts (SANU) inquired: why "in wars we die so willingly for freedom and in peace we lose it?"[260] This, and similar perceptions of Serbs as being, first and foremost, proud and honorable warriors, has been a recurring theme of the Ćosić's work. In this regard, this book concludes that victimization profoundly characterizes First Serbia's answers to questions of identity. The rise of the nationalistic intelligentsia's discourse on victimhood was initially motivated by publication of the book *The Woollen Times* in 1982 and the prison sentence Bosnian Serb poet Gojko Djogo received as a result of that publication.[261] In the late 1980s, the victimization narrative was enhanced by the use of language such as *genocide* and *ethnic cleansing* to refer to events in the Second World War. Since then, such terms have been a constant feature in public debate, and links have frequently been made between the Serbian struggle in 1941–1945 and the sufferings in Kosovo in the 1980s and 1990s.

These victimization themes can be traced to the time of the increased general mobilization of popular nationalism and the publication of the *Memorandum* in 1986. The first part of the *Memorandum* elaborated on the disparity between the economic and political systems prevailing in Yugoslavia at that time while the second part was concerned with the conditions being experienced by Serbs in Kosovo and Croatia. Guzina notes that in the 1990s the narratives of victimization, which were employed in strict ethnic terms in the text, were used as a catalyst for the exclusive rhetoric that characterized the public speech of many nationalist politi-

---

[259] Dobrica Ćosić is a Serbian writer, and Serb nationalist political theorist. He was the first President of the Federal Republic of Yugoslavia from 1992 to 1993. Admirers often refer to him as the "Father of the Nation" due to his influence on modern Serbian politics and the national revival movement in the late 1980s.

[260] The inaugural speech to the Serbian Academy of Sciences and Arts (SANU) quoted from Dejan Jović, *Yugoslavia: The State that Withered Away* (Budapest, Central European Press, 2008), p. 234.

[261] Gojko Djogo is a Serb poet and dissident who was imprisoned in Yugoslavia in the 1980s for defaming the memory of former president Josip Broz Tito. In December 1989, he was one of the founders of the Democratic Party in Serbia. He is a member of the Academy of Sciences and Arts of the Republika Srpska.

cians.[262] The *Memorandum* ended with a fervent message to the Others of Yugoslavia. Guzina notes that the rhetoric of the *Memorandum* revolves around the concepts of socialism, Serbia, genocide, the Others of Yugoslavia as an enemy, conspiracy, betrayal and traitor politicians.[263] Among other themes, the keywords which appeared in this and similar texts were *proud*, *innocent* and *soldier* and they fitted within a broadly abstract message about victim identity, as is largely to be expected within the terms of the *Memorandum's* meaning in the public sphere. It is worth quoting an excerpt which refers to the necessity of national renaissance:

> In less than fifty years, for two successive generations, the Serbs were twice subjected to physical annihilation, forced assimilation, conversion to a different religion, cultural genocide, ideological indoctrination, denigration, and compulsion to renounce their own traditions because of an imposed guilt complex … the Serbian people must be allowed to find themselves again and became an historical personality in their own right, to regain a sense of their historical and spiritual being, to make a clear assessment of their economic and cultural interests, to devise a modern social and national program which will inspire present generations and generations to come.[264]

Morus finds that frequent use of terms such as *annihilation, assimilation, conversion*, and *genocide*, placed together with the assertion that Serbs have lost their identity and as such must reassert it, brought the politicization of Serb national identity to its zenith.[265] Similarly, Živković finds that the main message of this discourse, which was first launched by poets and then disseminated widely through the state media, was to cast the Serbs historically as the archetypal victim.[266] This poetic narrative of how "they" slaughtered "us," and of "monumental evil" done to "innocent victims" resulted in a widespread call for revenge.[267] In this respect,

---

[262] Dejan Guzina, "Socialist Serbia's Narratives: From Yugoslavia to a Greater Serbia," *International Journal of Politics, Culture and Society*,17, no. 1, Fall 2003, p. 101.

[263] Ibid., p. 102.

[264] *Memorandum from Serbian Academy of Sciences and Arts* (Serbian Academy of Sciences and Arts, Belgrade, Serbia, 1986), p. 138.

[265] Christina Morus, "The SANU Memorandum: Intellectual Authority and the Constitution of an Exclusive Serbian 'People' ," *Communication and Critical/Cultural Studies*, 4, no. 2, (June 2007), p. 142–165 at 157.

[266] Marko Živković, *Serbian Dreambook: National Imaginary in the Time of Milošević* (Bloomington, IN: Indiana University Press, 2011), p. 183.

[267] Ibid., p. 183. For the media dissemination of this discourse, see Jovanka Matić, "The Media and Ethnic Mobilization: The Formula of Kosovo," in *Ethnicity in Postcommunism* (Belgrade: Institute of Social Sciences, Forum for Ethnic Relations, 1996).

the Serbian Academicians implied, as Jović notes, that nowhere is the tragic past more closely linked to the present than in respect of Kosovo.[268] In the years immediately prior to the wars, the victimization rhetoric made its way from academic debate to the common cultural lexicon through repeated use by prominent intellectuals who in the meantime became politicians.[269] Besides issues of victimization and Kosovo, the central theme in the discourse of First Serbia was the subject of external and internal enemies and conspiracy. Guzina states that external enemies including "the West, the Vatican, the United States, Germany, Turkey, and the Freemasons" had their internal collaborators and their "agents" among the Serbs in the form of "rootless cosmopolitans," "anti-Serbs" and "domestic aliens."[270] Many authors have agreed that this xenophobic discourse dominated Serbian public life in the late 1980s through the early 1990s.[271]

Between 1991 and 1995, the discourse of First Serbia was built on these themes from the *Memorandum* consolidated through the use of symbols and historical myths which were, as Thomas notes, already deeply ingrained in society.[272] Such positioning reveals that the nature of the First Serbia discourse is as a nationalist discourse, isolationist and turned inward. The in-group bias in predication is remarkable; First Serbia affiliates mention only what they consider to be the positive aspects of Serbian history and culture, while denying, rejecting or simply ignoring the harmful or undesirable aspects of the present and the past. Such a narrative was re-emphasized in many texts published in the af-

---

[268] Dejan Jović, *Yugoslavia: The State that Withered Away* (Budapest: Central European Press, 2008), p. 234.
[269] Ibid., p. 235.
[270] Dejan Guzina, "Socialist Serbia's Narratives: From Yugoslavia to a Greater Serbia," *International Journal of Politics, Culture and Society*, 17, no. 1, (Fall 2003), p. 105.
[271] See Glen Bowman, "Xenophobia, Fantasy and the Nation: The Logic of Ethnic Violence in Former Yugoslavia," in Victoria A. Goddard, Josep R. Llobera and Cris Shore, eds., *Anthropology of Europe: Identity and Boundaries in Conflict* (London: Berg, 2004), p. 152; and Dejan Guzina, "Socialist Serbia's Narratives: From Yugoslavia to a Greater Serbia," *International Journal of Politics, Culture and Society*, 17, no. 1, (Fall 2003); and Sabrina Ramet and Vjeran Pavlaković. eds., *Serbia Since 1989: Politics and Society under Milošević and After* (Seattle: University of Washington Press, 2006).
[272] Robert Thomas, *Serbia under Milošević: The Politics of Serbia in the 1990s* (London: Hurst, 1999), p. 22.

termath of the *Memorandum*, however its deeper roots lie in the idea of populism and anti-modern, anti-European sentiment. The narrative was promoted widely by the political and social actors of First Serbia who dominated publishing and the media in Serbia and who were openly hostile to what were seen to be Western European values. Among them were many very distinguished scholars, artists, painters, writers, architects, philosophers and SANU members who were considered to belong to this cluster, such as the poet Matija Bećković, the philosopher Mihajlo Marković, the Siminovci group, the writer Brana Crnčević, the psychiatrist and politician Jovan Rašković, the academic Nikola Koljević, the writer and historian Dejan Medaković, the philosopher Mihailo Djurić, the painters Bata Mihailović and Petar Omčikus, the writers and painters Momo Kapor and Dragoš Kalajić, and the flamboyant painter Milić od Mačve. As is often the case when exploring "fluid" social phenomena, the list of names mentioned here is not exhaustive. Yet, the "father of the nation" and well-known writer and academic Dobrica Ćosić[273] was considered to be the center and the core of attraction for First Serbia affiliates. These groups of pro-nationalist intellectuals steadily introduced the themes of Europe and the West configured as a particular kind of threat, which were mostly circulated in the *Politika* newspaper and were later to be severely exploited as part of the process of constructing the meaning of national identity within the First Serbia vocabulary.

Gagnon finds that these intellectuals played a critical role in the creation and legitimization of historical "injustices" through their own independent work which was steadily adopted by the state.[274] Yet, through the press and specific political channels, these First Serbia actors sought to identify specific principles of their crusade with the general beliefs and values of society. It is clear that these new theories of Serb

---

[273] For further investigation of Dobrica Ćosić's role and the role of the Siminovci in re-imaginings of Serbian nationhood see three works by Nicholas J. Miller: "The Children of Cain: Dobrica Ćosić's Serbia," *Eastern European Politics and Societies*, 14, no. 2, (2000), p. 268–287; "Postwar Serbian Nationalism and the Limits of Invention," *Contemporary European History*, 13, no. 2, (2004), p. 151–69; and *The Nonconformists: Culture, Politics, and Nationalism in a Serbian Intellectual Circle, 1944–1991* (Budapest and New York: Central European University Press, 2007).

[274] Valère Philip Gagnon, *The Myth of Ethnic War: Serbia and Croatia in the 1990s* (Ithaca, NY and London: Cornell University Press, 2004).

identity embraced a specific type of cultural ethnocentrism.[275] As Rossi notes, First Serbia ethnocentrism is far more exclusionary than others, especially due to the delineation of membership along religious lines and by shared historical memories of victimization during the Communist period.[276] In addition, Janjić demonstrates that the First Serbia narrative also embraces certain traditional Serbian values which are rooted in the extended familial relations of Slavic, Byzantine and Ottoman customs that serve to emphasize group solidarity and collective freedom, in sharp contrast to Western concepts of individual liberty and social justice.[277] In this sense, these actors conveyed some sense of an anti-modern sentiment and anti-enlightenment spirit, demonstrating a new type of identity vocabulary. One can notice a strong anti-Atlanticism being employed as the means to establish connections with other Slavic and former Third World countries in the hope that Serbia can revive its past influence. This alliance is very much embedded in the psyche of First Serbia political and cultural elites. The armed conflict in Croatia and Bosnia, and the highly critical Western television news reporting of it, served to sustain the residual sense of anti-Western identity that could be drawn on by the Serbian nationalist rhetoric whenever it was needed. Of course, the Eastern animosity toward Western pragmatism, empiricism and superficiality, in contrast to the depth of Slavic culture, was always prevalent among Serbian intellectuals. A fascination with the Russian 19th century novel is still sustained and is presented in today's Serbia as proof of Slavic depth and worth. Given this special relationship with the East, it is not difficult to see some intrinsic authenticity in the cultural interactions between Serbians and Russians, even under the changed circumstances in which we find ourselves today.

---

[275] Michael A. Rossi, "Resurrecting the Past: Democracy, National Identity and Historical Memory in Modern Serbia," PhD thesis, New Brunswick Rutgers, (2009).
[276] Ibid., p. 18.
[277] See Dušan Janjić, ed., *Serbia Between the Past and the Future* (Belgrade: Institute of Social Sciences Forum for Ethnic Relations, 1995).

"First" Serbia vocabulary

Self-ascribed victimhood and suffering appears to be the consistent theme among self-identified First Serbia actors. Jansen finds that the themes of victimhood and martyrdom originate from the defeat of the Christian armies at the Battle of Kosovo in 1389 and continue as the embodiment of Serbian suffering and sacrifice.[278] Moreover, during the wars in Bosnia and Kosovo in the 1990s, the theme of Serbs defending Christian Europe against Islamic expansionism were repeatedly used. Jansen finds that the tale of victimization continues with five centuries of oppression "under the Turks," reaching its climax in the Second World War genocide at the hands of German and Croatian Fascists and their collaborators.[279] It was not so much that traditions of inter-ethnic antagonism were "invented" but, as Bowman notes, a discursive shift effectively allowed these muted memories of the Second World War to become the central point of new definitions of identities.[280] The usual strategy of inventing enemies was, in the case of the Yugoslav ethnic conflict, as Jusić points out, a primary strategy of polarization.[281] Alongside this, was employed, as the core of communication strategy, the simplification of the narratives and the facts of the Second World War, in order to promote further the perception of national homogenization. To the same end, the First Serbia affiliates propagated the ideas of the uniqueness and antiquity of the Serbian nation. The prominent First Serbia painter Milić od Mačve writes:

---

[278] Stef Jansen, "Victims, Underdogs and Rebels. Discursive Practices of Resistance in Serbian Protest," in *Critique of Anthropology*, 20, no. 4 (2000), p. 402.

[279] Ibid., p. 403.

[280] Glen Bowman, "Xenophobia, Fantasy and the Nation: The Logic of Ethnic Violence in Former Yugoslavia," in Victoria A. Goddard, Josep R. Llobera and Cris Shore. Eds., *Anthropology of Europe: Identity and Boundaries in Conflict* (London: Berg, 2004), p. 152.

[281] Tarik Jusić, "Media Discourse and the Politics of Ethnic Conflict: the Case of Yugoslavia," in Pål Kolstø, ed., *Media Discourse and the Yugoslav Conflicts: Representation of the Self and Other* (Farnham, UK: Ashgate, 2009), p. 35.

> The Serbs are the autochthonous people of the Balkans. Emperor Constantine was a Serb, as were so many other Roman Caesars. We are still defending the so-called old [Julian] calendar named after one of them, Julius. Only, those Caesars were more or less deracinated Sorabs, Etruscans because the Roman and Latin tribes committed a terrible genocide against the Etruscans, just as the Croats are doing to modern Serbs. One day everything will be clear when Sorabian consciousness prevails.[282]

As Gojković notes, different types of discursive practices served as justification for participation in the Yugoslav wars, such as the *Antemurale Christianitatis*[283] motif, which sees the Serbs as the defenders of the gates and the bearers of true civilization.[284] The wars in Croatia and Bosnia were often explained and justified by recourse to the argument that Serbian men were defending variously themselves, their wives and children, their homesteads, the entire Serbian nation, Yugoslavia and, ultimately Christianity itself. What is more, Gojković suggests that the international isolation and UN sanctions which followed were mostly read by the First Serbia elites as being indicative of victimization by, and lack of understanding from, the West.[285] The strategy of inventing enemies gave way to the *Memorandum's* emphasis on the fate of Kosovo, as the primary strategy of polarization. Kosovo "had become a matter of life and death for the Serbian people"[286] and served to greatly advance the cause of national homogenization. To illustrate this premise, here is a quote from poet and national tribune Matija Bećković's article on the meaning of Kosovo:

---

[282] Milić od Mačve, the eccentric painter, became one of the main disseminators of the various theories of Serbs as the most ancient people. Quoted from Marko Živković, *Serbian Dreambook: National Imaginary in the Time of Milošević* (Bloomington, IN: Indiana University Press, 2011), p. 144.

[283] Latin for the "Bulwark of Christianity." This myth comes in many different guises and under different labels: *christianitatis, Europe, the defenders of the gates, the bearers of true civilization*, etc.

[284] Drinka Gojković, "The Birth of Nationalism from the Spirit of Democracy: The Association of Writers of Serbia and the War" in Nebojša Popov, ed., *The Road to War in Serbia* (Budapest: Central European University Press, 2000), p. 402.

[285] Ibid.

[286] Kosta Mihailović and Vasilije Krestić, *Memorandum: odgovori na kritike* (*Memorandum: the Answer to Criticism*) (Beograd: SANU, 1995), p. 99–149.

> Kosovo is the most expensive Serbian word. It has been paid for with the blood of the whole people. With that price in blood it became enthroned on the throne of the Serbian language. Without blood it couldn't have been bought, without blood it couldn't be sold. Kosovo is the equator of the Serbian planet … Kosovo is a Serbianised story of the flood: the Serbian New Testament. Kosovo is a hearth that assembles, a pillar that congregates the Serbian people. Kosovo is the crossroads on which the Serbs found themselves and found their path. Kosovo is the deepest wound, the longest remembrance, the most vivid memory, the most beloved ash—the spiritual cradle of the Serbian people.[287]

The First Serbia cultural elites managed to take from the reservoir of symbolic material from history, both recent and distant, and put the issue of Kosovo, as "the most expensive Serbian word," at the front of the political debates. First Serbia actors made frequent and very clear references to Kosovo, and to Orthodox Christianity, as symbols of Serbian national identity and as indicators of entrenched Serbian uniqueness. The rhetoric on Kosovo directly leads us to the glorification of the East, of Russia and of Orthodox Christianity. This argumentation continues the notion of the spiritual bankruptcy and corruption of the West which was promulgated in particular by theologians and high-ranking Serbian Orthodox Church officials including Bishop Nikolaj Velimirović.[288] Leading members of the Serbian Orthodox Church often expressed opinions such as "Western Europe has abandoned the path of Christ and has become the great evil, which poisons the environment in which the European part of humanity is dying, and Western Europe, having based its culture on man, has made man a slave to things."[289] These themes and

---

[287] Matija Bećković, "Kosovo je najskuplja srpska reč" in *Glas crkve: časopis za hrišćansku kulturu i crkveni život*, (1989), p. 19–28. The quote is taken from Marko Živković, *Serbian Dreambook: National Imagary in the Time of Milošević* (Bloomington, IN: Indiana University Press, 2011), p. 178.

[288] Nikolaj Velimirović (1981–1956) was an influential theological writer. When the Germans occupied Yugoslavia in the Second World War, Velimirović was imprisoned and eventually taken to Dachau concentration camp in Germany. After being liberated by the Allies at the end of the war, he chose not to return to Yugoslavia (which had a Communist government by that time). Instead, he spent some time in Europe and moved to the United States in 1946, where he remained until his death in 1956. A degree of controversy surrounds him in relation to his anti-Semitism. For more on Velimirović see Jovan Byford, *From "traitor"' to "saint": Bishop Nikolaj Velimirović in Serbian Public Memory* (Jerusalem: Hebrew University of Jerusalem, 2004).

[289] Nikolaj Velimirović, quoted from Byford, J. *From "traitor" to "saint": Bishop Nikolaj Velimirović in Serbian Public Memory* (Jerusalem: Hebrew University of Jerusalem,

ideas are still considered to be highly relevant to post-2000 political discourses in today's Serbian society. I postulate that First Serbia's attitudes encompassed the totality of perspectives in which the concept of national identity is projected through ethnic, primordial and spatial cultural lenses. Such discourse draws heavily on medieval Byzantine mythology designed and preserved through the centuries mainly by the Church. A considerable part of this is the so-called *patriotic discourse* that delves into several major motifs including, as Ejdus notes, the ideal of the warrior, martyrdom, treason, conspiracy, notions of victimhood, antiquity and uniqueness.[290] As an illustration of this, in the summer of 1994 Belgrade hosted a Gathering of the Cultures of Spiritually Kindred, Eastern Orthodox Peoples attended by various representatives hailing from sixteen Orthodox countries as far afield as Armenia and Belarus. The event was attended by a number of prominent First Serbia intellectuals, such as Kalajić, who wrote expansively on the topic of the "specific kind of Western decadence." Živković notes that Kalajić combines the views of the Western elitist right wing and of the Russian "Euroasianists," his opinions dominated by "conspiracy theories in which Freemasonry, the Trilateral Commission and the Vatican led by the "high priests of supranational capital," helped by the fifth column of domestic "mondialists" and "decadent cosmopolitans" try to undermine the "spiritual vertical" of the Serbian and other Orthodox cultures of the Byzantine Commonwealth.[291]

In this type of in group favoritism, Serbia is constructed as the home of genuine ancient values and antediluvian high culture. This

---

2004). For further insight into this matter see Mylonas, "Serbian Orthodox Fundamentals: The Quest for an Eternal Identity," *The American Historical Review*, 109, no. 3, (2004); and Vjekoslav Perica, "The Sanctification of Enmity: Churches and the Construction of Founding Myths of Serbia and Croatia," in Pol Kostø, ed., *Myths and Boundaries in South-Eastern Europe*, (London: Hurst, 2005); and Ivan Iveković, "Nationalism and the Political Use and Abuse of Religion: The Politicization of Orthodoxy, Catholicism and Islam in Yugoslav Successor States," *Social Compass: Review of Socio-religious Studies*, 49, no. 4, (2002), p. 523–536.

[290] Filip Ejdus, *"Security,* Strategic *Culture and Identity in Serbia,"* in *Western Balkans Security Observer*, No. 7, (Belgrade, October–December 2008).

[291] Marko Živković, *Serbian Dreambook: National Imaginary in the Time of Milošević* (Bloomington, IN: Indiana University Press, 2011), p. 144.

book concludes that these intellectuals have played, and continue to play, a pivotal role in codifying the cognitive structure of national identity by defining the cultural material without which the national narratives, consciousness and national memories of First Serbia would not exist.

The message of First Serbia regarding the Yugoslav conflicts was simple and constantly reiterated in the media: the villains of the story were variously the Croatians, Albanians, Bosnians, and the West, but never themselves. The heroes were those who fought against them, including Bosnian Serbs, but also Serb volunteers and militias from Serbia proper. The First Serbia message for posterity was not "never again" but, rather, "perhaps again if history repeats itself as it tends to do in this region." The public presentation of the number of victims in the wars was dramatically under-represented, and disproportionately so in the case of victims of the Serbian forces. The reasons given for the dissolution of Yugoslavia have repeatedly evoked the need for constant vigilance, for the waging of a continual battle, and have created a sense of belonging in adversity, where "We" are united in our recognition that we are surrounded with enemies. The more extreme early First Serbia actors sought to present history in a way that could be used for political benefit. Ever since then, these core First Serbia scholars and public intellectuals have presented the history of the wars in a way that is almost completely lacking in any responsibility or guilt on the part of Serbia. This simplified version of history is highly effective in sustaining an official historical consciousness free of collective responsibility and consequently shame. Such narratives bring about absences in the historic books and the absence of sensitivities in popular consciousness. The media's frequent and compelling reports featured almost exclusively Serbian victims and, while tales of cruelty and death are always touching and poignant, once emotions against the Others involved in the dissolution of Yugoslavia were stirred, then the audience was led to the unavoidable conclusion of loyalty to First Serbia's version of history. What we find here is the combination of the non-internalization of the official story "portrayed by the Western media," while not even accepting Serbia's defeat in the Yugoslav wars. Unsurprisingly, behind such a narrative of proud nationhood is a message for posterity that there is no need to be ashamed to be Serbian.

At this point I would like to shed some light on the dominance and control of the regime over television and print media. The rhetoric of First Serbia actors during and after Milošević's ascent to power was widely propagated by the state media, which was fully under the control of Milošević's bureaucrats by the end of 1990. Both Milošević's rise to power and the path to war were made easier by the control which the regime exercised over the daily newspaper *Politika*, the weekly magazine *NIN* and the national broadcasting service *Radio Television of Serbia (RTS)*. Gordy notes that maintaining control over sources of information was a key element of the regime's strategy for staying in power.[292] Although independent newspapers, television and radio stations such as Studio B and B92, who painted a very different picture, emerged following a brief wave of pluralism, most of them were rarely available outside Belgrade.

"First" Serbia after 2000

"First" Serbia discursive continuity with Milošević-era narratives has manifested in two different ways. First, it is evident that the pre-2000 discourse on "victims and perpetrators" continued to function in the post-2000 historical framework. Second, the persistence of the contested image of "Europe" resulted in the development with Russia of what Heuser and Buffet call a myth of special relationships.[293] According to these authors, assumptions of a special relationship can operate in either a positive or negative form, as an especially good relationship or as a contrasting relationship.[294] The First Serbia case reveals an open political orientation toward Russia and the Orthodox Commonwealth. After the end of the Milošević regime in 2000, the new president Vojislav Koštunica maintained a political orientation that drew on discursive continuity

---

[292] Eric Gordy, *The Culture of Power in Serbia: Nationalism and the Destruction of Alternatives* (University Park, PA: The Pennsylvania University Press, 1999), p. 41.

[293] For the myths of special relationships see Beatrice Heuser, and Cyril Buffet, *Haunted by History: Myths in International Relations* (Oxford: Berghahn, 1998), p. 260.

[294] Ibid.

with the previous government's rhetoric on Russia and Europe. Within the framework of a discourse of victimization, the First Serbia account has endured and renewed itself, principally through DSS's general manifesto and Koštunica's speeches. Koštunica's ideological position, as Cohen notes, was close to the moderate nationalists at the time of the 2000 elections.[295] He was also in general quite critical of Western involvement in the Balkans and this position was crucial for the 2000 elections, as consequently he could not be accused of being a "foreign stooge" in the way the regime often described opposition leaders.[296] Koštunica stated that he would pursue "neither attachment to the West, nor attachment to Russia," but rather a rational foreign policy.[297] In his inaugural address in 2000, Koštunica gave a clear warning to the international community "not to interfere in Yugoslavia's internal affairs."[298] The strategy of the DSS was clear already in the first months of their mandate. Koštunica's speeches were concerned with the issue of national dignity: "There are those who did us wrong, who bombed us. We cannot forget the damage or the crimes against us; Serbs will lose their identity if they forget those crimes."[299]

The post-2000 pro-nationalistic elites, as Subotić notes, greatly resented European attempts to make them take responsibility for the reputation of the "architect of the Yugoslav breakup and the biggest perpetrator of wartime atrocities" and saw this as another humiliation at the hands of the Europeans.[300] Subotić further notes a clear continuation of the victimization discourse, in this vision of the Serbian people as victims of crimes committed against them, and never by them.[301] The basic moral of First Serbia's message is, for all the differences of topic and style, essentially simple. The Serbian people, peasants and working peo-

---

[295] Lenard J. Cohen, *Serpent in the Bosom: The Rise and Fall of Slobodan Milošević* (Boulder, CO: Westview Press, 2001), p. 430.
[296] Ibid.
[297] "Koštunica's speech: Dear Liberated Serbia," *B92 News*, (October 6, 2000). http://news.bbc.co.uk/1/hi/world/europe/959312.stm
[298] Ibid.
[299] Ibid.
[300] Jelena Subotić, "Europe is a State of Mind: Identity and Europeanization in the Balkans," *International Studies Quarterly*, 55, (2011), p. 309–330 at 321.
[301] Ibid.

ple, were innocent people and the ills of Serbian history did not arise from the peculiarities of any specific Serbian doings, whether defined in cultural, political or socioeconomic terms, but from oppressing foreign forces, namely, in earlier history the Ottomans and at the end of the twentieth century, the international community. Thus, in First Serbia discourse Serbs continue to be portrayed merely as victims and never as perpetrators. As a direct consequence, the First Serbia elites and the public opposed cooperation with the Hague tribunal from the outset.[302] They perceived the court as a Western legal imposition, which predominantly tried Serb nationals, and, most importantly, which institutionalized a version of recent history that painted the Serbs as the main perpetrators of the war.[303]

The political hostility toward Europe was evident from the First Serbia elite's persistent insistence that Europe was responsible for the breakup of Yugoslavia and the wars that ensued. Certain actors suggested, as an alternative to joining the European Union, that Serbia instead forge a closer connection with Russia. The Progressive Party (SNS) is seen as the political wing of First Serbia, and is the strongest party in Serbia in the time of publication of this book. Before its transformation into a party of Euro-enthusiasts in 2008, certain elements of that party had been known for showing an openly anti-European and Euroskeptic orientation, and for promoting closer ties with Russia.[304] Tomislav Nikolić asserted that "when it comes to foreign policy, Serbia should focus on the Russian Federation, China, India, Brazil and the Arab countries. Right now, (President) Boris Tadić is more on the side of the EU, but life will teach him that he should pay more attention to Russia. Tadić's public evolution has already become evident."[305] According to Gallup research from 2011, as many as 69 percent of the Serbian population favor

---

[302] See Milivoj Despot, *The Hague Tribunal: Discord Between us and the World* (Belgrade: Helsinki Committee for Human Rights in Serbia, 2001).

[303] Jelena Subotić, "Europe is a State of Mind: Identity and Europeanization in the Balkans," *International Studies Quarterly*, 55, (2011), p. 309–330.

[304] Nikolić stated that he would be happy if Serbia became one of Russia's guberniyas. See "Europe or Russia" in *Radio Free Europe*, March 2, 2008.

[305] See "Nikolić Bemoans 'Unbalanced Priorities' since 2000" in *B92 News* (December 17, 2008). http://www.b92.net/eng/news/politics.php?yyyy=2008&mm=12&dd=17&nav_id=55798.

forging the closest ties with Russia, whereas only 31 percent think of the EU as friendly toward Serbia, and 15 percent consider the EU as openly hostile.[306] Thus, the Serbian public has been well known for showing a certain antagonism toward the idea of joining the European Union.

The post-2000 "Kosovo or Europe" debate

This section briefly tackles the post-2000 "Kosovo or Europe" debate, the complexities of which are explored in finer detail in later chapters. To recapitulate, the First Serbia discourse on identity understands Europe as a polity that seeks to take away from Serbia the territory of Kosovo, which is and will always be Serbian. On the same side of this ideological spectrum, despite being a member of the Democratic Party until 2012, former Serbian foreign minister Vuk Jeremić argued that it is obvious that Serbian national and religious identity means attachment, belonging and historical connection to Kosovo as "Kosovo is the cradle of Serbian national identity."[307] According to Jeremić, this historical premise evidences Serbia's legal and political claims to the province.[308] The "Europe or Kosovo" political debate became the predominant political narrative within the public sphere after Kosovo's declaration of independence in 2008. It is clear that, in large part by drawing heavily on the Kosovo case, the political and cultural elites of First Serbia have promoted a vision of Serbian identity which is divergent from any European identity and is built on fiercely alternative identity narratives. These narratives form a convincing Euroskeptic mode of identity which is already strong and clearly articulated, and, as Subotić argues, exists within its own

---

[306] According to Gallup Balkan Monitor, the role of the international community over the last twenty years was depicted as extremely harmful by 40.6% of surveyed participants. Moreover, half of the Serbian population thinks NATO is still extremely hostile toward Serbia and 69% disapprove of US leadership in the region (Gallup Balkan Monitor, 2011, Survey on Geopolitics).

[307] Here, Jeremić refers to the foundation of the first Serbian state on the territory of Kosovo in the 12th century. *HardTalk*, BBC, September 1, 2010.

[308] Vuk Jeremić, *HardTalk*, BBC, September 1, 2010.

discursive space, and strong political and cultural coalitions continue to promote them.[309]

Even the most fervent and zealous anti-European stances are not marginalized but are effectively included in the debate on Europe. These discursive strategies, as Volčić notes, presented a simplified and culturally inferior image of the West as supermarket culture, Disneyland, Britney Spears and insurance companies.[310] Additionally, the views of the ultra-nationalistic right toward Europe can be summed up by the slogan: "The EU is a grave for the Serbian people."[311] Such views can be found among groups such as the *Obraz Fatherland Movement* and *Dveri* which perceive the EU as a "body that has abandoned all the basic principles of the old European civilization—God, nation and family."[312] Now banned, *Obraz* stated that Western orientation in Serbia should be contrasted with the "nationalism of Saint Sava that puts meaning in place of godless internationalism."[313] *Dveri*, a pro-Christian right-wing group, is another influential discursive actor in Serbian public space that understands the history of Serbia in the following way:

> The misfortunes of the Serbian people in the 20th century have largely been caused by forced, hasty, and badly calculated integrations, starting with Yugoslavism, via the communist quasi-brotherhood and unity, to a push for Euro-Uniate integration at any cost. This forces us to adjust our 21st century policies fully and absolutely only to Serbian interests. Even though we (Serbs) ended up as the last believers in Yugoslavism and communism even when these two utopias were in the middle of a bloody collapse in front of our very eyes, we cannot allow ourselves to be the last followers of a collapsed ideology of Euro-Uniatism.[314]

---

[309] Jelena Subotić, "Europe is a State of Mind: Identity and Europeanization in the Balkans," *International Studies Quarterly*, 55, (2011), p. 309–330 at 314.

[310] Zala Volčić, "The notion of 'The West' in the Serbian National Imaginary," *European Journal of Cultural Studies*, 8, no. 2, (2005), p. 155–175 at 165.

[311] See "EU is a Grave for Serbian people," *Obraz*, (August 9, 2010). http://www.obraz.rs.

[312] Marko Stojić, "Between Europhobia and Europhilia: Party and Popular Attitudes Towards Membership of the European Union in Serbia and Croatia" in *Perspectives on European Politics and Society*, 7, no 3, (2006), p. 325.

[313] See "The EU is a Grave for Serbian people," *Obraz*, (August 9, 2010). http://www.obraz.rs

[314] "Political Manifesto: Foreign Policy," *Dveri*. http://www.dverisrpske.com/sr-CS/nasa-politika/izborni-program/spoljna-politika-dveri.php.

Certain radicalized groups entreat their audience never to forget the past. Rather than forget the past they relocate it. The perpetrators, who bear the guilt for the war are "Them," and the victims are still "Us," and the new resistance fighters to this New World Order are living on and striving for power in modern Serbia. Thus, the discursive practices of First Serbia narratives throughout the 1990s internalized the heroic victim, and externalized the more powerful enemy, be it the Turks, the West or Europe. This main narrative was established in the early 1990s and has now been re-shaped and re-interpreted, but remains the key framework within which is presented Serbia's impalpable past.

The next section focuses solely on the beginning of the Other Serbia anti-war movement from 1991 onwards. During the conflicts of the 1990s, the Serbian public sphere was heavily dominated by debates between groups that still remain at opposite ends of the ideological political spectrum. I intend to set out the manner in which these groups performed the role of "constitutive outside" for each other in the early days of their reconstitution. However, one can immediately detect a problem. Do First and Other Serbia envision Serbian collective identity as a shared historical legacy, a shared fate and destiny? The analysis will show that the two ideological strata are opposed in respect of the legacy of Yugoslavia, the role of religion in political affairs, and the identity of the common enemy. There is no shared view of the Other and therefore no sense of a common perceived future. The debates analyzed here demonstrate how the processes of othering, and consequently the notion of a divided society, are continually being remodeled, reinvented and reconstructed.

"Other" Serbia: beginnings and self-identification

This work reflects a constructivist perspective in which different actors drawing on history and each other's role in it, may come to view "belonging" in different ways. This section explores the establishment of "Other" Serbia and the principles of their manifesto. From 1992 to 1995 horrific atrocities were perpetrated in Croatia and Bosnia in a systematic manner, however, those events occurred outside Serbian territory. As a result of the Milošević regime's policies, the elites were further polarized, and existing ideological divisions were further emphasized. The Serbian political scene was partitioned into "defenders" and "attackers" of these policies. Other Serbia exemplified the voices of dissent and of attackers of the Milošević regime who claimed that the war in general, and specific incidents of barbarity in particular, were not taking place in their name. The concept of Other Serbia can be said to have first come into being when the non-governmental organization *Belgrade Circle* published a journal in 1992 with the same name. On January 25, 1992 the *Association of Independent Intellectuals Belgrade Circle* was founded. According to their manifesto, *Belgrade Circle* was intended to be a critical voice that openly fought against the militaristic politics of the Milošević regime and especially against ethnonationalism, populism, war crimes and ethnic cleansing.[315] In the period between 1992 and 1995 the *Belgrade Circle* conducted the *Saturday Sessions* project, public lectures and discussions attended by both members and non-members, which hosted approximately 140 intellectuals from all former Yugoslav republics and abroad. As the result of these seminars two books were published, *Other Serbia* and *Intellectuals and War*, which brought together around fifty texts. Ivan Čolović notes that these books were the products of the alternative voices of intellectuals, professors, architects, writers, journalists, film and theatre directors, among others, who were "engaging in the long-term fight with political apathy in Serbian society."[316] These public gatherings, which represented a vital hub for the political and cultural life of the so-called Other — in this sense *different, non-nationalistic* — Serbia, were envisioned as opposition to the militaristic nationalism of the Milošević regime, and to its "xenophobia and populism" which, in their view, had taken over Serbian society in the early 1990s.[317] Čolović also argues that Other Serbia, during these sessions, revisited the legitimization of the wars in Slovenia, Croatia and Bosnia, thus sending a powerful message to Europe and the world that not all citizens of Serbia stood united in support of bloodshed and genocide.[318] Notable partici-

---

[315] For the collected essays and their political contexts in the early 1990s, see Aljoša Mimica, ed., *Druga Srbija* (*Other Serbia*), (Beogradski Krug, Borba, 1992).
[316] Ivan Čolović, *Belgrade Circle Journal Online,* 2002. http://web1.uct.usm.maine.edu/~bcj
[317] Ibid.
[318] Ibid.

pants in these *Saturday Sessions* included philosopher Radomir Konstantinović, professor Latinka Perović, scholar Ivan Čolović, well-known writer and dissident Milovan Djilas, ballerina Jelena Santić, film-maker Živojin Pavlović, professor Obrad Savić, theatre-director Borka Pavičević, feminist Saska Stanojlović, sociologist Aljoša Mimica, professor Filip David, former mayor of Belgrade Bogdan Bogdanović, and sociologist Dušan Janjić among many others. Dragović-Soso considers that many of these individuals' political origins can be found in the dissident activism of the "Belgrade critical intelligentsia" of the 1970s and 1980s, with its various committees for the defense of free thought and expression and its petitions for respect of human and civil rights.[319] This view is supported by Bilić, who adds that various Yugoslav activism in the 1990s utilized social networks created through student, feminist and environmentalist engagement in socialist Yugoslavia and in that way enabled the establishment of many of the organizations devoted to human rights which still exist today across the post-Yugoslav space.[320]

From their early 1990s debates, through the concept of First and Other Serbia, the identity narratives of the national Self and Serbian radical or amicable Others, started to reveal themselves. This is why I first investigated the structures of the dominant discourse of First Serbia, which acted both to constrain and to enable the other political actors/discursive agents. My aim was to clearly identify this basic discourse upon which the discourse of Other Serbia and the discourses on Europe and identity were built. In this respect, professor Ljubiša Rajić,[321]

---

[319] Jasna Dragović-Soso, "Collective Responsibility, International Justice and Public Reckoning with the Recent Past: Reflections on a Debate in Serbia" in Timothy Waters, ed., *The Milošević Trial—An Autopsy*, (Oxford: Oxford University Press, 2013).

[320] Bilić, Bojan, *We Were Gasping for Air: [Post-]Yugoslav Anti-War Activism and Its Legacy* (Baden-Baden: Nomos, 2012), p. 12.

[321] Professor Ljubiša Rajić established and developed the Department for Scandinavian Studies at the University of Belgrade. Interestingly, for most Norwegians he is remembered as "The voice from Belgrade," reporting in fluent Norwegian from Serbia in the late 1990s, conveying the values of another, democratic and liberal Serbia. He was elected a member of the Norwegian Academy of Sciences. Rajić was appointed Knight of First Class of the Royal Norwegian Order of Merit in 2009 for the promotion of Norwegian-Serbian relations, particularly in the field of language, literature and culture. "The death of Dr Ljubiša Rajić," is on *Norway – the official site in Serbia* http://www.norveska.org.rs/News_and_events/The-death-of-Dr-Ljubiša-Rajić/.

one of the main *Belgrade Circle* session participants, explored in more detail the resistance to the dominant values of First Serbia. A central question of this chapter, then, refers to the process of nomination: how are the social actors linguistically constructed by being named? In Rajić's view, Other Serbia means different Serbia.[322] The analysis of these defiant texts reveals the ways in which Other Serbia understood, imagined and created itself. Rajić asks what kind of Serbia is wanted, how far can that ideal be achieved, and who will create this different Serbia:[323] "the [Milošević] government is unlikely to do it as it has created exactly the kind of Serbia it needs and has no need for a different one. Would the main opposition parties that are trying to rehabilitate Milan Nedić[324] (while paying lip service to Slobodan Jovanović[325] at the same time), that are trying to resurrect Dimitrije Ljotić's[326] ZBOR, that are building monuments to Draža Mihailović,[327] and that are asking for the return of

---

[322] Ljubiša Rajić, "Srbija iz početka" (Serbia from the Beginning), in *Druga Srbija deset godina posle: 1992–2002 (Other Serbia Ten Years Later: 1992–2002)*, edited by Aljoša Mimica, (Helsinski odbor za ljudska prava, 2002), p. 58.

[323] Ibid.

[324] Milan Nedić was a Serbian general and politician who was the Prime Minister of the Nazi-backed government during the Second World War. Nedić was chief of general staff of the Yugoslav Army and Minister of War in the Royal Yugoslav Government. The controversy surrounding him relates to the fact that the Serbian Academy of Sciences and Arts named him as one of the 100 most significant Serbs. Nedić's portrait was included among those of Serbian Prime Ministers in the building of the Government of Serbia. In 2008 the Minister of Interior and Deputy Prime Minister Ivica Dačić removed the portrait after neo-Nazi marches were announced in the country.

[325] Slobodan Jovanović (1869–1958), Serbian jurist, historian, and statesman, Prime Minister and Deputy Minister of War in the Yugoslav government-in-exile (in London) during the Second World War. When, after the Second World War, the Allies recognized the communist government of Yugoslavia, Jovanović became President of the Yugoslav National Committee in exile. In July 1946 he was condemned in absentia to twenty years' hard labour. "Slobodan Jovanovic" in *Encyclopaedia Britannica* online (last updated July 31, 2015). http://www.britannica.com/EBchecked/topic/306826/Slobodan-Jovanovic

[326] Dimitrije Ljotić was a Serbian fascist politician and Nazi German collaborator during the Second World War. In 1935, he was elected President of the newly-formed party ZBOR which is often compared to fascist movements in other countries.

[327] Dragoljub "Draža" Mihailović was a Yugoslav Serb general during the Second World War and the leader of the notorious Četnik detachments of the Yugoslav Army. After the war, Mihailović was tried and convicted of high treason and war crimes by the authorities of the Federal People's Republic of Yugoslavia, and executed by firing squad.

Momčilo Djujić[328] be able to do it? Their version of "Other Serbia" would be even worse than the current one. Could it be the portion of the Serbian intellectual elite that has no issues with nationalism but considers its members more intelligent than those that are running the country; those that are not against war per se, but are against the notion of starting a war and then proceeding to lose it? Or would it be us, the so-called independent intellectuals?"[329]

By analyzing First Serbia's historical heroes, Professor Rajić directly positions Other Serbia against them. Thus, what is Other Serbia in the discourse of the Belgrade liberal intelligentsia? Is an Other Serbia even possible? As noted above, the process of nomination refers to how actors are constructed by being named. Čolović suggests that "the expression Other Serbia became a motto for all those who sooner or later came to see the dangers of the nationalist policies of the past five or more years."[330] The guru of Other Serbia, Radomir Konstantinović, noted in a similar vein that Other Serbia is "the one that does not reconcile with the crimes."[331] Writer László Végel[332] recalls "I admit when I first heard about the "Other" Serbia paradigm I thought of a liberal state free from the

---

[328] Momčilo R. Djujić was a Serbian Orthodox priest who became a Croatian Serb Četnik commander and led a significant proportion of the Četniks within the Independent State of Croatia during the Second World War. After the assassination of King Alexander of Yugoslavia in 1934 he joined the Četnik movement led by Kosta Pećanac. After defending local Serbs against the Ustaše, he collaborated with the Axis against the Yugoslav Partisans throughout the remainder of the war. Djujić survived the war, surrendering to the British and eventually emigrating to the United States. He was instrumental in perpetuating Četnik ideas in the United States, and controversially appointed Vojislav Šešelj as a Četnik vojvoda in 1989.

[329] Ljubiša Rajić, "Srbija iz početka" ("Serbia From the Beginning"), in Aljoša Mimica, ed., *Druga Srbija deset godina posle: 1992–2002 (Other Serbia Ten Years Later: 1992–2002)*, (Helsinški odbor za ljudska prava, 2002), p. 58.

[330] Aljoša Mimica, ed., *Druga Srbija—deset godina posle: 1992–2002 (Other Serbia: Ten Years Later: 1992–2002)*, (Helsinški odbor za ljudska prava u Srbiji, 2002), p. 364

[331] Ibid., p. 34.

[332] László Végel is a writer, and a theatre critic. He writes in his mother tongue, Hungarian, and is part of Hungarian, as well as Serbian, literature. In 2009 he received the highest prize for literature in Budapest.

grip of ideology and nationalism and retrograde doctrines of historical mythology."[333]

Professor Rajić notes, "While *we* were arguing ("Other" Serbia), *they* were busy distributing weapons ("First" Serbia)."[334] This naming and positioning clearly points to the origins of the internal social cleavages in Serbia as being the pro-war and anti-war positions adopted by the various social groups. In the immediate aftermath of communism, and in the times of conflict and authoritarian regimes which followed, one can see the feeble initial stages of creation of the movement of liberal intelligentsia. Mirko Tepavac[335] envisioned Other Serbia as a *new country*:

> I do not view the "Other" Serbia as an alternative to the present one in which we are stuck and whose destiny we share whether we like it or not. I also do not view this "Other" Serbia as some sort of noble utopia, or as a country that does not yet exist and needs to be outlined as a plan. I do not imagine it as a future country, one that will inevitably appear but not as "Other" Serbia, but one of much iteration. This would be Serbia in a certain period, different from both past and future iterations.[336]

The main question here is: what is the strategy of the discursive construction of collective Serbian identity in the Other Serbia discourse? By calling themselves other, different, something that comes second, is "Self-Othering" the dominant strategy in this discourse on identity? Also, is this difference toward the Other (First Serbia or Europe) constructed as having been acquired, or as an inherent difference? The historian Ćirković[337] noted in 1992 that Other Serbia is new and educated

---

[333] Lásló Végel, "Šanse liberalne katarze" ("The Chance of Liberal Catharsis"), in Aljoša Mimica, ed., *Druga Srbija deset godina posle: 1992–2002 (Other Serbia Ten Years Later: 1992–2002* (Helsinski odbor za ljudska prava, 2002), p. 49.

[334] Ljubiša Rajić, "Srbija iz početka" (Serbia From the Beginning), in Aljoša Mimica, ed., *Druga Srbija deset godina posle: 1992–2002 (Other Serbia Ten Years Later: 1992–2002)* (Helsinski odbor za ljudska prava, 2002), p. 59.

[335] Mirko Tepavac was a distinguished Yugoslav politician and an officer in the Second World War.

[336] Mirko Tepavac, "Da li je moguća Druga Srbija?" ("Is Other Serbia even Possible?") in Aljoša Mimica, ed., *Druga Srbija deset godina posle: 1992–2002 (Other Serbia Ten Years Later: 1992–2002)* (Helsinski odbor za ljudska prava, 2002), p. 45.

[337] Sima M. Ćirković (Osijek, 1929–Belgrade, 2009) was a Serbian historian and member of the Serbian Academy of Science and Arts. His work focused on medieval Serbian history. In 1986 Ćirković criticised the *Memorandum* of the Serbian Academy of Sciences and Arts when, during the Siege of Dubrovnik, he and other Yugoslav histori-

and should represent "the cultured layer of Serbian society that should try to impose its value hierarchy which is quite different from the prevailing one [First Serbia]."[338] It is clear that these activists and actors reiterate and acknowledge the differences between "European, liberal values" and "patriotic values." The essentialist conception of the national identity is discredited, but what remains is very powerful. Still, the pattern is not clear, nor is whether Other Serbia is still an ongoing project, a positive end to aspire to bring about in the future or, in other words, a political promise. If it is ongoing, this begs the questions of what ideas this project promotes, and how these actors understand and evaluate their own Serbianness. In the shadow of the Yugoslav wars, any notion of Serbian national identity was uniquely problematic, uniquely tortured. Due to its partial responsibility for causing the wars, Serbian nationalism was considered unacceptable, totally discredited. Other Serbians could not even bear to called themselves Serbs or to be in any way patriotic without arousing anxiety and horror among their neighbors or the wider world. In this respect, sociologist Pešić[339] asks if perhaps Other Serbia is just a phantasm:

---

ans sent an open letter to the Yugoslavian and Croatian forces asking them to not damage the historic district of the city.

[338] Sima M. Ćirković, "Srbija od zabluda i obmana," ("Serbia from Delusion to Illusion"), in Aljoša Mimica, ed., *Druga Srbija deset godina posle: 1992–2002 (Other Serbia Ten Years Later: 1992–2002)* (Helsinski odbor za ljudska prava, 2002), p. 47.

[339] Pešić is a prominent member of the democratic opposition and was member of the Serbian Parliament from 1993 to 1997 and from 2007 to 2012. She was a founder member of the Yugoslav Helsinki Committee (1985), the Association for the Yugoslav Democratic Initiative (1989), the Yugoslav European Movement (1991) and the Centre for Anti-war Action (1991). From 1992 to 1999 she was the President of the Civic Alliance of Serbia, and from 1993 until 1997 she was one of the leaders of the Zajedno (Together) coalition, with Vuk Drašković's Serbian Renewal Movement and Zoran Djindjić's Democratic Party. At the moment she is a senior scientific associate at the Institute of Philosophy and Social Theory.

> Is "Other" Serbia the same intelligence in a different mind, as the opposition politicians would like to see it; or a new direction, as moral critics would like to see it? Or is it the creation of a new cultural space, as independent intellectuals would like to see it? "Other" Serbia is built around the porousness of its concept, or better put, it deliberately creates this porousness by doubting *that it is Serbia at all*. Its culture used to be created by people marked with a stamp of Europe, the stamp of universality and uniqueness of the continent on which Serbia lies. That stamp also marks these pages describing the "Other" Serbia that we are inventing today.[340]

I find that the Other Serbia identity of the 1990s was to a large extent role-specific and derived from the fact that post-communist Serbian intellectuals, amidst the war and authoritarianism of the Milošević regime, were searching for a common historical consciousness, and a sense of common perceived future, that would give a sense of collective identity and community. But, by doing that, they positioned themselves in contrast to the stronger nationalist Other; their position was one of anti-position, their identity is one of distinction, disparity and divergence. Pešić defines and nominates what others have failed to notice, namely that Other Serbia gathers around the doubt that they even pertain or belong to Serbia at all. In this respect, I note that Other Serbia affiliates produce and construct their own identity discourses, but at the same time these Other Serbia actors are themselves products of the values, norms and social exclusion they actively create in those discourses. In this way, Other Serbia political and societal actors help construct and further strengthen the normative framework of exclusion and Self-othering in which they operate. It is clear that their anti-First Serbia identity constitutes the behavior of these actors but, at the same time, it also constrains their behavior when they desire to create new myths of common past and collective identity. Therefore, when Other Serbia actors doubt whether or not they want to be associated with, be considered relevant to, and belong to, "Serbia" at all, these actors intensify and further strengthen the discourse of othering. The emphasis is often placed on their anguish over the responsibility attributed to Serbians for the dissolution of Yugoslavia, and over the international stigma suffered as a result, and on their concern for the victims. How was the difference

---

[340] Vesna Pešić, "Istorijski i drustveni akteri" ("Historical and Social Actors"), in Aljoša Mimica, ed., *Druga Srbija deset godina posle: 1992–2002 (Other Serbia Ten Years Later: 1992–2002)* (Helsinski odbor za ljudska prava, 2002), p. 59.

between First and Other Serbia public engagement understood and assumed in the texts from the establishment of Other Serbia in 1992? Anthropologist Gordana Logar[341] explored it further:

> This Other Serbia currently runs in parallel to the one that has all the regalia of state power: army, police and press. But that is not where differences end. "Other" Serbia is at a very early stage but shows all the signs that she will live and grow, and she does not call for hatred and war. She does not feel inferior and isolated, as she does not fear the rest of the World. She is not stuck in ignorance, and does not see an enemy in people who think differently, who are from a different nation, or who practice a different religion. This "Other" Serbia will not start wars, especially not using the excuse that all Serbs must live in one state. However, she will ring the alarm bells at any signs of human rights and freedoms being endangered, both those of Serbs outside of Serbia and those of all the nations that live in Serbia. She will not allow people's houses, whether they belong to Serbs or any other people, to be burned in the name of Serbdom.[342]

The Other Serbia has consistently demonstrated a degree of self-consciousness in the eyes of the world, but also between individual actors within its membership. I suggest this is because their national identity expresses the curious combination of their strong sense of pacifism together with a certain stigma felt in respect of their nation's past misdeeds. However, the Other Serbia grouping have unfailingly held a strong sense of who they were: who was included and who was excluded from their number. To define who "the Serbs" were in 1992 is difficult owing to First and Other Serbia differences, but what is even more problematic is the task of giving the Serbian nation a value, a meaning. Were the Serbs, by their nature, warriors or were they prepared to fight for peace among Balkan nations? The construction of the enemy mentality was central to the nationalism of the 1990s. The main difference between the First and Other Serbia groups remained their pro-war and anti-war positions, but further difference also derived from the fact that the war was waged in the name of ethnic superiority. First Serbia positioned itself, falsely, as superior in its moral values, its love of freedom, and its independent and rebellious spirit. The alterative voices of Other

---

[341] Gordana Logar is an anthropologist and a columnist for Danas, a daily newspaper published in Belgrade, which was established in 1997.

[342] Gordana Logar, "Druga Srbija na univerzitetu" ("Other Serbia at University"), in Aljoša Mimica, ed., *Druga Srbija deset godina posle: 1992–2002 (Other Serbia Ten Years Later: 1992–2002)* (Helsinški odbor za ljudska prava, 2002), p. 68.

Serbia can be seen as acts of resistance to the dominant narrative of confrontation.

In the process of post-communist redefinition, anti-war inclined writers, professors and public intellectuals questioned not only what Other Serbia consists of, but in whose interests and for what purpose it exists. One of this book's central questions refers to the processes of self-identification of Other Serbia actors. I attempt to outline the values and boundaries, positive and negative traits, qualities and features, which Other Serbia attributes to its own discourse. To this end, I note that in Other Serbia's so called political manifesto, Rajić quite clearly defines their socio-cultural goals:

> Different Serbia requires a long-term struggle and changes in the mindset of its population. It's almost as if we have forgotten the causes of civic revolutions and the reasons for the creation of civic society. The main cause was and remains the fight against absolutism. This fight is continuous and it is fought through the creation of interest-based organizations, and by the creation of a political citizen that knows what his real interests are, how to achieve them and who is in the way of them being achieved.[343]

Although the domination of the public sphere by First Serbia identity discourses spread by the Milošević regime, which relied on themes of national euphoria and victimization, was almost absolute Other Serbia actors maintained that they had positioned themselves as the "synonym of dissent to the nationalistic craze, criminality and war, pogroms and the meaningless destruction of villages and towns."[344] To this end, the participants in the *Belgrade Circle* continuously sought an alternative to violence, war and destruction. Lazić argues that Other Serbia actors were "de-totalizing the socialist system, which existed within the ideological field, and promoting the intrusion of new alternative thinking" in the public sphere.[345]

---

[343] Ljubiša Rajić, "Srbija iz početka" ("Serbia From the Beginning"), in *Druga Srbija deset godina posle: 1992–2002 (Other Serbia Ten Years Later: 1992–2002)*, edited by Aljoša Mimica, (Helsinski odbor za ljudska prava, 2002), p. 59.

[344] Ivan Čolović, "Introduction," in Aljoša Mimica ed., *Druga Srbija deset godina posle: 1992–2002 (Other Serbia Ten Years Later: 1992–2002)* (Helsinski odbor za ljudska prava, 2002), p. 1.

[345] Mladen Lazić, "Od klasnog i nacionalnog monologa ka dijalogu" (From Class and National Monologue to Dialogue), in Aljoša Mimica, ed., *Druga Srbija deset godina*

Traitors and heroes

The primary significance of Other Serbia actors lies in the fact that many of them helped to propagate particular perceptions of Serbia and Serbian identity during the dissolution of Yugoslavia and, as a result, of Serbian relations toward Europe. To illustrate how these perceptions were mediated, it is pertinent to consider that certain First Serbia actors perceived, and still perceive, Other Serbia anti-war activists as "anti-war profiteers," as "anti-Serbs" and therefore as traitors. Public figures from the liberal end of the political spectrum and civil society typically enter such narratives cast as *traitors, foreign mercenaries* and *sell-outs*. I note, however, that the word *traitor* is placed at the center of both discourses. The uses of terms such as *hero* and *traitor* are inextricably correlated and span the entire history of this region. Certain Other Serbia actors accept the accusation of being actively opposed to the regime and to the war but at the same time overturn the concept of heroes and traitors. Filip David[346] responds to the accusations of treachery: "The only remaining option for us is to become traitors. That means that we should betray the system that invokes war and hunger, where people live in a fever, constantly fed by hatred, while being paranoid and obsessed with their own grandeur at the same time ["First" Serbia]. To be a traitor in that kind of system is the least that any moral and honorable man should do."[347]

On the theme of patriotism and traitors, Lazić notes that a monopoly of patriotism is the worst kind of monopoly, because it directly implies judgments on who can be called a respectable citizen and who a

---

posle: 1992–2002 (Other Serbia Ten Years Later: 1992–2002) (Helsinski odbor za ljudska prava, 2002), p. 8.

[346] Filip David is a Serbian Jewish author and was a long standing drama editor of Serbian National Television (RTS). He is one of the founders of Independent Authors, a writers' association founded in 1989 in Sarajevo. He was also one of the founders of the Belgrade Circle. David currently works as a professor of drama at the Faculty of Dramatic Arts of Belgrade University. He has co-authored the script for the film "When day breaks" which was Serbia's Academy Award candidate for 2012.

[347] Filip David, "Biti Izdajnik" (To Be a Traitor), in Aljoša Mimica, ed., *Druga Srbija deset godina posle: 1992–2002 (Other Serbia Ten Years Later: 1992–2002)* (Helsinski odbor za ljudska prava, 2002), p. 5.

traitor.[348] The motive of treason is endlessly cited in inter-Serbian political struggles and, as Živković points out, it resonates with the Kosovo-inspired epic-ethos, as the "traitor" takes an archetypal role.[349] In the nationalist discourse the archetypal traitor is linked with the urban liberal intelligentsia who are "deracinated traitors to the nation and the mercenaries of the West."[350] But, as a form of anti-identity, Other-Serbians willingly position themselves as traitors to nationalism. Other-Serbians understood themselves as the only voice of conscience and reason in the public sphere at a time of complete collapse of the value system, and when the only other voices to be heard were those of nationalistic warmongering.

The ultimate rejection of nationalism by Other Serbia affiliates at that time is representative of their attitudes toward Milošević's policies. Professor Davidović, writing in 1992, suggests that "nationalism became our curse, and until we rid ourselves of that misfortune, we cannot expect to get out of the present state of chaos and senselessness."[351] Therefore, Other Serbia affiliates comprehend Milošević and the outcome of his nationalistic policies as a tangible treachery committed against the Serbian state and consequently the Serbian nation. In the same publication, Inić,[352] one of the main voices of Other Serbia, notes that

---

[348] Mladen Lazić, "Od klasnog i nacionalnog monologa ka dijalogu" (From Class and National Monologue To Dialogue), in Aljoša Mimica, ed., *Druga Srbija deset godina posle: 1992–2002 (Other Serbia Ten Years Later: 1992–2002)* (Helsinški odbor za ljudska prava, 2002), p. 8.

[349] Marko Živković, *Serbian Dreambook: National Imaginary in the Time of Milošević* (Bloomington, IN: Indiana University Press, 2011), p. 187.

[350] Ibid., p. 241.

[351] Milena Davidović, "Srbija nade" (Serbia of Hope), in Aljoša Mimica, ed., *Druga Srbija deset godina posle: 1992–2002 (Other Serbia Ten Years Later: 1992–2002)* (Helsinški odbor za ljudska prava, 2002), p. 59.

[352] Inić was a well-known political analyst and a one of the founders of the Democratic Party in 1989.

all nationalisms are dangerous, there is no such thing as a less dangerous nationalism. In that respect, the greater-Serbian nationalism is even more extreme than others in terms of the consequences it brought to the Serbian people. It stems from the fact that by destroying Yugoslavia and bringing the Serbian people to the verge of bare survival, the greater-Serbian ideologues destroyed the territorial integrity of Serbia itself. I know not of any other nationalists who were prepared to do something as evil as that to their own people.[353]

In the 1990s Serbia, even though the media were under the tight scrutiny and control of the regime, Other Serbia actors openly refuted hate speech and called for the use of an alternative vocabulary. This particular movement, as Dević notes, was a mobilization of the more articulate segments of pan-Yugoslav, urban, cosmopolitan and genuinely non-ethno-nationalistic cultural identity.[354] The written work which resulted, in the form of publications and statements, identified the main difference between people as resting on moral and ethical grounds rather than ethnicity. Therefore, Other Serbia actors do not speak or write in the name of "the nation," or address the "nation" but instead address "the citizens." Thus, at a time when the words such as *Serbian nation, enemies* and *genocide* had gained currency, Popov notes that these groups distinguished themselves from the ruling regime, as well as from the main opposition parties, even in their vocabulary.[355] From this one can deduce that the spectrum of meaning constructed by the Belgrade critical intelligentsia at that time relates to political and societal pluralism, at least in normative terms. Their efforts had a tendency to create a parliamentary democracy and to develop a real democratic political culture in Serbia. An important characteristic of the Other Serbia actors is their actual and truthful civic orientation: most of the initiatives in the early 1990s were instigated by ordinary individuals, which is indicative of the democratic strength of the public sphere at that time. As Fridman observes, political opposition was fragmented and those parties which openly challenged

---

[353] Slobodan Inić, "Tako smo duboko pali" (We Have Fallen so Deep) in Aljoša Mimica, ed., *Druga Srbija deset godina posle: 1992–2002 (Other Serbia Ten Years Later: 1992–2002)* (Helsinski odbor za ljudska prava, 2002), p. 89.

[354] Ana Dević, "Anti-War Initiatives and the Un-Making of Civic Identities in the Former Yugoslav Republic," *Journal of Historical Sociology*, 10, no. 2 (June 1997).

[355] Nebojša Popov, ed., *The Road to War in Serbia* (Budapest: Central European University Press, 2000), p. 505.

the regime were rather weak.[356] The anti-war and anti-regime activism came from the so-called independent intellectuals, comprising various anti-nationalist groups who organized a pacifist network which bound this anti-Milošević struggle together.

The organizations and social actors until 2000

Other Serbia signifies "different Serbia" as it represents "all those individuals whose war this is not."[357] These groups and individuals organized differently at various stages in response to the regime's policies. As argued above, "Other" Serbia groups initially dealt mostly with peace initiatives, campaigns, forums, centers and movements. Their activities passed through two stages from their emergence in 1992 until 1994. The first stage was characterized, as Fridman notes, by a variety of street protests and cultural-artistic activities against warmongering, while in the second stage the street protests disappeared and many anti-war groups transformed into a variety of NGOs including documentation centers engaged in collecting data on war crimes and violations of human rights, institutions providing humanitarian aid, and counselling centers for refugees.[358] This stage coincided with a steady influx of financial support from NGOs and various peace and women's groups based in Western Europe. The best example of this is *Women in Black* (Žene u crnom) which came into being at the beginning of October 1992, at the time of armed hostilities against Dubrovnik. From the group's founding these women, led by feminist Staša Zajović, gathered every Wednesday to express their protest against the war and militarism, appearing peacefully and silently in public spaces, dressed in black. They used strategic political action in order to pressurize the regime, mostly by staging public disturbances. As a way of illustration, after the bombing of Sarajevo

---

[356] Orli Fridman, "It was like fighting a war with our own people: anti-war activism in Serbia during the 1990s," in *Nationalities Papers*, 39, No. 4, July 2011, p. 511.

[357] Ivica Petrovic, "Simbioza nacionalizma i komunizma" (Symbiosis of Nationalism and Communism), in Aljoša Mimica, ed., *Druga Srbija deset godina posle: 1992–2002 (Other Serbia Ten Years Later: 1992–2002)*, (Helsinski odbor za ljudska prava, 2002), p. 228.

[358] Orli Fridman, "It was Like Fighting a War with our Own People: Anti-war Activism in Serbia During the 1990s" *Nationalities Papers*, 39, no. 4 (July 2011), p. 507–522 at p. 511.

in May 1992, a 1,300 meter-long black ribbon was carried by a procession. It stretched from the Albanija building in the central Terazije square to Slavija square in Belgrade, symbolizing protest, solidarity and mourning for the thousands of victims of the war in Bosnia. The independent press reported some 50,000 participants,[359] although the state media ignored these protests. Such events were covered sporadically in the independent media by the quality weekly newspapers, *Borba* and *Vreme*, and the TV station *Studio B*, although its audience was limited. The only media that followed the anti-war protests and activities fully and regularly were the weekly *Republika* and the independent radio station *B-92*, started in 1989 by a dozen students and young journalists. At that time, *B-92* aired talk shows and critical commentaries on the nationalist policies of the regime and their partisan politics and became a symbol of media resistance in the late 1990s, and a prominent participant in the Other Serbia struggle.

Toward the end of 1992 the *Fund for Humanitarian Law*, a non-governmental organization founded by Nataša Kandić, a sociologist by training, was established as a documentation center involved in the collection and classification of information about various war crimes and human and minority rights abuses in the former Yugoslavia. At the end of 1994 Sonja Biserko, a former Yugoslav diplomat, founded the *Helsinki Committee for Human Rights* in Belgrade. *The Centre for Cultural Decontamination*, founded by dramatist Borka Pavičević in 1994, was the first such institution for promoting voices of dissent and alternative culture. Since 1992, major support for the activities of these groups have come primarily from two sources: the *Open Society Fund*, or *Soroš Foundation*; and several Western European peace and women's rights groups that have visited Belgrade. Certain individuals reappear as the founders of new organizations. Sušak points out that this duplication of initiatives and groups contributed to the fragmentation of existing organizations and causes.[360]

---

[359] Bojana Sušak, "An Alternative to War," in Nebojša Popov, ed., *The Road to War in Serbia* (Budapest: Central European University Press, 2000), p. 479.

[360] Ibid., p. 480.

The next two phases of intense mobilization are linked to the 1996–97 student protests, and to the period beginning in the lead-up to the September 2000 elections and continuing up to the October 5, 2000 demonstrations. As noted in Chapter 2, during the opposition protests in 1996–97, demonstrators expressed the belief that Serbia needed to return to Europe and requested the adoption of European standards and practices of government. Thomas suggests that it was evident from their banners bearing slogans such as "Belgrade is the World" that these protesters expressed an internationalism which was in line with the desire of *Zajedno* opposition leaders to emphasize to the outside world their pro-Western orientation.[361] Regardless of the failure to create a wider movement gathered around a similar political platform, the mere existence of these organizations created a path toward civil society, social networks, institutions and the values that are essential ingredients of the Other Serbia network. In the years after the fall of Milošević, Other Serbia associates and civil society organizations focused on dealing with the past, and with Milošević's ideological legacy, in continued reliance on their fiercely anti-nationalist positions.

"Other" Serbia's rift after 2000

After 2000, well-known Belgrade writer Vladimir Arsenijević,[362] who is associated with "Other" Serbia, argued that taking partial responsibility for what the Milošević regime had done to the democratic opposition and the other nationalities in Bosnia and Kosovo almost made him into an *inverted nationalist*.[363] Arsenijević therefore implied that a consequence of the change of regime was that the Other Serbia network and the new

---

[361] Robert Thomas, *Serbia under Milošević: The Politics of Serbia in the 1990s* (London: Hurst & Company, 1999), p. 178.

[362] Arsenijević won the 1994 NIN-award in January 1995 for his first novel *In the Hold* (U potpalublju). This anti-war novel, which takes place during the Battle of Vukovar in autumn 1991, was the first work of art in Serbia which openly discussed the violent disintegration of the country from the perspective of those who lived in Belgrade at the time. This slim novel was soon translated into twenty languages and placed Arsenijević almost instantly among the most translated Serbian writers.

[363] Vladimir Arsenijević and Andrea Pisac, "An Accidental Serb," *Index on Censorship,* 38, (2009), p. 140.

democratic government have taken the full responsibility for the acts of the Milošević regime during the 1990s. According to Arsenijević, this means that Other Serbia has been dragged into the nationalistic narrative again: "I have always refused to be identified by my national identity, I am only a Serb by accident, that is my premise."[364] Many liberal and fiercely anti-war intellectuals had similar concerns, and feelings of distress and unease around the subject of "what it means to be a Serb" in post-Milošević Serbia. In other words, some Other Serbia affiliates wanted to defend themselves, pointing to the fact that they were part of the extensive network that had fought fiercely against the regime, and so deny any responsibility for Milošević's wrongdoings. In this respect, Fridman notes that during the 1990s the democratic coalitions were formed on the unifying idea that people were against Milošević, however, civil society groups needed to start negotiating over what they would fight for in the aftermath of the demise of the regime.[365] As this challenge emerged, of what to fight for immediately following the demise of Milošević on October 5, 2000, and in particular after the assassination of PM Zoran Djindjić in 2003, it became increasingly difficult to reach general agreement on the matter.

A brief analysis of the 2002 Point of Departure debate in Chapter 5 helps us explore the reasons for a rift in Other Serbia. The justification for including such analysis is that it provides the setting for an extensive consideration of the 2003 Missionary Intelligentsia debate in the same chapter. These debates reveal that the main ideological struggles within the civil society public sphere and network were connected to the creation and shaping of collective memories of the Yugoslav wars of the 1990s. These struggles included discussions in the public sphere in Serbia of responsibility for the conflicts and for war crimes, and of the role of the Serbian Orthodox Church (SOC) in everyday politics. By 2006, the central focus was shifting to the field of human and minority rights, such as the struggle for more tolerance between different ethnicities in the region, women's rights and the issues of Roma and LGBT visibility.

---

[364] Ibid., p. 141.
[365] Orli Fridman, "It was Like Fighting a War with our Own People: Anti-war Activism in Serbia During the 1990s" *Nationalities Papers*, 39, no. 4 (July 2011), p. 515.

Yet, from the debates, one can see how First and Other Serbia differences on national identity were very much part of the overall discussions on Europe, on the future of Serbia and on the role Europe had played in the dissolution of Yugoslavia.

In the aftermath of the early reforms, the lack of a consensus over how to confront the past and the Yugoslav wars created difficulties within Serbia's liberal intelligentsia. Disagreement came as result of different approaches to the position on "collective responsibility" for the wrongdoings by the Milošević regime, or in simple terms, the extent of Serbian responsibility and guilt. In those early days, new ICTY indictments, arrests, trials at the Hague Tribunal, and the establishment of the special local courts provoked grand public spectacles. Various Other Serbia intellectual groupings, including a loose coalition of NGOs and independent media outlets, as Dragović-Soso notes, had built a collection of publicly available records and created a foundation for future examination of the legacy of the Milošević years.[366] Some individuals, such as *Vreme* journalist Dejan Anastasijević and human rights activist Nataša Kandić, contributed to judicial processes through their own testimony or by supplying evidence. This work follows Dragović-Soso's argumentation on the split within the Serbian liberal intelligentsia on questions of the Hague Tribunal and its prosecution of Milošević, and therefore, on questions of Serbia's recent past. She notes that disagreements on these subjects provoked intense emotional fallout among the members of the Other Serbia grouping, and also among some individuals who were not members, as the lines of allegiance after 2000 became more unstable and changeable.[367] This passionate fallout and the subsequent discussion are outlined in the later section on Point of Departure debate. Following Dragović-Soso, I suggest that the debate about the Milošević trial revealed that the underlying source of discord in Serbia's liberal intelligentsia resided in the deeply divisive experience of the 1999

---

[366] Jasna Dragović-Soso, "Collective Responsibility, International Justice and Public Reckoning with the Recent Past: Reflections on a Debate in Serbia" in Timothy Waters, ed., *The Milošević Trial—An Autopsy*, (Oxford: Oxford University Press, 2014), p. 34.

[367] Ibid., p. 35.

NATO intervention.[368] Additionally, intense discord existed on the questions of Serbian collective responsibility for the wars, the so-called Serbian guilt. The discussion, which is still taking place, revolves around the question of whether the Serbs are both perpetrators and victims, or just the victims, of the Yugoslav wars. Two divergent conceptions of the reasons and justifications behind the 1999 NATO intervention emerged from the Other Serbia camp, and two very different explanations of the behavior of the intellectuals and media during this period were offered.

Ramet identifies this inner Other Serbia division as being between two groups, the first being the *hard liberals*,[369] who subscribe to civic values and in many cases also advocate gender equality and tolerance of sexual minorities.[370] According to Ramet, the second group consists of *soft liberals*,[371] or flexible realists, and the adherents of this group avoid dogmatism, although the politicians in this group such as Boris Tadić and others from the DS party frequently made nationalistic statements in connection to the "loss of Kosovo."[372] Ramet considers soft liberals to be moderate nationalists, closer to the liberals than to the ultranationalists, however, my work approaches Ramet's conception critically, noting that soft liberals take both sides within the liberal/national discourses. This premise is tested in Chapter 5 which further considers this fallout and analyzes the textual debate behind the split. The analysis of various debates during the decade following October 5, 2000 is used as a study to illustrate these assertions.

Further discord in Other Serbia could be seen in the irreconcilable stances which emerged in respect of the role of the West/Europe in the Balkans and the neo-liberal politics of "humanitarian interventions." The hard liberals supported the politics of conditionality of the EU and US toward Serbia, especially in terms of the ICTY process, financial aid and

---

[368] Ibid.
[369] Two prominent organizations can be identified as hard liberals: The Fund for Humanitarian Law, and the Helsinki Committee for Human Rights.
[370] Ramet et al., eds., *Civic and Uncivic Values: Serbia in the Post-Milošević Era* (Budapest: Central University Press, 2011), p. 5.
[371] Soft liberals are gathered around *Vreme* magazine. Also included are Democratic Party members and members of the 2004–2008 government.
[372] Ibid., p. 6.

the bid for EU candidacy. Others condemned the 1999 NATO intervention, as well as the Yugoslav army's ethnic cleansing and the KLA's violence against the Serbs. Radović's letter to *Vreme* magazine in 2002 outlines the stance adopted within Other Serbia in respect of, and expresses her personal criticism of, the NATO and US military interventions:

> Democracy can be achieved only by difficult and patient work, the creation of the atoms of a democratic society, the rules and procedures of democratic decision-making. The United States and NATO have reversed the evolution of democratic relations, made worthless the decade-long effort of our nongovernmental organizations, and rendered senseless the Gandhi-like resistance of the Albanian people for which I have the greatest respect.[373]

More importantly, these disagreements about state politics toward the Hague Tribunal and the legacy of the 1999 NATO intervention further contributed to the Other Serbia debate on national identity and joining the EU. The analysis of this debate in the next chapter reveals that political affiliates of Other Serbia, mostly politicians from the democratic camp, have failed to create an efficient model of democratic community that would ascertain and shape a favorable link between Serbia and Europe. This failure has, since 2000, been an enduring impediment to achieving European integration. The perceived harshness of the conditionality attached to Serbia's EU candidacy made Other Serbia elites doubt the wisdom of promoting Europeanization as an achievable prospect and a suitable goal. Neither pro-European political parties nor Other Serbia actors managed to successfully tap into the existing pro-European public sentiment in order to promote Europeanization. Their appeal to follow the European road was also endangered by the democratic elites deciding to build their political programs and manifestos around the line of the Other Serbia rift. This division was similarly apparent in the party politics of the democratic bloc. At that time, the soft liberal view was best represented politically by Boris Tadić's Democratic

---

[373] Nadežda Radović, "Pismo pod bombama" (Letter under Bombs), in *Vreme*, no. 610 (September 2002).

Party, and the hard liberal position by the Liberal Democratic Party of Čedomir Jovanović.[374]

Joining the European Union was the official national preference and was on the agenda of civil society. On the other hand, the European idea in Serbia was never completely developed into a coherent narrative and European values never fully internalized and thus Serbs always remained rather reluctant Europeans. Following Subotić, I note that this came as a consequence of Other Serbia's inner disagreements over the role played by the EU, and the West in general, in Serbia's democratic transition.[375] The post-Milošević political and cultural elites of Other Serbia have attached various meanings to Europe, as well as to the Self (the Serbian state), in new political discourses which are rearticulated from older discourses from the 1990s. In Other Serbia texts, the Serbian state (the Self) is represented as not European (and therefore not civilized), and the favorable link between Europe and Serbia is absent. As argued above, these particular identity narratives originate from the discourses on identity that dominated during the Milošević years. Nonetheless, positive references to European politics and life remain potent and these help to buttress both the "Europe as historical ally" and "Eu-

---

[374] Jovanović became involved in politics as a leader of the student protests in Belgrade during the winter of 1996–97. He officially became a member of DS in 1998, and quickly rose up the party ladder, eventually becoming its Vice-President in 2001. He was elected to the Serbian Parliament in the 2000 parliamentary elections, on the list of the Democratic Opposition of Serbia (DOS). On March 31, 2001, after a masked government unit stormed the fortified Villa Mir in an attempt to arrest its resident Slobodan Milošević, Jovanović was at the scene, negotiating with the former Yugoslav president and urging him to surrender. In March 2003, following the assassination of Prime Minister Zoran Djindjić, Jovanović advanced to the position of Deputy Prime Minister in the government of the new Prime Minister Zoran Živković. Dissatisfied with the party's new direction under the leadership of Boris Tadić, Jovanović criticized him publicly, most notably for his policy of political cohabitation with Prime Minister Vojislav Koštunica's government. Finally, on November 5, 2005, Jovanović and his supporters founded the Liberal Democratic Party (LDP). In the 2008 presidential elections, the LDP finished fifth with 5.34% of the total votes, well behind Boris Tadić and Tomislav Nikolić . Ahead of the second round vote, contrary to expectations from some circles, Jovanović decided not to throw his support behind Tadić, opting instead to stay neutral.

[375] Jelena Subotić, "Europe is a State of Mind: Identity and Europeanization in the Balkans," *International Studies Quarterly*, 55, (2011), p. 309–330 at 320.

[375] Ibid., p. 321.

rope as natural objective and strategic goal" narratives. Still, Serbia's recent past became a threat to Serbian identity, and an obstacle to the positive embrace of European values and thinking. In this respect, the only remaining source of legitimacy of "being European" has been measured against the criteria of fulfilling the EU conditions for candidacy and membership.[376] Consequently, Serbia's persistent failures to fulfill the EU's conditions have convinced the Other Serbia affiliates and spectators that Serbians have failed to "became European." This study asserts that the political elites constantly reinterpret and rearticulate elements of extreme forms of negative polarization and radical othering, Other Serbia continuously "Others" the existent political community, as well as an imagined political system of Serbian national identity: belligerent, intolerant, isolated, jingoistic and xenophobic. However, it is important to stress that the attempts of liberal intellectuals to view Serbia's relationship with Europe as a kind of battle between good and evil are unrealistic in that they readily ignore the continually dominant roles played by those liberal intellectuals themselves, and by the local population and the national governments. Such identity narratives, even put into new political contexts, just serve to strengthen the First and Other Serbia ideological positions within the discursive/political field.

Conclusion

It is clear that post-Yugoslav Serbian collective identity was forged during the time of the general mobilization of popular nationalism in the 1990s. As a result, it was dependent on the cyclical and perpetual image of the unjust treatment of the Serbs. The highly intrusive Milošević regime forged a very real sense of nationalist identity among its citizens, who were bounded by it in a physical sense due to economic hardships. This was the identity of the "proud Serbians" but, at the same time, harbored an element that can be called a *despite-identity*, that is, an oppositional identity toward Europe. This identity also meant passivity, withdrawal, resistance, opposition, and unthinking conformity, and these traits prevail even today in the Serbian political culture. However,

---

[376] Ibid.

an Other Serbian identity of Other Serbian citizens who were prepared to express their own views became more apparent in the weeks after the 2000 elections, when hundreds of thousands found the courage to come out on the streets of Belgrade and proclaim that they were against the regime, and that they are not prepared to allow Milošević to speak in their name any longer. Serbian politicians arguably became most aware of their collective identity when they realized, after the demise of the regime, how poor their relations with Western Europe were. Even when the new democratic system was established, the old system remained in people's minds. Most Serbians were never ashamed to be Serbians and the notion of national identity remained available for widespread popular democratic mobilization in the aftermath of the regime's dissolution.

Moreover, this chapter stressed the importance of investigating the extent to which there is discursive continuity between the Milošević era narratives of First and Other Serbia on national identity and those prevalent in post-Milošević Serbia. I submit that the Other Serbia discourse constructs "the Serbs" as being collectively responsible for Milošević's policies, but not individually responsible, as they are the ones who fought fiercely against the regime. On the other hand, First Serbia actors continue to engage with the nationalist trope of Serbs being the ultimate victims of Yugoslavia, and to adopt an enemy mentality in respect of their various regional neighbors, Europe and the West. Despite the centrality of the concept of national integrity in current First Serbia discourses, which remains unchanged, there is a significant departure from the previous Milošević-era discourses. In fact, in post-2000 First Serbia political discourse, ethnic nationalism was not constructed as being necessarily central to the interest of the Serbian state and nation, but instead a difference was drawn between "good" (patriotic) and "bad" (radical) nationalism. As a result, one can see the emergence of liberal-nationalists, the moderate nationalists, the so-called Progressives, as well as of the more fundamentalist nationalists of "Third" Serbia. Additionally, I argue that such discourse can be traced back to the rhetoric of the soft liberals and the moderate nationalist stance of former Minister of Foreign Affairs Vuk Jeremić during his time in the Democratic Party. Comparatively, an analogous rift occurred in Other Serbia discourses on the nation and the past: hard liberals of Other Serbia persuasively encouraged lustration and a radical break with the ideological heritage of the Milošević years, while soft liberals accepted the politics of "cohabitation" with elements of First Serbia. This is evident from Boris Tadić's 2008 coalition with Dačić's SPS, Dačić having formerly been spokesperson for Milošević's party. The next chapter will explore how "Europe" is constructed in the identity narratives of First and Other Serbia. I will show that, in contrast with EU countries where Europe might be perceived as a choice, in the Serbian case, the West in general and Europe in particular is seen as a necessity for the construction of the national Self.

Chapter 4:
The Construction of "Europe"

I consider Europe to be a symbolical space where Serbian ideas about themselves are reflected, yet where no single interpretation of Europe is precise and accurate. Hence, the aim of this chapter is to reveal how different and opposing perceptions of Europe are played out in the public sphere and what this tells us about the nature of Serbian national identity. From the literature on European identity, it is clear that Europe has absorbed many different identities. Europe, articulated from the center, refers to growth and progress, personal freedoms, human rights and individuality.[377] This book examines the way that Europe is perceived from its periphery, specifically from Southeast Europe. Eastern Europe's post-1989 discourse on "return to Europe," featured frequent employment of family metaphors and reconstituted a new form of emotion-laden Westernism across that region.[378] In the Serbian public sphere, Volčič notes that, after 2000, statements about "giving Europe a second chance" were also recurring themes. However, within five years of regime change, images of the West had deteriorated and become less positive.[379] In contrast to using family symbols and metaphors, Western Europe is addressed, as Volčič points out, along the lines of the "Fortress Europe"—a reference to restrictive laws, policies and practices which result in the exclusion of non-citizens of Europe.[380] Similarly, post-Milošević elites have attached several adverse meanings to *Europe*, and the *West* in general, as well as to the Self (the Serbian state), which are rearticulated from older discourses into new political ones. This, then, is an inquiry about discourses on civilizational identity, on notions of "be-

---

[377] Gerard Delanty, *Modernity and Postmodernity: Knowledge, Power, the Self* (London: Sage, 2000), p. 32.
[378] For further insight into this topic, see Alan Smith, *The Return to Europe: The Reintegration of Eastern Europe into the European Economy* (Basingstoke: Macmillan Press, 2000), p. 11.
[379] Zala Volčič, "The Notion of 'The West' in the Serbian National Imaginary," *European Journal of Cultural Studies*, 8, no. 2 (2005), p. 158.
[380] Ibid.

ing civilized" or "belonging or not belonging to civilization," including how these discourses on identity are used in contemporary Serbian politics. This chapter concentrates exclusively on how Serbian elites approach "Janus-face Europe,"[381] that is, how these intellectual communities engage with conceptions of European and Western civilization, and with representations of these particular civilizational identities, in framing their own identities.

The debates on Europe span a wide range of topics and arguments. Prominent among these are arguments concerning the cultural and historical similarities or differences between Serbia and Europe, the EU's democratic deficiency, Serbia's human rights violations and war crimes, and the national interest and strategic goals. Some arguments that have developed around these issues, mostly to be found in the soft liberal "Other" Serbia discourse, can be seen as technical, functionalist evaluations of Serbia's preparedness for EU accession. The extreme "First" Serbia discourse is dominated by questions of the essential, inherent differences between Serbia and Europe. By way of illustration, I will analyze various representations of Europe by First Serbia, starting with the cultural-essentialist understanding of the national Self. Thus, the following section explores the main discursive strategies used in the right-oriented Euroskeptic DSS's political manifesto and by their political ally, the nationalist *Dveri*,[382] which has been a registered political party since 2010. The DSS, the SRS and *Dveri* feature prominently in my analysis because, after the demise of Milošević regime, themes including the "anti-Serb" West and Russia as the closest ally, so often present in

---

[381] See Zoran Milutinović, *Getting Over Europe: The Construction of Europe in Serbian Culture* (Amsterdam, New York: Rodopi, 2011).

[382] Various extreme right-wing associations are involved in well-organised publishing activities. The most active of these, with its own Belgrade bookshop, is *Srpski sabor dveri*. The most popular titles among young right-wingers are the Protocols of the Elders of Zion (whose authenticity they strongly defend on their websites), the nine-volume collected works of Dimitrije Ljotić and books by Nikolaj Velimirović. See the article by Jovana Gligorijević, "Mladi I ultra-desnica: bal pomracenih umova" (The Youth and the Far-right: A Ball of Deranged Minds), in *Vreme* Issue 744, (April 2005). *Dveri* became a political party and participated in local and presidential elections in 2012, only to be left out of the parliament due to having received only 4.34% of the vote.

the patriotic discourse, were adopted by these conservative political parties. These sources are included to represent the opinion of the majority of the Serbian population. The second part of the chapter tackles the Other Serbia questions of the nature of Serbian democracy and its international obligation to recognize its recent past. By de-ideologizing existing identity categories, the final section tackles the discursive position which could imply that Europe is not the ultimate radical Other but instead is an element of "Us" (the Serbian subject). The question remains: can Serbia be presented as part of Europe and could Serbian public discourse construct an inclusive and affirmative "Europe"?

The "Idea of Europe": Inclusion and exclusion

The Serbian political and cultural discourses of "First" and "Other" Serbia on national identity and "who the Serbs ought to be" reflect the place that Europe occupies in the Serbian social and political imaginary. Delanty understands the theme of Europe as essentially a unifying theme existing within a cultural framework of values.[383] Does Europe unite Serbia? I argue that in the Serbian public sphere Europe is used in the opposite way—as a theme of perpetual threat and fragmentation. The differences, which appear in the First and Other Serbia discourses, that set Europe and Serbia apart are constructed as inherent and exclusionary. The literature has revealed that an inclusive national identity results in a greater tendency for identification with broader social groups.[384] This chapter examines the implications of inclusive and exclusionary identities of the Serbian Self for attitudes toward Europe.

---

[383] Gerard Delanty, *Modernity and Postmodernity: Knowledge, Power, the Self* (London: Sage, 2000), p. 32, p. 3.

[384] Lauren M. McLaren, *Identity, Interests, and Attitudes to European Integration* (Basingstoke, UK: Palgrave Macmillan, 2006), and Samuel Bowles and Herbert Gintis, "Persistent Parochialism: Trust and Exclusion in Ethnic Networks," *Journal of Economic Behaviour and Organization*, 55, no. 1, (2004), p. 1–23, and Jack Citrin and John Sides, "More than Nationals: How Identity Choice Matters in the New Europe," in Richard K. *Herrmann*, Thomas *Risse*-Kappen and Marilynn B. *Brewer*, eds., *Transnational Identities: Becoming European in the EU* (Lanham, MD: Rowman and Littlefield, 2004), p. 161–85.

The inclusive and exclusive discourses are defined, as Hansen notes, as the positions which discursive actors take toward Others: they set political, economic, cultural or geographical limitations.³⁸⁵ But which roles do these discourses play when defining Europe's and Serbia's collective identity? Do they tend to emphasize the differences between "us" and "them," or to focus on the commonalities which bind these two entities? I contend that both First and Other Serbia consider that the Serbian Self is constituted within those discourses through the constant delineation of others, and principally "Europe." As Hansen points out, whereas the Self is constituted through the constant delineation of Others, that Other can be articulated as an superior, inferior or equal. ³⁸⁶ Identity formation inevitably evolves around constructions of inferiority and superiority and hence a particular distribution of discursive and political power. As this study illustrates, the encounter between Europe and Serbia is not one between two equally powerful parties. Since the age of Enlightenment, Europe embodied notions of Reason and Progress and, as Brisku notes, those values are inexorably linked with core European identity narratives of constant betterment. ³⁸⁷ In contrast with other EU member states, Serbia's peripheral position vis-à-vis the EU necessitates the appropriation of such national identity narratives. Serbia's asymmetrical position toward the EU has practical implications in the day-to-day politics of readjusting and rearticulating certain themes. This phenomenon is not unusual. In Passerini's words, the image of Europe necessarily contains a demarcation of the non-European, as Europe is always seen in the mirror of the Other.³⁸⁸ Thus, it must be recognized that Europe can also emerge as the Other from within, that is, what the Other considers

---

[385] Lene Hansen, *Security as Practice. Discourse Analysis and the Bosnian War* (London and New York: Routledge, 2006), p. 51.

[386] "It might also be constituted as threatening, but it might be an ally, a stranger or an undeveloped subject in need of help." See Lene Hansen, *Security as Practice. Discourse Analysis and the Bosnian War* (London and New York: Routledge, 2006), p. 54.

[387] Adrian Brisku, *Bittersweet Europe: Albanian and Georgian Discourses on Europe: from Berlin 1878 to Tbilisi 2008*, (Oxford: Berghahn Books, 2013), p. 20.

[388] Luisa Passerni, *Europe in Love, Love in Europe: Imagination and Politics in Britain Between the Wars*, (London: Tauris, 1999), p. 3

Europe to be, as a *self-imposed* exclusion.[389] As a result, one can see how images of Europe act as self-induced marginalization across a variety of texts and media.

Representation of Europe in the "First" Serbia discourse

> The church is a guardian of the collective experience of being of the Serbian people and the Serbian state. The church honors our saints who were also often our greatest statesmen, but also honors the victims of Jasenovac, Jadovno, Kragujevac, Kočevje and the NATO bombing every year. If the church were reformed, and there were external pressures for that to happen, it would forget and lose the historical and convocational experience of the Serbian people. The church has been an irreplaceable and unchangeable spiritual and moral guidepost for our people for almost one thousand years.[390]
>
> Vojislav Koštunica, former President of Serbia

This section examines the discursive strategies employed in the representation of Europe within the "First" Serbia discourse on religion and modern identity. The final part of this section will examine the attempts made by First Serbia to create a form of "new patriotism," and what this means for Serbian state identity as well as for the construction of post-Milošević political identities. Particular attention will be paid to how these terms are constructed in relation to the dissolution of Yugoslavia, to processes of transition, to European integration in general and how "Europeanization" as a process of modernization is understood in particular, and finally to the question of Serbia's culture, its history and its geography.

Nation and Church

Among the openly essentialist arguments that shape the "First" Serbia discourse, there can be discerned three closely-interrelated clusters of perspectives which have had an overwhelming influence in the debates. These consist of arguments referring, in broad terms, to the question of Serbia's culture (the Orthodox religion), its history (its recent troubled

---

[389] Bo Strath, ed., *Europe and the Other and Europe as the Other* (Brussels: Peter Lang, 2000), p. 11.
[390] Vojislav Koštunica, *Speeches and Analysis* (DSS). http://dss.rs/category/govori-i-analize

relations with Europe) and its geography (its connections with Russia). Although these topics are so strongly interrelated in the First Serbia reflection on the Serbian Self and the European Other that their frontiers are often blurred, I prefer to analyze them separately, in order to better accentuate the way each specific argument has been developed. To the extent that the Serbian Self is linked to Europe, the obsession with preserving the values of the Self has been translated in First Serbia identity discourses as the preservation of something distinctively "ours." From the following words, taken from the DSS web page, one can grasp the spirit of Koštunica's creed.

> The Serbian church is the first, the oldest and an ever-present institution of the Serbian people. Morality, literacy, art, culture and eventually the state are all achievements that the Serbian people reached through the church. There are countries that were created very recently and that find it easy to have no relationship with the church, and in countries like these churches can function like numerous civic associations. However, that simple and easy route is closed for *us if we intend to stay what we are*. There are those who believe that the year in which Serbia joins NATO and the EU should be our year zero and that Serbian history should be restarted in that year. In that kind of calendar there would naturally be no need for the Serbian Orthodox Church.[391]

Even in the aftermath of the revolutionary events of October 5, 2000 Koštunica encouraged spiritual restoration, and openly joined forces with remnants of the defeated nationalist elites. He continues to hold the position that the Church is the most relevant institution for the Serbian national identity, holds the nation together and provides it with the psychological "we" feeling. Serbia has been a republic since 1945, but the symbols of national identity such as the Serbian flag, with the anachronistic symbol, a crown, and the national anthem, the hymn Bože Pravde,[392] are all suggestive of monarchic influences. Jovanović notes that

---

[391] Vojislav Koštunica, *Speeches and Analysis* (DSS). http://dss.rs/category/govori-i-analize
[392] The national anthem *Bože Pravde*, adopted by the Serbian dynasties of Obrenović and Karadjordjević in the late nineteeth and early twentieth centuries, was a symbol of unity which transcended dynastic rivalries as well as all the rifts among the people. A century later, the anthem was used by opposition leader Vuk Drasković during his anti-regime protests. For that reason, Milošević refused the adoption of the anthem, and favoured *Mars na Drinu* (March to the Drina River), a military marching song, and the elegiac *Tamo Daleko* (Far Away). On the occasion of the referendum in May 1992, the marching song had a slight advantage but the referendum failed due to a poor turnout. *Bože Prav*de finally found its way into the 2006 Constitution as the offi-

Serbia in this way simulated continuity by putting together old symbols charged with strong national and religious content, but with new meaning and usage.[393] At the center of this political and cultural debate is Europe, but most First Serbia discursive actors make frequent use of culturalist-essentialist arguments. I argue that as a result of a particular cultural-essentialist understanding of the Self, contemporary nationalism in Serbia has become increasingly preoccupied with the defense and preservation of national values. Below I will attempt to classify the variations of each dominant theme of Church, military neutrality and affiliation to Russia.

Geography: "East for the West, and West for the East"

Koštunica suggests that Serbia has often found itself in exceptional situations in which the Great Powers have asked Serbia to forgo some of its state interests, such as Kosovo, in the name of some allegedly higher cause.[394] He argues that accepting such requests is not the politics of compromise but the acceptance of self-renunciation and self-abolishment.[395] Koštunica clearly defines the role of the "foreign factor" as one of enmity. For him "there is no doubt that the West and Europe had a key role in the destruction of national unity in Serbia in 2008 for the sake of its own interests."[396] Such language is at the heart of the discourse analyzed here, especially the constant emphasis on preserving the "national interest", e.g. over Kosovo. Koštunica's argumentation is as follows:

---

cial anthem, but with the lyrics about the "Serbian king" replaced with "Serbian lands." See Vladan Jovanović, "Serbia and the Symbolic (Re)Construction of the Nation," in Paul Kolstø, *Strategies of Symbolic Nation-building in South Eastern Europe*, (London: Ashgate, 2014), p. 94/5.

[393] Ibid., p. 96.
[394] Ibid.
[395] Ibid.
[396] Ibid.

> The Western countries have received an amnesty and were freed from any responsibility for their actions in bringing about the illegal secession of Kosovo, including the NATO aggression against Serbia in 1999. The consequence of all of this is that instead of national unity, foreign influence started to dominate. This was devastating both for national interests and the progress of Serbia, and for the preservation of basic self-respect and national dignity.[397]

Effectively, here he expresses the importance of the continuation of Milošević-era narratives regarding the relationship with the West. In such ethical and political context, Europe is continually strategically replaced by an aggressor, a bully and an entity that wants to eradicate and abolish Serbian national dignity. This replacement is neither neutral nor innocent, but is a rhetorical move that creates a hierarchy through the construction of a binary opposition of a positive Self against a negative Other. In contrast to Serbia, which is, in Jeremic's words, "small and proud,"[398] Germany and Europe are portrayed as having no respect for Serbia's brave history. But at this stage, the exchange is made, and Serbia will not only join the EU but NATO's EU. In other words, using *European* and *Atlanticist/NATO* interchangeably does not arise from the simple fact that "Europe" is seen as a continuation of the main aggressor against Serbia, namely the NATO Alliance. This representational mechanism simply helps the tangible construction of the power relation between the Serbian Self and the European Other, seen here as a continuation of the NATO forces. Below are Koštunica's words, using a geo-strategic argument widespread in First Serbia argumentation schemes: "Serbia is an old European state, and she was never outside of Europe in her entire history, in the same way that Europe itself is much older than the European Union."[399] Koštunica has built on the idea that Serbia is in fact part of the old Europe, but not of the new decadent one. Erjavec and Volčič point out that this discourse emphasizes the struggle for the "re-

---

[397] Ibid.
[398] Vuk Jeremić, "Ovation, Then Apology, for Serbian Song," in *New York Times* (January 17, 2013). http://www.nytimes.com/2013/01/18/world/europe/united-nations-apologizes-over-serbian-song
[399] Vojislav Koštunica, *Speeches and Analysis* (DSS). http://dss.rs/category/govori-i-analize

al" Europe.[400] In this way First Serbia appropriates the "European discourse" in order to create their own political-historical context in which to legitimize Serbia's image as protecting the real West from Islam in a manner reminiscent of the Ottoman invasion.[401] The image of Serbia as standing on the frontiers of East and West has a powerful echo in the First Serbia discourse:

> ... in the past the Serbian people found the means and measures that allowed it to keep its national identity. At the same time there was also a consciousness of the identity of the Serbian people and a strong will to protect the basic national values. Somewhere in that range between the attractiveness of economically developed Europe and national consciousness about protecting our identity was the best formula for Serbia's place in Europe. Throughout our history it has been commonly perceived among our people that Serbia is the East for the West, and West for the East, which further testifies that that is where the right place for Serbia in Europe was sought.[402]

As argued in discussions about collective identity, cultural-historical identity is a recurrent concept. However, the heritage of the crudest past stereotypes of the European and Islamic Other(s) prevails in the nationalistic and Church-orientated First Serbia discourse. The prejudices from the past are constantly at work: centuries-old clichés, repertories, codes and metaphors are reproduced in today's First Serbia discourse.

Military neutrality: Russia as part of the Self?

In the DSS agenda it was suggested that Serbia should embrace political and military neutrality by not joining any formal state or military alliances and thus keep military sovereignty intact.[403] However, what the DSS and Koštunica in fact propose is that neutrality could greatly improve Serbia's economic cooperation with Russia, particularly through free trade agreements.[404] Such cooperation could, it is hoped, be one of the backbones of Serbia's economic development. In any case, Koštunica understands that a politically neutral Serbia would have significantly

---

[400] Karmen Erjavec and Zala Volčič, "The Kosovo Battle: Media's Recontextualization of the Serbian Nationalistic Discourses," *Harvard International Journal of Press/Politics*, 12, no. 3, (2007), p. 78.
[401] Ibid., p. 77.
[402] Vojislav Koštunica, *Speeches and Analysis* (DSS). http://dss.rs/category/govori-i-analize
[403] Vojislav Koštunica, *Speeches and Analysis* (DSS). http://dss.rs/category/govori-i-analize
[404] Ibid.

better relations with Russia than a Serbia that joined the Euro-Atlantic community.[405] In the DSS's geo-strategic evaluation, Russia and China represent strong alternatives to Europe. The Russian Federation is seen as a potential security ally. Europe exercises an increasing assertive role, and Serbia should besides create new security alliances outside of Europe in order to remain with the established ones. This position also understands Russia in terms of its historical and cultural linkage with Serbia. However, the multiplicity of the Other in the First Serbia discourse has an ordered classification. It is important to understand where Russia stands in the hierarchical listing of Others. All anti-Europe debates configure the Russian Federation as friendly Other, even as a part of the Serbian Self. In doing so, these actors play on the fundamental role of this Slav connection by frequently demonstrating the importance of retaining this association. Moreover, the countries from the Non-alignment Movement are positioned as "old friends," an economic alliance embedded within a historical setting. Europe, on the other hand, is positioned as the radical Other. Through an evident process of binarization, the Serbian Self is victimized, freedom-loving and innocent, and battling against the EU, seen as a malevolent giant whose practices are undemocratic and meddling. Such characterizations are extended to the European Other with its history of bloody wars and authoritarian power, of which Germany and Britain are the primary suspects. Paradoxically, in the post-communist Eastern European context, the right-wing politicians would by default oppose the Russian influence or pro-Russian sentiment, but in Serbia the support for such politics mainly comes from the nationalist right-wing political spectrum.

Below, I illustrate how essentialist arguments are used in the opposing First Serbia discourses. The following quote from Tanasić is helpful in understanding the core geo-strategic arguments for getting closer to Russia:

---

[405] Ibid.

> It is only when our political elite manages to make a calculation based on which we will rely on our eastern brethren, and which guarantees their interests in our country, that we will deserve the right to count on their support. Only then are we going to have the right to be angry if we do not get as much support as we feel we require. At the same time such a calculation would nullify the arguments of those that are against closer relations between Serbia and Russia, since it would unequivocally show that such close relations are based on principles that they themselves accept as universal and that it is worth more to Serbia to be close to Russia and in one piece than as a rump in the EU.[406]

As well as the economic and strategic reasons for political closeness to Russia, Tanasić also evaluates the geo-strategic opposition to Serbia's EU membership through a wide range of considerations of the consequences of accession. The argument is mainly based on Serbia's military neutrality, or on saying a "historic no" to NATO affiliation. Second, what makes Russia much closer to Serbia than Europe is explained primarily on the grounds of religion and culture. In these comparisons, the closeness of Russia to Serbia is supported most of the time by making overt references to their shared religious heritage. This observation supports my finding that Orthodox Christianity appears to be a major constitutive element of Serbian identity as seen in the conservative First Serbia discourse. In this respect, it is evident that religious differences contribute greatly to the Otherness of Europe in First Serbia vocabulary. However, this religious and cultural connection does not necessarily mean that religious distinctiveness is the single decisive factor in the Otherness of Europe, as economic factors and military neutrality also inhabit the Serbian collective imaginary. The strategy offered in the First Serbia discourse is to claim that entry to the EU would mean the unavoidable separation of Serbia from anything Russian, as Vukadinović argues that it would also inevitably weaken other ties, such as cultural ties.[407] In his words, "Russia and Serbia have always been friendly countries. We have to stick to Russia, tie our boat to the Russian ship and calmly sail through the global storm."[408] As presented above, Russia plays a pivotal role in the First Serbia identity narrative, as this discourse establishes

---

[406] Nikola Tanasić, "Sta sve Rusija nije: dve Srbije I dve Rusije" (Things that Russia is not: Two Serbias and two Russias) in *New Serbian Political Thought* (January 13, 2005).

[407] See *Serbia needs to chose: the EU or Russia,* in *B92* News (February 23, 2012).

[408] Djordje Vukadinović, "Srbija I Velike Sile" (Serbia and Great Powers). http://www.studnel.com/fakulteti/srbija-i-velike-sile.html (Accessed March 31, 2012).

Russia simultaneously as part of the extended Serbian Self, both in the past and also in recent history. First Serbia discursive actors[409] often compare the Otherness of Europe with that of Russia, finding Russia much closer to the Serbian Self.

Srpski Sabor Dveri

As argued, the constellation of arguments used in the "First" Serbia discourse pertains to questions of history, geography and culture/religion. The basic demarcating feature of these clusters of arguments is that they all relate to the construction of "inherent, essential characteristics" of Serbia that are presented as unalterable. Beyza notes that the usage of these inherent and unchanging criteria is an exercise in inclusion and exclusion.[410] Vladan Glišić, now former *Dveri* spokesman[411] suggests that, before entering the European Union, Serbia needs to be crystal clear about which values and institutions are dispensable, and which values, rights and institutions must be kept at any cost in order to avoid irreparable damage which would amount to the destruction of the Serbian nation. [412] Glišić develops his argumentation further by arguing that this

> challenge also implies that missing that chance might even bring about the disappearance of our people. That will depend entirely on the EU as it generally does not care whether there will be such a thing as the Serbian people participating in the processes inside the Euro-empire, or a mass of consumer-inhabitants without identity, a section of the Euro-population which will be the object and not the subject of these processes.[413]

---

[409] Bishop Nikolaj Velimirović, an anti-modernist and opponent of the Enlightenment and secularism, understood "Europe" as individualism, atheism, rationalism, egoism, science and imperialism. In his view, because Europe has abandoned its faith, it has sunk into illness and death. Velimirović believed that Serbia needed to choose "either Europe as Death or Christ" as Europe was decadent and in need of spiritual rebirth. See Zoran Milutinović, *Getting Over Europe: The Construction of Europe in Serbian Culture* (Amsterdam and New York: Rodopi 2011), p. 148.

[410] See Tekin C. Beyza, *Representations and Othering in the Discourse: The Construction of Turkey in the EU Context* (Amsterdam: John Benjamins, 2010), p. 34.

[411] Vladan Glišić is a politician and a former spokesman of *Srpski Sabor Dveri*.

[412] Vladan Glišić, "Pitanja srpskog identita," *Srpski Sabor Dveri*. http://www.dverisrpske.com/sr-CS/index.php

[413] Ibid.

For Glišić, being Serbian does not mean being simultaneously European as Serbian values have their own distinct weight and significance. In the same sense, this motif of authentic values happens to be intensively present as the main political value in terms of the "ethics of Kosovo," as Antonić maintains.[414] It refers to "the higher human values of virtue and love, and to the belief that this mortal world is not only made for selfish individuals. The battle for Kosovo is the battle in our souls, and it is a battle of sacrifice for the other."[415] Glišić proposes that entry into the EU does not depend on the Serbs, but Serbian survival and progress inside the EU does. He argues that

> it depends on how we position ourselves with regards to the question of what makes us Serbs—a conscious community that wishes to be active in European events as an active subject and not a passive object. For me—as a Christian believer inside the true Christian community, i.e. Orthodox Christianity which is always concrete, in other words the community of Orthodox Serbs, the community of St. Sava[416]—it is very easy to assess what it is that makes the core of Serbian identity, or better put the Serbian essence, or as Kosovo Serbs say the "Serbian being."[417]

Albanians are constructed, by Glišić, as non-Westerners and Serbian lands are constructed as "Old Europe." Erjavec and Volčič argue that religious discourse is used in terms of the "defense or wall of Christianity."[418] One important point here is that the theme "Serbs were defending Christianity against Islam" is associated with nationalistic ideology and the idea of "Kosovo as the cradle of Serbia."[419] Furthermore, the distinctively Serbian values which Glišić offers as the core of the Serbian are

---

[414] The term "ethics of Kosovo" was coined by political analyst Slobodan Antonić in the *Politika* newspaper, see Slobodan Antonić, "Kosovo i tinejdzeri" (Kosovo and Teens), in *Politika* (February 28, 2008). http.//www.politika.co.yu/pogledi/Slobodan-Antonić/KOSOVO-I-TINEJDZERI.sr.html.

[415] Ibid.

[416] Of all the Serbian saints, St. Sava is accorded primary authority as the patron saint of the nation.

[417] Vladan Glišić, "Pitanja srpskog identita," *Srpski Sabor Dveri*. Retrieved from http://www.dverisrpske.com/sr-CS/index.php

[418] Karen Erjavec and Zala Volčič, "The Kosovo Battle: Media's Recontextualization of the Serbian Nationalistic Discourses," *Harvard International Journal of Press/Politics*, 12, no. 3, (2007), p. 78.

[419] Ibid.

represented by St. Savism[420]—the Serbian incarnation of Orthodoxy, or Orthodoxy as true Christianity.[421] Glišić suggests that "it is what separates us from other 'nations' as a community of pledge, from nations that were created through state power, borders and violence. That is why the Serbs are above all not a historic or political community, but a spiritual community of a pledge to Christ, a pledge made by St. Sava."[422] In Glišić's opinion this is why Serbian patriotism is not nationalist or imperialist but defensive and social.[423] In relation to being European, he in fact understands there is a difference between making a contract with Europe and saving Serbia's unique cultural appeal: "That means that Serbia is in Europe and that it always was in Europe. Europe is our first natural port of destination. There isn't a single reason that should preclude the Serbs from making their contribution to this modern, contemporary Europe as they did until now. But they cannot accept either the triumphalist church nor social Darwinism as European teachings."[424]

Although *Dveri* accepts Serbia inside Europe, they understand the "spiritual experience of Europe inside the Serbs"[425] as being wrong. These tightly-interknitted arguments raised about Europe—its constructed traits, mainly politico-historical, but also some cultural-religious—reveal a choice of Europe that is in collision with the perceived construction of what "Serbian identity" means. *The Obraz Movement*,[426] banned in 2012, expressed their views in the slogan: "the EU is a

---

[420] St. Savism is a teaching which regards the nation as holy. It is a fusion of Orthodox theology with nationalist values, with traditional elements from the Serbian Church reinforced by the influential teaching of inter-war theologian Nikolaj Velimirović and communist period religious dissident Justin Popović. Robert Thomas, *Serbia under Milošević: The Politics of Serbia in the 1990s*, (London: Hurst, 1999) p. 37.

[421] Vladan Glišić, "'Pitanja srpskog identita" (The Questions of Serbian Identity), *Srpski Sabor Dveri*. http://www.dverisrpske.com/sr-CS/index.php, accessed February 10, 2006.

[422] Ibid.

[423] Ibid.

[424] Ibid.

[425] Ibid.

[426] The far-right organization Obraz is notorious for inciting violence against gays, and in particular for their 2001 attack on the first ever Belgrade Gay Pride parade which left several marchers and police officers injured. Obraz was banned by the Serbian Constitutional Court in June 2012. The group defines its basic principles as patriotism and faith in the Serbian Orthodox Church. They see themselves as defenders of the purity

grave for the Serbian people," as they perceive the EU as a body that has abandoned all the basic principles of the old European civilization — God, nation and family.[427] Another common practice in the hard-line nationalistic First Serbia discourse is to construct the European Other as a secularist, godless society. In this stereotyped construction, "the European" emerges as a secularist fundamentalist who, without the constant supervision of the Orthodox Church, would certainly defy the existing Serbian qualities, such as family and traditional values. In the above statement, the actor overtly refers to Serbia as a "land of Orthodox religion" at the same time calling Europe a "Catholic" unity, and declaring European culture to be "Christian but different." Also, Serbian authority is threatened by an institutionalized and largely meddling European leviathan. As a result, independence from European decadent value systems is considered a protection; the idea being that a threat to Serbian judiciary is simultaneously a threat to every Serbian citizen. Will Serbs be allowed to make their own *rakija*, hit their kids or their women, if they wanted to, it is often asked. This view highlights the organic nature of Serbian laws and practices and posits a relativist view on the universal agenda on human rights. In this sense, to be European is often too narrow and it limits what Serbs are and can attempt to be. Instead, the Serbian nation has an open door to Eurasia and Asia. In this sense, Serbian national identity once again contains an exclusive Serbian vision that cannot be constrained by the obsession with becoming just one more European peripheral state.

Anti-occidentalism: The West as decadent

The most striking feature of the nationalist discourse is the rearticulation of key moments/identities of the anti-occident discourse, which criticizes

---

of the Serbian language, of the Cyrillic alphabet and of family values. In its 2005 report, the Serbian Ministry of Interior dubbed Obraz a clerofascist organization. See "Serbia Bans Far-right Organization 'Obraz'" in *Balkan Insight*, (June 12, 2012).

[427] See Marko Stojić, "Between Europhobia and Europhilia: Party and Popular Attitudes towards Membership of the European Union in Serbia and Croatia, "*Perspectives on European Politics and Society*, 7, no. 3, (2006), p. 312–35 at 325.

Western education, reason, and the idea of progress.[428] The construction of the Western era as a decadent period is not unprecedented. Wilson notes that the ideas of growth and progress, personal freedoms and individuality, rational inquiry and scientific and technological progress have been seen as dehumanizing for the population.[429] By investigating this pre-modern feature of "First" Serbia, Milutinović puts forward that modernization is perceived as something that will "destroy the pastoral idyll of the traditional peasant society" as well as a social, political and cultural model that is not worth emulating.[430] Ruralism is perhaps most readily identified with decency, candidness and goodness by First Serbia. Often, it is seen as the real society of the village as opposed to the unnatural or "unreal" society of the town. Milutinović finds that Serbian anti-Occidentalism glorifies the Slav-barbarian superiority and natural generosity of the Serbian people and their inherent spirituality, idealism and traditional wisdom.[431] Such anti-modern sentiment, already comprised in the SANU *Memorandum,* clearly resonates strongly with First Serbia intellectuals. In this sense, the argumentation continues with the notion of the "spiritual corruption of the West," which is clearly directly influenced by the views of Serbian theologians and high-ranking Serbian Orthodox Church officials, particularly the well-read Bishop Nikolaj Velimirović, an anti-modernist and opponent of the Enlightenment and secularism.[432] However, after the Church's extreme politicization of Velimirović's attitudes, this strategy of othering "Europe" found its place among the broader socio-cultural structures, Perović notes.[433] First Serbia identity narrative, especially prominent in DSS and *Dveri* vocabu-

---

[428] See Jovan Byford, *Teorija zavere: Srbija protiv 'novog svetskog poretka'* (Conspiracy theory: Serbia vs. "the New World Order"), (Belgrade: Beogradski centar za ljudska prava, 2006).

[429] David Wilson, "Defending our Decadent West: The Meaning of Contemporary Atlanticism," *The European Journal: The Journal of the European Foundation*, 4, no. 3, (1996), p. 22–23.

[430] Zoran Milutinović, *Getting Over Europe: The Construction of Europe in Serbian Culture* (Amsterdam and New York: Rodopi, 2011), p. 12.

[431] Ibid.

[432] See Jovan Byford, *From "Traitor" to "Saint": Bishop Nikolaj Velimirović in Serbian Public Memory*, (Jerusalem: Hebrew University of Jerusalem, 2004).

[433] Latinka Perović, "The Flights of Modernization" in Nebojša Popov, ed., *The Road to War in Serbia* (Central European University Press, 2000), p. 116.

lary, does not simply provide an outline of the ethno-religious features of the Serbian nation, but also the basic features of the political organizations of the future Serbian modern state. Brubaker finds that every discourse of the nation includes elements of discourses of both ethnic nationalism and civic nationalism and the difference between the two is often ideologically constructed.[434] The political elites of First Serbia constantly rearticulate and renegotiate a particular ethnic myth/narrative of national identity which provides not only the history, but also the rationality and the argumentative structure, for future policy. Such new post-2000 Euroskeptic discourse obtains authority by reference to the older one; at the same time, this rearticulation reifies the identity of the older anti-West Milošević discourse.

The "Europe or Kosovo" dilemma

"First" Serbia is self-identifying as a defeated nation whose enemies were partially aided by that same Europe and are at the present moment part of that European framework. Kosovo is lost because of Europe. Indeed, Subotić notes that First Serbia political and cultural elites perceive European support for an independent Kosovo as the ultimate betrayal, and that this image fitted and resonated well with the Kosovo political mythology which is an important part of the nationalist discourses.[435] In the aftermath of Kosovo's declaration of independence in 2008, the dilemma of "either Kosovo or Europe" began to take a prominent place in the public sphere. Subotić finds that support for Kosovo's independence by the EU, the US and the West irritated Serbia and significantly influenced its desire to Europeanize.[436] In the aftermath of 2008, former president Tadić outlined Serbian policy as "both Europe and Kosovo."[437] Tadić claimed that "this policy ensures a European future for

---

[434] Rogers Brubaker, *Nationalism Reframed: Nationhood and the National Question in the New Europe* (Cambridge: Cambridge University Press, 1996).

[435] Jelena Subotić, "Europe is a State of Mind: Identity and Europeanization in the Balkans," *International Studies Quarterly* 55, no. 2 (2011), p. 309–330 at 314.

[436] Ibid.

[437] Tadić was referring to Serbia's efforts directed to both purposes: fighting for European Integration as well as seeking to prevent Kosovo from gaining full independence. See Boris Tadić, "Both Europe and Kosovo," in *Politika*, (February 24, 2012).

Serbia while protecting our national interests. It also shows that Serbia is a factor of stability in Southeast Europe."[438] This standpoint was supported by Patriarch Irinej who argued that "both Europe and Kosovo" was not an impossible policy, but that losing Kosovo would be too high a price to pay for EU membership.[439] In the aftermath of the 2012 elections, the First Serbia discourse became even more evident. Newly-established President Nikolić set out that if it were made an official condition of EU membership for Serbia to choose between Europe or Kosovo, the European path would be abandoned: "I have not changed my mind. I said that if we have to give up on Kosovo then we might as well forget Europe, and I stand by what I said."[440] The articulation of the prospect of "losing Kosovo," following the declaration of the independence of Kosovo in 2008, is suggestive of deep national crisis. Since the Yugoslav wars, the Kosovo issue had the effect of catapulting identity into the forefront of the political debate and compelling the elites to again try to answer the quasi-metaphysical question of who the Serbs would be without Kosovo.

Paradoxically, Kosovo is both the "Serbian highest value," but at the same time, it is constructed to be a radical Other. Although historically regarded as a part of Serbia, Kosovo is also regarded as a threat, a "land of criminals, corruption, drugs and blood revenge"[441] and constituted as menacing and hostile. There is also a secret European agenda on Kosovo. Kosovo is considered to be undemocratic and ruled by the "criminals and mafia bosses," but this is a static configuration and there is no capacity for reform and modification. Among right-wing opponents of the EU/Europe, most evident are the cultural arguments that were often instrumentalized to reject Kosovo's place in Europe, on the

---

[438] Ibid.

[439] Patriarch Irinej, "Politika 'i Evropa i Kosovo' nije nemoguća" (The policy "Both Europe and Kosovo" is not impossible) in *Politika*, (December 30, 2012).

[440] From the interview with Tomislav Nikolić "President: Srebrenica crime was no genocide" published in Italian daily *Corriere della Sera* (October 9, 2012).

[441] "Kosovo, the land of criminals, corruption, drugs and revenge," *Vestinet.rs, Spiegel* (January 26, 2013). http://www.vestinet.rs/pogledi/kosovo-zemlja-kriminala-korupcije-droge-i-krvne-osvete; "All the drugs are coming from Kosovo," B-92 (December 20, 2011). ww.b92.net/info/vesti/index.php?yyyy=2011&mm=12&dd=20&nav_category=16&nav_id=567129

grounds that it does not share all of the European culture which is common to all the nations of Europe. In the aftermath of the 2008 declaration of independence, the cultural dimension of these essentialist strategies was powerfully reinforced by the political dimension.

If Kosovo is recognized, Antonić writes, "one of our values (i.e. Kosovo) has already been sacrificed in the name of our highest aim (i.e. Europe). It will be very bad if we have reached a point where we have to sacrifice another value—democracy."[442] Therefore, in the First Serbia discourse, "entering the EU" is linked to losing sovereignty, and to the loss of democracy. This process of linkage is quite contrary to most discourses on Europe in Central and Eastern European EU integration, in which Europe is directly linked to the foundations of democracy. In the aftermath of 2008, the word *integrity* was overlexicalized in word connections such as *territorial integrity, sovereignty*, etc. In this respect, in the article "A voice against the EU," Milanović notes that Europe is the issue that divides the Serbs more than any other.[443] Milanović puts forward that this is not because they do not believe in the advantages of European unification, but because they are not prepared to give Kosovo away.[444] Thus, in this argumentational scheme, the First Serbia discourse on Serbia's EU membership is first and foremost built on a specific essentialist understanding of Serbian history in relation to Kosovo, in all its cultural, social and political dimensions. Koštunica suggests that there are important and compelling reasons that make us think about Kosovo as a breaking point that determines the future of Serbia as "it is only a matter of time when the new requests to surrender territory will be made." [445] Kosovo has always been framed in terms of a sacrifice and once more that sacrifice to Europe will influence the future of the Serbian state. Koštunica goes on to refer to famous poet Milovan Danojlić: "Kosovo is a lump of earth that is being torn away from Europe and

---

[442] Slobodan Antonić, "Srbi I Evro-Srbi" (Serbs and Euro-Serbs), in *Politika* (March 4, 2007).
[443] Branko Milanovic, "Glas protiv pregovora sa EU" (A voice against negotiations with the EU) in *Politika* (April 17, 2008).
[444] Karmen Erjavec and Zala Volčič, "The Kosovo battle: Media's Recontextualization of the Serbian Nationalistic Discourses," in *Harvard International Journal of Press/Politics* 12, no 3, (2007), p. 75.
[445] Vojislav Koštunica, *Speeches and Analysis* (DSS). http://dss.rs/category/govori-i-analize

from Serbia as a European nation, for the sake of globalist plans. After that kind of robbery there is less Europe and less life in all of us."[446]

Identity markers such as victimhood and martyrdom are always included in the spatial construction of "Kosovo," but these identities are often constructed as a mixture of the territorially bound, yet abstract, political meaning. Kosovo is frequently used by Serbian intellectuals and politicians to re-contextualize the epic genre in an ordinary political message. Re-contextualization is often used to refer to the process by which a dominant text assimilates, for some strategic purpose, elements of another genre, in this case epic poetry.[447] In a timespan of only a few years since Kosovo's independence, the cultural/essentialist arguments have been widely used across the political spectrum, as the identity dimension of European membership has become more prominent in the First Serbia discourse. In contrast to this, Vuk Drašković, leader of the SPO, maintained there were two paths available for Serbs, both excluding Kosovo. Drašković suggested that one of the choices is "Serbia in the EU, meaning Serbia without Kosovo but with Kosovo Serbs having the strongest possible links with Serbia, whereas the other one is Serbia outside of the EU, and in a hostile relationship with the EU, which means Serbia without Kosovo and no Serbs left in Kosovo."[448]

Regarding the independence of Kosovo, it has been said that membership of the EU would be a fair trade-off for a lost province. Europe is presented here as a sort of substitute for Kosovo. In this and similar views, identities are changeable and Serbs should not accept that outdated model of traditional and territorial identification. Here, the emphasis is on the ability of Serbia to distance itself from its belligerent history and to position its national identity in progressive terms. But more importantly, one can see the inevitability of the recognition that it should focus on partnership, rather than enmity and conflict, with other

---

[446] Ibid.

[447] Paul Chilton, and Christina Schäffner, "Introduction: Themes and Principles in the Analysis of Political Discourse," in Paul Chilton and Christina Schäffner, (eds.), *Politics as Text and Talk: Analytic Approaches to Political Discourse* (Amsterdam: John Benjamins, 2002), p. 36.

[448] Vuk Drašković, "Imamo dva puta, oba bez Kosova" ("There are two paths we can take, both without Kosovo") in *Politika* (November 29, 2012).

such national identities. The extracts presented above are only examples, among many, of the way culture and history have been instrumentalized in simultaneously assessing Serbia's and Kosovo's Europeanness, their belonging or not belonging to "Europe."

Thus, one can see how, in the aftermath of 2008, the main argumentation strategies put forward were formulated in the form of the "either/neither Europe or/nor Kosovo" dilemma. Vukadinović argued that the correct choice is neither Europe, nor Kosovo, and suggests the concept of "self-reliance" in order "to cool off the hot heads of local Europhiles at the peak of Serbian Euro-fanaticism."[449] He makes constant references to detachment from Europe and the romanticized view of going it alone, subsequently positioning Serbia's identity as isolationist rather than internationalist. This thinking includes an obsession with myths of balance of power and is emblematic of an isolationist sense of idealism. Vukadinović points out, "if there was ever any dilemma, today it has become clear that Kosovo and the European integration of Serbia are not separate processes and never were. It is now clear that we will never be allowed into the EU until we resolve the issue of 'neighborly relations' with Kosovo."[450] Therefore, discursive actors and debate participants who belong to the right of the Serbian political spectrum depict Europe as not only culturally divergent but also a threatening entity: Europe is dangerous as it "took a part of Serbian territory"; Europe is once again represented as a tormentor, an oppressor that forces Serbia to obey its rules. In this context, extensive references are made to historical conflicts, such as the Second World War and the 1999 NATO intervention, or misapprehension between Serbia and Europe on the independence of Kosovo or the dissolution of Yugoslavia. These are given as obvious evidence of the incompatibility of the "two cultures."

---

[449] Djordje Vukadinović, "Srbija I Evropska Unija: mamuzanje mrtvog konja" (Flogging a dead horse) *Vreme*, Issue 1037 (November 18, 2010).
[450] Ibid.

Discursive constructions of in- and out-groups in the "First" Serbia

In terms of the Self and Other nexus, I argue that the main discursive strategy utilized in the "First" Serbia discourse is one which equates the values of the First Serbian Self with the "real" Serbian Self. In this way, it is constructed as representing the same image: only First Serbia is the real Serbia. Although several argumentative and rhetorical tools such as topoi of culture, Orthodox vocation, faith etc., and metaphors, especially Kosovo spatial metaphors, have been instrumental in the construction of in-group sameness, most activity has been done through selective use of the third person plural pronoun *they* when writing about Europeans, and the first person plural *we* when speaking about "defenders of national values," Serbians or occasionally Russians. The study of the relationship between these pronouns has been shown to be extremely important in studying political discourse, as they are at the border of syntax and semantics.[451] According to Chilton and Schäffner, "pronouns, especially the first person plural (we, us, our), can be used to induce interpreters to conceptualize group identity, coalitions, parties, and the like, either as insiders or outsiders."[452] Hansen finds this exclusion between "insiders" and "outsiders" takes place not only on the basis of spatial construction of identity, but also on temporal grounds.[453] However, there are no final definitions of what constitutes the *we*, the *other*, *inside* or *outside* in relation to Europe, as these terms can change over time.

The widespread use of first or third person pronouns to denote the First Serbian Self as a large part of the all-encompassing Serbian Self is remarkable. In many utterances it is possible to find expressions such as *Our Serbia, We, the Serbs, the Serbian nation, nationhood, We, the Orthodox,*

---

[451] Van Dijk, "Discourse, knowledge and ideology," in Teun A. van Dijk et al., (eds.), *Communicating Ideologies* (Berne: Lang, 2004), p. 5–38 at 7.

[452] Paul Chilton, and Christina Schäffner, "Introduction: Themes and Principles in the Analysis of Political Discourse," in Paul Chilton and Christina Schäffner, (eds.), *Politics as Text and Talk: Analytic Approaches to Political Discourse* (Amsterdam: John Benjamins, 2002), p. 30.

[453] Lene Hansen, *Security as Practice: Discourse Analysis and the Bosnian War* (London and New York: Routledge, 2006) p. 48–49.

defenders of Serbdom and so on, employed together. In this way, the First Serbia Self is constructed as a large part of the Serbian Self, if not the only part, and as holding First Serbia values as an extension of Serbianness. "Europe" and the "Other" Serbia Self are conceptualized as an extension of the "foreign hand" and a fragment of the foreign another, the European Other, the Western Other. These utterances can be found especially in the texts of Slobodan Antonić about Other-Serbians. For example: "They [home-grown missionaries, missionary intelligentsia] become embittered toward their surroundings, they start to despise society as a whole, and then eventually they start to hate it. …. They even send an open invitation to "civilized foreigners" to come and occupy the country."[454] In his text "Serbs and Euro-Serbs," Antonić employs this strategy to spatially construct Other-Serbians as belonging to another locality: "Welcome. Europe has been waiting specially for all those of you who can't stand Cyrillic, who can consider a nation narrow-minded and primitive, and who believe that any kind of national pride has an unbelievable stench."[455] It is therefore obvious that the selective use of the first person plural pronoun *we*, and the third person plural pronoun *they*, provides the speaker with an opportunity to put his discourse into perspective. Antonić rightly identified the forms of discursive clashes and conflicts, of First and Other Serbia by putting them into the context of post-Milošević Serbia but he also encapsulates the manner in which the Serbian national identity has been configured in terms of the exclusion of diversity in the light of these clashes and conflicts.

Positive self-presentation and national self-glorification

Positive and unblemished presentation of Serbian culture and "civilization"—principally represented by the Church and by Orthodox byzantine historical heritage—is a dominant strategy of predication in "First" Serbia political discourse. It is not unusual for members of groups to "think of themselves in human terms as better than the oth-

---

[454] Slobodan Antonić, "Misionarska inteligencija u današnjoj Srbiji" (Missionary intelligentsia in today's Serbia) in Vreme, no. 631 (February 5, 2003).

[455] Slobodan Antonić, "Srbi I Evro-Srbi" (Serbs and Euro-Serbs), in *Politika* (March 4, 2007).

ers," as Elias puts it, and to appear to establish boundaries between groups by stigmatizing outsiders.[456] However, one can suggest that in the context of the First Serbia discourse about Europe, positive Self-presentation manifests itself as an emphasis on one's own values, which Elias calls the social prejudice or "the feeling of their own superior virtue."[457] The in-group bias in predication is remarkable; First Serbia actors often mention only what they consider to be the positive aspects of Serbian history and culture, while denying, obfuscating or simply ignoring the negative aspects of the present and past. Such in-group bias is a very common form of "ideologically based strategies" of positive self and negative other presentation.[458] To illustrate this we do not need to go further than former Serbian PM Dačić who argued in 2012 that "the Serbs must stay proud of their fight against fascism and their freedom-loving history and they must not allow the fact that Serbia lost half of its male population in the First World War and that the Serbs made huge sacrifices in the Second World War to be forgotten."[459] According to Dačić, the Serbian victims have been forgotten and history has been skewed in such a way as to make the Balkan nations that were defeated in the World Wars more important than Serbia and the Serbian people.[460] The discourse that constructs Serbia as always innocent and "being on the right side"[461] for centuries makes little or no reference to the Balkan enmities of the recent past or responsibility for the war crimes committed in the name of the Republic of Serbia by the Milošević regime. In this type of First Serbia in-group favoritism, real Serbia is constructed always as the home of "real," genuine and authentic values. Such in-group bias in this particular sub-type of predication, as Beyza notes, often leads to the assertion of the superiority of one's own culture and civilization.[462]

---

[456] Elias, Norbert, *The Established and the Outsiders: A Sociological Enquiry into Community Problems* (London: Sage, 1994), p. 23.
[457] Ibid.
[458] Ruth Wodak and Teun A. van Dijk, (eds.) *Racism at the Top: Parliamentary Discourses on Ethnic Issues in Six European States* (Klagenfurt: Drava Verlag, 2000), p. 90.
[459] "The Serbian Prime Minister commemorates" in *Tanjug* (October 14, 2012).
[460] Ibid.
[461] Ibid.
[462] See Tekin C. Beyza, *Representations and Othering in the Discourse: The Construction of Turkey in the EU Context* (Amsterdam: John Benjamins, 2010), p. 65.

The difference attributed to Europe and Other-Serbians

First, it should be noted that in the "First" Serbia discourse, Serbia is constructed as always having been part of Europe, meaning part of Old Europe, which concept differs from that of Western Europe. And this difference toward Western Europe is emphasized and put forward as important in terms of identity. I argue that First Serbia actors understand the "European Other" and "Other" Serbia as being fundamentally different from the "real and true" Serbian Self. The difference attributed to the Other-Serbians and Europe is almost natural and essential, and is deeply rooted in history, religion, culture and civilization. Second, the construction of the European Other and Other-Serbians by First Serbia is typically fueled by xenophobic stereotypes. In this right-wing discourse, the European Other is quite often constructed as *arrogant*, *brutal*, and *aggressive*, and "it repeatedly forces conditionality." This is a portrayal that gives away a stereotypical image of the Other.[463] The historicity of this particular image of "arrogance" can also be observed in the lexicals Serbian discursive actors strategically employ to revive the image of the "arrogant" European bully in connection to the 1999 NATO intervention. Added to this is a sub-discourse that constructs European practices as being totalitarian, supremacist and meddlesome, and in which the idealistic rhetoric of Europe is overshadowed by the realist world of nation-states.

The representation of Europe in "Other" Serbia discourse

> All of my life I had this urge not to forget. This feeling that one has started to forget things is the first step towards death, so I want to live and remember. But if I remember then I cannot accept all of this. Yes, we're talking about Europe, fuck it, let's wait a bit and then re-join the queue later, I don't know. It just cannot be my goal if it means that I have to be in the same train with these people ("First-Serbians"). The train stinks and I don't feel like going anywhere. I prefer to walk, slowly.
>
> Petar Luković, *The Train to Europe*, Peščanik Series, September 2008

---

[463] Ibid, p. 67.

This section analyzes the main argumentative strategies employed in official state discourses and civic society discourses. The official state discourses were constituted by reformers and soft liberals mostly from the Democratic Party, including former president Tadić, who has repeatedly stressed that Serbia will join the EU but will "enter Europe with our identity: We spent twenty years legitimizing our national politics, and by that I don't mean just the civic one. Even today we are trying to enter Europe with our identity, which implies legitimizing our national goals."[464]

On the other side of the democratic political spectrum, Vesna Pešić, considered to be a hard liberal, expressed the view that decisions on Europeanization were never made and that Serbian society is not ready to modernize.[465] She named the Serbian Orthodox Church as the main culprit for this state of affairs:

> The Serbs have looked into history and do not recognize any of the current events. They have lost the connection with modern civilization and hope that by some miracle this civilization would collapse. The pillar of this kind of thinking is the Serbian Orthodox Church. It has become an institution that decides which citizens can and cannot exercise their civic rights. The banning of the Belgrade Pride parade in 2011 is good evidence.[466]

Zoran Ostojić[467] recognized that "Europe" is not about "whether we will have inflation of two percent or whether VAT will be fourteen percent, or if we have a broadcasting management agency, or bonds and shares or a good money market."[468] Ostojić puts forward that reconciliation and recognition of Serbian wrongdoings is impossible to achieve if the president, the prime minister and the heads of all the main political parties

---

[464] Tadić, Boris, "Entering Europe with our identity," in *B92*, (December 12, 2009).

[465] Vesna Pešić, in the debate "Is Serbia Giving up on European Integration—Let's Show the Politicians our 'Civic Teeth'," at Hotel Zira in Belgrade, hosted by the *Fund for Humanitarian Law and the Independent Association of Journalists of Vojvodina* (March 12, 2005). Participants included intellectuals, civic activists, representatives of the non-governmental sector and politicians. http://www.e-novine.com/srbija/srbija-tema/51630-Pokazati-politiarima-graanske-zube.html.

[466] Ibid.

[467] Zoran Ostojić, "Beograd Stanislava Vinavera" (Belgrade by Stanislav Vinaver), in *Hourglass Series* (June 22, 2007). Ostojić was an LDP parliamentarian, journalist and politician.

[468] Ibid.

and the majority of the media avoid dedicating considerable time to these issues:

> Above and below it the essence is the value system—8000 people (in Srebrenica) were murdered and if the International Court of Justice said that that was genocide there should be no debate, we should just draw lessons from it. By doing that we will just make life easier for the next generations, those who were not even born when it all happened. They should not be forced to face this just because we were too cowardly to admit our own guilt.[469]

One can see clearly how Serbia's recent past became a threat to Serbian identity, and blocked the positive embrace of European values and thinking. Dimitrijević inquired what is meant by the word *West* and adds "if we are talking about the cultural model and values such as democracy, rule of law, human rights and economic liberalism, there is no need to refer to it as Western as these are ideals that have by now been accepted by almost everybody in the east of Europe as well."[470] In the same vein, Dimitrijević questioned the significance of the adjective in the phrase *pro-Western intellectual* when viewed in the context of the complementary *pro-Eastern intellectual*.[471] He, additionally, posed the question of whether the pro-Eastern intellectual would be against all the values listed earlier,[472] concluding that this would make pro-Eastern intellectuals only those who support values based on non-European civilizations.[473] Dimitrijević concludes that what is really referred to is the political West (or the Western Bloc), a concept that became obsolete in 1989.[474] The statement above, made by a respected human rights lawyer, is exemplary of the Other Serbia discourse on identity and Europe, in which Serbia is expected to become part of the EU/Europe through convergence of democratic values and culture over the next few decades. The activities of civic NGOs have shown the more activist and emancipatory character of the Serbian intellectual position. The Europe-

---

[469] Ibid.
[470] Vojin Dimitrijević, "Greske u koracima" (Walking in the Wrong Direction), in *Vreme*, no. 636. (March 13, 2003).
[471] Ibid.
[472] Ibid.
[473] Ibid.
[474] Ibid.

an symbolic geography was, Živković notes, the "most proximate source of 'civilization'."[475]

The disagreement between soft liberals and hard-liners

In the Other Serbia discourse which advocates Serbia's EU membership, the use of value-oriented arguments is considered simply irrelevant and Serbian culture is constructed as something that is constantly evolving, i.e. not a historically given object. But there is a collision between two ways of thinking, as regards how Serbia can go forward from here. The EU embodies transformation including the enlargement, further democratization, and tackling corruption and climate change. In the moderate soft liberal view, Serbia is close to the EU, it belongs to Europe and currently is moving even closer to Europe. In this discourse, then, there is a strong possibility not only for Serbia to incorporate the values of the European Other through constant betterment and improvement, but there is a strong case for the reconciliation of the countries of the Balkan region. I suggest that in the soft liberal "Other" Serbia discourse, change and transformation are seen as attainable, although through a very painful and arduous process. Also, the discourse on Serbian national identity is articulated in a more instrumental than primordial sense. Former Director of the Office for European Integration, Milica Delević, has repeatedly stressed that Serbia needs to make an assessment of the Serbian self-serving national interests,[476] that the EU is its biggest economic partner as the largest foreign investments come from there. "We are in Europe, we are surrounded with those countries that wish to be there, and Europe is our destiny."[477] On the other hand, hard liberals understand change as slow, even unattainable, as the Serbian Self might be undeniably inferior to the European Other. Žarko Korać, a professor and former

---

[475] Marko Živković, *Serbian Dreambook: National Imaginary in the Time of Milošević* (Burlington, IN: Indiana University Press, 2011), p. 44.
[476] "Delević: Početak pregovora u skorije vreme," *Blic* online (May 9, 2013) http://www.blic.rs/Vesti/Politika/381653/Delevic-Pocetak-pregovora-u-skorije-vreme
[477] "Delević: Rešenje za krizu samo u EU," *Blic* online (April 25, 2012) http://www.blic.rs/Vesti/Politika/319039/Delevic-Resenje-za-krizu-samo-u-EU

member of the democratic opposition has this to say about Serbian identity and Europe:

> Yes, I am in favor of Europe. But what does that really mean? Nothing. I am against corruption. Yes, and? What does that mean exactly? We are in favor of Europe, but we are not in a hurry as we will go there 'with our identity.' That sentence means absolutely nothing. It is one of the most pointless sentences ever spoken. Take Europe today. Now, can someone really tell me that the Spaniards and the Swedes have become one and the same? Or the Greeks and the Irish? Are Bulgarians and Danes now completely the same in today's Europe? What kind of nonsense is that? Of course, it is not that easy to change popular and national identities. They are something that changes in a gradual, extended process, and God only knows how. But identity always stays specific because it is a characteristic of a society.[478]

Hard-liberal Other Serbia actors do tend to focus on the lack of democracy within the Serbian institutional structures, and the unchangeable character of the Serbian national identity. The narrative of Central and Eastern European states which have successfully shaken off their communist past and embraced liberal democracy is startlingly absent. In this respect, Jovan Byford, discussing First Serbia's refusal to accept certain European values on the *Hourglass* radio show, argued that the central concept of the patriotic wing of the contemporary Serbian establishment is exemplified by Ratibor Djurdjević's[479] words "Europe as a source of untold evil—Serbs in Europe, yes, Europe in Serbia, God forbid."[480] Byford describes this argument as a calculation: "Serbia will enter Europe in order to gain all the consequent economic benefits, but our spiritual being must be defended to the last from these European ideas that they are trying to impose on us."[481] First Serbia's message here is clear: Europe positions itself as a bearer of democratic values and, by "democratizing" the rest of Eastern Europe, it further regulates the behavior of these states for the purpose of its own political and commercial interests. Within their anti European debates, Europe is accused of hypocrisy and treason. Other Serbia, on the other hand, views democracy as an essen-

---

[478] Žarko Korać, "Loše" (Bad), in *Hourglass Series*, (December 11, 2009).
[479] Owner and editor of the Ikhtios publishing house. His words are quoted from *Pravoslavlje* magazine, which is owned by the Serbian Orthodox Church.
[480] Jovan Byford, "Evropa u Srbiji? Boze sacuvaj!" (Europe in Serbia? God forbid!), in *Hourglass Series* (December 23, 2005).
[481] Ibid.

tial requirement for the peace and political stability of the whole region. Yet, Serbia does not possess the political and social capital required in order to establish a more mature form of democratic structure and institutions. Other Serbia actors do not understand Serbian democracy as possessing an organic, home-grown and democratic structure in which politicians work for the people and play the role of their guardians. Thus, EU membership is seen as a way of strengthening Serbia's depleted sense of Self and by which it may regain its former sense of dignity.

On Serbia's duty to recognize its past

LDP president Čedomir Jovanović, speaking at the "Serbia in Europe" rally, argued that there will be no European Serbia if "we do not defeat those who turned us into the Nazis of the 21st century." Jovanović has found that the only difference between the photos from Srebrenica and those from Auschwitz is that the former are in color: "People, we stand covered in the blood and gunpowder of the 1990s because no one has bothered to clean it off."[482] Jovanović, like many in the LDP, has refused the idea that Ratko Mladić held Serbia hostage by not turning himself over to the police for so long, but instead considers that Serbia itself is a hostage of the ideology that allowed Mladić to do what he did.[483] That ideology, Jovanović claimed, came from the Academy of Sciences and Arts, from the Church, from the government, from the parliament, from the secret services.[484] The *we* in the "Other" Serbia discourse is often constituted by the rest of the Serbs, the ones that are *the disappointed*: "We are many thousands of people who were never asked about anything, because the state is holy and anything can be done in its name."[485] Dawson rightly notes that that these "disappointed" citizens of Serbia did not become disillusioned with the idea of democracy, liberal ideology or human rights, but the political choices in Serbia; the individuals

---

[482] Čedomir Jovanović, president of Liberal Democratic Party, at the rally "Srbija u Evropi" (Serbia in Europe), October 5, 2011. http://istina.ldp.rs/Liberalno-demokratska-partija
[483] Ibid.
[484] Ibid.
[485] Ibid.

who represented those political options were not acceptable, as they were considered corrupt or untrustworthy. [486] In its party manifesto, the Liberal Democrats put forward that "only a Serbia that can face its past can successfully face its future."[487] Srdja Popović, the lawyer, insists that "Serbia cannot deal with European Integration if it does not first tackle the crimes committed in our name."[488] The preferred Serbia that is put forward in the LDP manifesto is not Other Serbia as the goal, but "different Serbia, different from the country that became the most backward and disgraced place in Europe in the 1990s."[489] In this view, the new Serbia should be "different from the country that believed in the values which brought about wars and dictatorship and different from the country that had no respect for its youth, its women and its minorities, and therefore for the majority."[490] On the theme of lessons learned, Korać asks in what way Serbia needs to understand what happened and to learn more about the crimes that have been committed:[491] "After all, Europe has learned in the most dramatic way about the power of fanaticized masses and their destructive anger. Perhaps this is the first and the most important lesson that we must learn if we want to understand our present situation."[492]

Broadly speaking, two major variants exist on different argumentation about dealing with the past, recognizing the Srebrenica genocide and the independence of Kosovo. I argue that the hard-line variant of the Other Serbia discourse refers to the Srebrenica and other brutal and inhuman atrocities as providing a clear indication that Serbia is clearly brutal and barbarian and in that way, insufficiently European. It is often repeated that the scale of severe atrocities committed by the Serbs reflects their incompatibility with European values and norms. In many instances, in debates among the hard liberals, incidents from the war are

---

[486] James Dawson, *Cultures of Democracy in Serbia and Bulgaria: How Ideas Shape Public*, (London: Ashgate 2014), p. 31.
[487] "LDP political manifesto"(March 4, 2012). http://istina.ldp.rs/Liberalno-demokratska-partija
[488] Srdja Popović, "Europe" in *Hourglass Series*, (December 11, 2009).
[489] Ibid.
[490] Ibid.
[491] Žarko Korać, "Lose" (Bad), in *Hourglass Series*, (December 11, 2009).
[492] Ibid.

depicted as historical evidence of the Serbs' prototypically barbaric character. Svetlana Lukić, Editor-in-Chief of *Hourglass*, contends that Serbia is a sick society:

> These are societies that on the one hand would like to become a part of Europe, but on the other do not believe in the basic principles on which the EU is founded. These are societies that are ruled by people that have broken the most basic civilizational and Christian norms, that are now supposed to take us into the fold of a union of civilized states, and who continue to kiss crosses wherever they can. This hypocrisy at the very top of the government, church and the army spreads like a virus across the whole society. The citizens express support for EU entry, but at the same time despise all the basic Western values except money. They consider tolerance as weakness, differences between people as a necessary evil, they hate the Roma people and homosexuals and are proud of their tribes, their authoritarianism and misogyny. Until we all agree that after the words of the fifth commandment—thou shall not kill—there is no but ... many people will continue to live like dogs in their sovereign, national, proud states.[493]

Essentialization of the nature of Serbian national identity is thus also present in the hard-line Other Serbia discourse, as well as in "First" Serbia. One can immediately detect the concept of "nestling orientalism," which describes the essentalization of groups with perceived "primordial qualities." Hayden suggests this orientalist discourse was internalized by the people in the former Yugoslavia.[494] Attitudes about the Serbs are, it turns out, an effective device for testing the strength of Other Serbia's Balkanist understanding of cultures, political traditions and the "national character." For if any national group stood to benefit from the power of rhetoric to divide a purportedly European or pro-Western "them" from a backward Balkan "us," it would without the doubt be the elites, of First and Other Serbia as their ideological repertories remain stable and secure. But what exactly was the magnitude of the atrocities committed in the Yugoslav wars? And how is this significant issue understood in the context of these divergent discursive variants?

---

[493] Svetlana Lukić, "They all make us go crazy" in *Monitor Magazine*, Issue 1082, (July 15, 2011). Lukić is editor-in-chief of the *Hourglass* radio show, political journal and webpage.

[494] Milica Bakić-Hayden and Robert M Hayden, "Orientalist Variations on the Theme 'Balkans': Symbolic Geography in Recent Yugoslav Cultural Politics," *Slavic Review*, Vol. 51, No. 1 (Spring 1992), p. 922.

The nature of crimes

In that respect, Dragović-Soso puts forward that in the Point of Departure debate,[495] the argument was not just about defining who the victims or perpetrators were in the Yugoslav wars, but about the more fundamental question of the extent and nature of the crimes committed: were Serb crimes of a different order to those of others?[496] Equally present in the Other Serbia discourse is another central way of approaching the issue, that of the soft liberals, who rarely essentialize the problem. Rather than regarding the atrocities committed by the Serbian side in the Yugoslav wars as an indication of Serbia's cultural and civilizational difference from Europe, this view considers the actual consequences of dealing with the truth in a newly-formed post-conflict society. In this light, Cerović has put forward that questions such as why Milošević enjoyed a high level of popular support in Serbia at one time, why the war took place at all and why Serbia came into conflict with "the whole world" deserved reckoning with.[497] In his view this reckoning could not be broached in what he saw as the one-sided and distorted way of Other Serbia hard-liners.[498] For him, their insistence on the ethnicization of the crimes effectively represented a "stubborn selection of facts and a refusal to think about anything other than "Serb guilt."[499] In fact, Cerović has argued, Serbs had not backed Milošević's policy in the 1990s to the extent that was being claimed, and the hard-liners were conveniently forgetting another part of the story—"the history of the Serbian resistance which finally toppled Milošević."[500]

---

[495] The 2002 Tačka Razlaza (Point of Departure) debate lasted three months and included discussions about the Yugoslav wars and Milošević's legacy. The end result was that the "Other" Serbia group split into two, hard-liners and soft liberals.

[496] Jasna Dragović-Soso, "Collective Responsibility, International Justice and Public Reckoning with the Recent Past: Reflections on a Debate in Serbia," in Timothy Waters, ed., *The Milošević Trial—An Autopsy*, (Oxford: Oxford University Press, 2011), p. 10.

[497] Stojan Cerović, "Tvrdoglava selektivnost" (Stubborn Selectivity) in *Vreme*, no. 610, (September 12, 2002), p. 33.

[498] Ibid.

[499] Ibid.

[500] Ibid.

This soft liberal approach to facing the past emphasizes democratic resistance and Serbia's potential for political change. The issue of facing the past and recognizing responsibility for crimes is presented as a problem of democratic deficiency. For those who hold this view, the present problem of the country's failure can be solved through goodwill and resourceful politics. According to this view, what is needed is more time to ensure greater political maturity and more democracy. EU integration is also seen as a part of the solution. As is evident in the literature about the construction of a common European identity,[501] Europe is constructed as being able to face its past errors. Recognizing its past errors, and coming to terms with its own history is taken to be a distinctly European value, a European lesson to the world, and a prerequisite for civilization.[502] By the same token, it has been suggested by Hansen and Wæver that temporal construction of European identity is exactly the reason why the EU is in general constructed not against an external Other, such as Russia or the Middle East, but rather against the temporal Other of its own violent past and the Second World War.[503] The community of European states were created as an answer to brutal atrocities of the Second World War and in the spirit of "never again." Thus, on a general level "the past" also plays a significant role in the construction of the EU's discourse on European identity.

The discursive construction of in and out-groups in "Other" Serbia

The production of negative self-presentation

Here, it should be noted that historicity does not operate only in the First Serbia discourse but also in that of the "Other" Serbia. The liberal intelligentsia also make frequent use of a selective reading of history, in lean-

---

[501] See Cathleen Kantner, "Collective Identity as Shared Ethical Self-Understanding: The Case of the Emerging European Identity," in *European Journal of Social Theory*, 9, no. 4, (2006), p. 501–524 at 504.

[502] Justin Gibbins, *Britain, Europe and National Identity: Self and Other in International Relations*, (Palgrave Macmillan, 2014), p. 21.

[503] Lene Hansen and Ole Wæver, (eds.) *European Integration and National Identity: The Challenge of the Nordic States* (London and New York: Routledge, 2001), p. 1–19.

ing on older positive images of the European Other which are still alive in the Serbian collective imaginary/memory. In such a context, this discourse often resorts to historical images of the European Other such as a "homeland of human rights," "tolerant of other religions" and a "functional multicultural society that exists peacefully." In these constructions, centuries-old respectful images of the "good European" are often made instrumental to support the stability of the discourse in which the "Serbs" could and are only portrayed in an inferior sense. For instance, former Mayor of Belgrade, Bogdan Bogdanović[504] habitually argued that Serbia betrayed not only European values but also itself during the 1990s. On the theme of civil Belgrade he explains that from 1991, "there is no Belgrade anymore":

> This civic Belgrade of mine has left Serbia in its entirety. People who once reacted to my words and perhaps understood them have scattered themselves around the world. But even that is better than the humiliation of living in your country that is no longer really yours. There is another thing that is horrifying and that is generally not written about: the fate of many people from former Yugoslavia who were not nationally affiliated because they were cosmopolitan, or were from mixed marriages, or have created mixed marriages. These people are condemned to perdition and oblivion, which is horrifying. .... These people are discriminated against in a way that would be unthinkable from the perspective of any democratic European state.[505]

Bogdanović openly puts forward the idea that he is a traitor of the Serbian people, at least of the Serbian people the way they are today. He plays with the well-known imprint of the traitor in the public sphere: "They all accuse each other of being traitors and the whole country is full of traitors. And in a way that is true. Serbia betrayed itself."[506] Bogdanović offers a different account of Serbian history:

---

[504] The architectural and literary work of Bogdan Bogdanović is well known, not only across former Yugoslavia but across Europe and globally. This great designer and philosopher of urban construction left the city of his birth in 1994 and emigrated to Vienna. He did this after a lifetime of achievements in Belgrade that brought him a professorship at the faculty of Architecture and a spell as mayor of Belgrade. He also resigned from the Serbian Academy of Sciences.

[505] Bogdan Bogdanović, "Srbija je samu sebe izdala" (Serbia Betrayed Itself) in *Dani* magazine, (December 21 1998). http://www.bhdani.com/arhiva/91/tekst291.htm

[506] Ibid.

> Serbia reappeared at the beginning of the 19th century and it was a small cute country of peasants that came out of a revolution and was received in Europe with romantic exuberance. …. For a small nation that was received in Europe with so much care and love to end up the way it has today, with the whole civilized world treating it as a monster, Serbia had to betray itself.[507]

The quotations above demonstrate how the supporters of the European idea in Serbia construct Europe as having a tradition of values such of tolerance toward other nations, religions and customs, all the values that Serbia persistently lacks itself. In this construction the emphasis is often placed on a demonization, dehumanization and intolerance of "ethnic other" groups, and images of horrific crimes in Srebrenica, these being the particular images prevailing in Other Serbia anti-nationalist discourse. It could therefore be argued that in Other Serbia discourses, the historical images of Serbians as following the European path until the 1980s and then choosing a cruel, vicious and uncivilized course with Milošević are overtly present and widespread in the Serbian collective imaginary/memory. Therefore, the Other Serbia discourse offers a concentrated, rigorous and reduced negative Self-presentation of Serbia but with a parallel, forceful, and positive presentation of the European Other which often instrumentalizes the image of "wicked, barbaric Serbia."

The Serbian Self is inferior to the European other

This study has shown that negative predication of the "Other" Serbia often comes in the form of binary oppositions, through negative presentation of the Serbian Self (e.g. "the people who have broken the most basic civilizational norms").[508] Other Serbia discursive actors put in contrast, and thus emphasize, the positive values attributed to the European Other. Serbia is often contrasted with Europe and is found to be undemocratic (as opposed to "democratic Europe"), intolerant, chauvinistic and xenophobic (as opposed to "tolerant and moderate Europe"), backward and poor (as opposed to "developed and prosperous Europe"), or irrational, aggressive and prone to violence (as opposed to "rational and peaceful Europe"). The negativity attached to Serbia coupled with the

---

[507] Ibid.
[508] Svetlana Lukić, "They all make us go crazy," in *Monitor Magazine*, Issue 1082, (July 15, 2011).

positive representation of Europe further generates hierarchical power relations which construct the superiority of the European Other and the inferiority of the Serbian Self. In other words, the Serbian Self is not only perceived as different, religiously fanatical or aggressive, but is also inferior when compared to the peaceful and tolerant European Other. Controversies around whether Serbia's history was progressive or stagnant contributed to the creation of such identity construction. Djurić's historical comparison between Europe and Serbia would be an exemplary utterance:

> It is impossible to talk about a market for anything in a country that has no understanding about its own position nor has ever developed it in its entire history. Recently while reading a book on the life of Van Eyck, I learned that oil painting as a technique was discovered around 1400 when Spain colonized Flanders. During the years of servitude the Flemish researched and discovered a technology that reached Italy around the same time and created a revolution in painting. Though we are just across the sea from Italy we had no idea about what was going on. At the time we were *living in forests* while Despot Stefan Lazarević was trying to free us from Sultan Bayezid. It is hard not to think about how someone over there who was sitting under occupation made great discoveries, while here there weren't even any real cities.[509]

In this negative predication, the Other Serbia continually compares the Serbian Self with the European Self, finding it undeveloped, backward and historically inferior. I note that eventually this particular form of Other Serbia's politics of producing negative Otherness has important political consequences for the sedimentation of the unwavering anti-European identity discourse of First Serbia.

The hard-liners' variant: Balkanist discourse

The extreme variant of the Other-Serbian hard-line discourse is Luković's argumentation against the "First" Serbia elites and the Serbian population. Luković is even against those institutions which dealt with

---

[509] Djurić continues with this thought, saying that in an interview with "Dani" from Sarajevo, Goran Bregović once described how he found the following hypothetical situation very strange: "Goethe and Vuk Karadžić sat and had a dinner as friends. Then each went his own way, Goethe to write Faust, and Vuk to put together the first Serbian grammar. That tells you all you need to know about the market of ideas." Uroš Djurić, "Skup neuklopljenih" (The Cluster of Unadjusted), in *Vreme*, Issue 759, (July 21, 2005).

the processes of European integration: "It just cannot be my goal if I have to be in the same train with these people, the train stinks and I don't feel like going anywhere. I prefer to walk, slowly."[510] In this view, complete institutional reform or even adoption of the acquis communautaire would not assist Serbia to be become a European state, or to be perceived as a country belonging to Europe. Thus, according to the hard-line variant of the Other Serbian discourse, even EU membership would not bring the Serbians closer to European values. What is needed is a full reconciliation in the region, honest and dealing directly with past crimes, as well as a sincere domestic and internal wich by the whole of society for extensive transformation—political, cultural and social. However, that change is not possible and it will never be. This position is held by a considerable number of "Other" Serbia hard-liners. It can be argued that this Balkanist discourse, as employed in the Other Serbia hard-line variant, links Serbia with the *primitive, barbaric, hateful* and *unreasonable* and conceives it as radically different from the modern Europe of *order, civilization* and *reason*. Hansen suggests that Balkanism is a construction of temporal Othernesss, in which "the Balkan," or in our case "Serbia," is constructed as incapable of inner change or transformation.[511] In Hansen's matrix, this first construction of temporal Otherness as incapable of change is further radicalized by a second temporal move which constitutes such uncivilized, violent, disgusting and barbaric identity as "inherent."[512] The alternative to such an identity matrix, on the other hand, is the identity construction that differentiates Serbia from Europe, yet links it with the quality of being undeveloped but still capable of change and transformation, which implies some sort of civilizing mission from "outsiders," e.g. Europeans.

---

[510] Petar Luković, "Voz za Evropu" (The Train to Europe), in *Hourglass Series* (September 19, 2008).
[511] Hansen, Lene, *Security as Practice: Discourse Analysis and the Bosnian War* (London and New York: Routledge, 2006), p. 61.
[512] Ibid.

Serbian identity (in)capable of change

Still, can an inferior non-European national identity created by the "Other" Serbia be perceived to be resolved through reform or good will? In the Other Serbia hard-line discourse, what makes Serbia so different is first and foremost its culture or civilization/religion/lack of culture; that is to say, the Serbian Self is primarily a civilizational Other to Europe. This variant of the discourse constructs Serbia as belonging almost exclusively to another cultural realm which is *abnormal, crazy, barbarian, primitive* and unable to change. Petar Luković, in *Hourglass*, used to argue that

> entering Europe has been presented here as some kind of abnormal effort to make us look normal so that it actually happens. But it's not like 'we want to be normal', it's just how it has to be. We have to whitewash our toilets so that they are not full of shit because that's what Europe demands, but otherwise we're happy just the way we are. There is no real desire to do anything here, at least so that we can say: Fuck Europe, let's live well, lead a normal life and try to make something for ourselves here. But no. The pressure from Europe will ensure that the sewage is sorted out. But sorting out the people, sorting out the lunatics, sorting out laws, there is no pressure from Europe to do that—that should be a normal thing.[513]

Hard-line variants of Other Serbia do differ from the soft liberal option on the question of the possibility of transformation. As Hansen notes, reading political identity through temporal constructions implies the existence of *progress* and *change* over time.[514] As a result, articulations of temporal identity such as *development*, *change*, *transformation* and *continuity* are crucial for analyzing constructions of identity such as First and Other Serbia debates on Europe. The idea that progress can be made by the strength of society itself, through the efforts of citizens of Serbia themselves, and not due to pressure from the outside appears to be a persistent theme in the soft liberal variant. Mijatović finds that the majority of political actors are trying to give the public the impression that "we are but a step away from Europe, even though we consistently fail to make it," and that just a "little extra effort is needed, just one more

---

[513] Petar Luković, "Voz za Evropu" (The Train to Europe in *Hourglass Series* (September 19, 2008).

[514] Lene Hansen, *Security as Practice: Discourse Analysis and the Bosnian War* (London and New York: Routledge, 2006) p. 154.

task to fulfill and Europe will take us into its fold."[515] Mijatović also suggests that it is not easy to be in favor of Europe in Serbia, as from the economic perspective the attractiveness of Europe and the European Union should lie more in a Serbian desire to Europeanize and improve conditions rather than in instructions and money which would be received during the process of accession.[516] Following the soft liberal position, Mijatović believes change is possible, however it solely depends on *us*: "It seems that it would be better for us if would just roll up our sleeves and try to make something out of Serbia than to depend on somebody else's goodwill."[517] Similarly, the view of Milica Delović, was that adoption and application of laws should be the heart of the story of Serbia's European path.[518] Vesna Pešić suggested, in the same vein, why she truly became a follower of the European idea: "A follower of people who want to live a normal life and who do not want to give up on this idea. And it's not just about Europe as such, but institutional change and change in the way of life that that needs to be organized."[519]

In this new articulation of European orientation, Delević and Pešić offer an affirmative variant of change and progress. True change is possible. They claim that the motivation to change Serbia could be the money that Serbia might receive from EU funds, however, Delević pointed out that "above all our motivation should be the fact that on its road to the EU Serbia will work to improve itself."[520] If an affirmative identity construction is created, a more positive image of Europe is shaped. In this way, I note, the ontological relationship between identity formation and difference is constructed as acquired and not inherent. Following this theoretical matrix, I argue that Serbia's difference from Europe is constructed here as acquired yet still exclusive, as the change "only de-

---

[515] Boško Mijatović, "Nije lako biti za Evropu" (It is not easy to be in favor of Europe), in *Politika*, (September 17, 2008), p. 32. The author is a member of the Center for Liberal-democratic Studies.
[516] Ibid.
[517] Ibid.
[518] Milica Delević, "Evropljanka" (The European) in *Blic*, (November 27, 2010). http://www.blic.rs/Vesti/ Tema-Dana/220062/Milica-Delević-Evropljanka
[519] Vesna Pešić, "Treća Srbija" (The Third Serbia) in *Hourglass Series* (May 12, 2005).
[520] Milica Delević, "Evropljanka" (The European) in *Blic*, (November 27, 2010). http://www.blic.rs/ Vesti/Tema-Dana/220062/Milica-Delević-Evropljanka

pends on us." In this sense, Delević reflected that the country has already changed a lot: "I hope that we will change even more once the negotiations start and will continue to change throughout our journey to the EU. The money we will receive is financial and technical aid."[521] Even when change is presented as achievable and probable, there is an articulation first and foremost of a motivation for societal reform solely as an obligation, and then immediately after this, the emphasis is put on the financial dimension. From the lens of a new positive identity narrative about Serbia, the integration with EU would be, therefore, before everything else ideological and not only historical. Europe is constructed as the means to further empower an internationalist notion of Serbian selfhood. We should call for a reformist role model not only with a view to the desired economic shift but also a reinvention of Serbian identity — into the "We" the Serbs want to become.

Positive identification of the European Other

In the "Other" Serbia discourse, especially that of the hard-liberal intelligentsia, but also in the soft liberal official state discourse which openly commits to EU membership of Serbia, the Serbian Self is not constructed to be an extension of the European Other, neither now nor in the future. Even within the discourse supporting EU membership, which employed certain traits of positive identification, the European Other is not constructed as a similar, close, non-threatening extension of the Self. Even within the soft-liberal stance, there were constant voices about infamous European betrayal. Jeremić, the former democratic government's Foreign Secretary, frequently repeated the foreign policy stance in terms of the "Europe or Kosovo" dilemma: "This place, Kosovo, is our Jerusalem; you just can't treat it any other way than as our Jerusalem; the big mistake of the West was expecting Serbia simply to acquiesce to the loss of the province, cowed in the face of American and Western European recognition for Kosovo."[522]

It is clear that even in the soft liberal discourse the positive message about Serbia belonging to Europe and the link that would inextricably

---

[521] Ibid.
[522] "Kosovo is Serbia's Jerusalem," *New York Times*, (January 17, 2010).

connect "Serbia" with "Europe" is non-existent. The emphasis is not remotely that Serbia shares the same set of values, historical references, cultural heritage or destiny with Europe. Instead, the constant focus was on the loss of Kosovo. In the case of Slovenian discourse of the 1990s and other Eastern European countries during the EU integration, these nations were depicted, as Purcell and Kodras note, to be on the road to their rightful "return to Europe."[523] In the light of that, the discourses of a return to "Europe," or the "West," illustrate that the Self can be constructed through an identity that is articulated as identical to it, but not there yet. However, as Hansen points out, such development discourse simultaneously indicated that those countries are identical with, yet temporarily separated, from Europe.[524]

Absence of development discourse

I suggest that, even within the explicit democratic "Other" Serbia discourse, Serbia did not immediately identify with Europe. Joining the EU was—and still is—the official state priority, but European values were never taken for granted in a manner that made them fully internalized. Serbia's post-Yugoslav identity, as Subotić notes, has developed in profound isolation from Europe because of Serbia's reputation as the architect of the Yugoslav breakup and as the greatest perpetrator of wartime atrocities.[525] She proposes that Serbian elites and the general public greatly resented this perceived "humiliation" by Europe and the harshness with which they felt European institutions had dealt with Serbia.[526] Nonetheless, I suggest that the absence of a development discourse in Serbian state and elite discourses is remarkable. Hansen notes that development discourse constructs a temporal distance between those states who have developed and those who have not; still, this distance is per-

---

[523] See Darren Purcell, and Janet E. Kodras, *Redrawing the Balkan Image of Slovenia* (Tallahassee, FL: Florida State University, 2001).

[524] Lene Hansen, *Security as Practice: Discourse Analysis and the Bosnian War* (London and New York: Routledge, 2006), p. 67.

[525] Jelena Subotić, "Europe is a State of Mind: Identity and Europeanization in the Balkans," *International Studies Quarterly*, 55, (2011), p. 309–330 at 311.

[526] Ibid.

ceived as something that can be bridged by development.[527] However, in the hard-line Other Serbia discourse, the European Other is constructed as the outright superior to the Serbian Self, but the development linkage that would involve concrete policies to be undertaken in order to progress is remarkably absent. As a result, I put forward that the inability of the Other Serbia liberal intelligentsia and their political associates to appropriate a viable and unified model that links "Serbian identity" with "Europe" and European values has been the greatest hindrance to achieving full democratic maturity and political stability. Other Serbia elites embraced the ideology of, what Dawson calls, liberal pessimism instead.[528]

The soft-liberal official state discourse, where Europe was repeatedly represented as one of the Great Powers and an entity that takes something away from Serbia, e.g. Kosovo, for instance by former foreign minister Jeremić, was heavily criticized at the time by the hard-liberal intelligentsia for not offering a greatly needed cultural and historical link to Europe. Lazar Stojanović points out that Serbia has lived in ambivalence between Europe and Russia for 200 years.[529] Stojanović argues that joining Europe means much more than just a signature for membership:

> We want to join a union that considers the occupation of Tibet as one of the biggest crimes, and feels that it needs to be corrected. On the other hand we don't think that way. We think that the occupation of Tibet is OK, that crimes can be perpetrated in Chechnya with impudence, and we also have nothing against the Russian invasion of Georgia. We never said a word about any of these things in spite of the fact that that is against our own policy. I don't know anyone that would let you in their own house, let alone an international organization if all you do is annoy everyone.[530]

It is obvious that the connection and the bond made in most other Central and Eastern European countries before the integration was based on the similarities with the Western Europeans, such as linkages to human

---

[527] Lene Hansen, *Security as Practice: Discourse Analysis and the Bosnian War* (London and New York: Routledge, 2006), p. 153.
[528] James Dawson, *Cultures of Democracy in Serbia and Bulgaria: How Ideas Shape Public*, (London: Ashgate 2014), p. 121.
[529] Stojanović, Lazar, extract from debate *"Is Serbia Giving up on European Integration— Let's Show the Politicians our 'Civic Teeth'"* (October 12, 2011). http://www.e-novine.com/srbija/srbija-tema/51630-Pokazati-politiarima-graanske-zube.html. 2012/03/03.
[530] Ibid.

rights, secularism, common cultural heritage and belonging and the pledge to a democratic set of principles. Contrary to this, in Serbian official state discourse, the legislative and judicial reforms conducted as part of preparations for further negotiations with EU were not legitimized through a narrative of self-development and improvement. The Serbian soft-liberal official state discourse did not legitimize these actions as in other Eastern European states, through the metaphor of steady betterment or progress, which would bring the Serbians closer to the Europeans, but it legitimized it solely as the result of the politics of conditionality conducted by the EU itself. In the same light, prior Minister of Justice Vladan Batić suggested in 2002 that the Serbian government has cooperated with the Hague Tribunal "out of necessity."[531] Former Serbian Deputy PM Božidar Đelić argued in 2011 that those who believe Serbia can be blackmailed into giving up its national interests in exchange for EU integration are wrong.[532] These statements are exemplary of the use of the construction of the Europeans as not having a similar set of explanations as Serbians in relation to the dissolution of Yugoslavia and to Kosovo, but as a supranational political entity, which only wants to take away something from and blackmail Serbia. This book has posed the question of whether, despite the absence of development and self-betterment discourse, Serbia, through adoption of European policies, can adopt and internalize the so-called European values. I put forward that this change is critically dependent on what image of "Europe" is constructed in the Serbian public sphere in the first instance. This section has illustrated that perspectivization of discourses on "Europe" creates a representational paradigm which has been continuously recreated to produce the ideologically determined demarcation between "Us" and "Them."

---

[531] Vladan Batić, *Ljudi i vreme: izjava nedelje,* (People and Time: Week Review) in *Vreme*, No. 587, (April 4, 2002).

[532] Božidar Đelić, *"We Won't be Blackmailed into Giving up National Interests,"* in B92 News, Kosovo Status, 30. (October 2011); http://www.b92.net/eng/news/politics-article.php?yyyy=2011&mm=09&dd=30&nav_id=76636 accessed March 3, 2012.

Conclusion

This chapter has set out to analyze how Europe is constructed in the texts of "First" and "Other" Serbia. Additionally, it opens a space for the following chapter's analysis of how Serbian identity is constantly recreated and reconstructed within First and Other Serbia discourses. Defining what Europe means in Serbian public discourses is fraught with problems, as Europe is, in general, a highly fluctuating idea and not self-evident. Similarly, I put forward that the idea of Europe in First and Other Serbia discourses is largely contested. Delanty also notes that the European idea has been more the product of conflict than of consensus in the great flux of history.[533] I consider "Europe" as a structuring discourse: "Europe" cannot be reduced to an idea, an identity or a reality since it is a structuring force itself.[534] What is real is the discourse in which ideas and identities are formed and constituted. Thus, in Serbia, the idea of Europe has been disengaged from the state tradition during Yugoslav times and was only used as the normative idea during the establishment of the post-Milošević modern state. In the Other Serbia discourse, there is a trace of the idea that Europe is not merely the Other, but can be seen as an element of "Us." However, this development is not the prevailing one. It is would be very difficult, in the Serbian case, to track down the process through which Europe became first a cultural idea, and then a self-conscious political identity, as Smith notes has happened in other Central and Eastern European countries, as well as all Western European states.[535] To illustrate this point, the Balkan region can offer a good example. Barbullushi has demonstrated that all post-communist Albanian discourses on state and nation have articulated Albanian national identity in terms of secularism and Westernism, and the identity of state elites in terms of nationalism yet, simultaneously, commitment to European integration.[536] Regarding the Serbian case, I draw from Kantner's assumption that a strong

---

[533] Gerald Delanty, *Inventing Europe: Idea, Identity, Reality* (Palgrave Macmillan, 1995), p. 2.
[534] Ibid., p. 3.
[535] See Alan Smith, *The Return to Europe: The Reintegration of Eastern Europe into the European Economy* (Basingstoke: Macmillan Press, 2000).
[536] Odeta Barbullushi, "The Politics of 'Euro-Atlantic Orientation': Political Identities Interests and Albanian Foreign Policy 1992–1997," PhD thesis, (University of Birmingham, 2009), p. 129.

European identity is not a functional precondition for legitimate everyday democratic governance in the EU.[537] However, more importantly, Kantner claims that in extraordinary situations, and in order to institutionalize integration in ethically sensitive fields, it is necessary that citizens discursively agree on an ethical self-understanding of their way of life,[538] which claim complies with the Serbian case.

My criticism focuses on the fact that, during the years of transition and the accompanying political shift, the idea of Europe always remained tied to the ethnic and national values, which had a reifying effect on collective identity formation. From my analysis, it also becomes apparent that the idea of Europe failed to became a cohesive collective factor in the Other Serbia discourse. Gilman finds that identities can take on a pathological form when they are constantly constructed against a category of Otherness.[539] In that case, instead of identity being defined by a sense of belongingness and solidarity arising out of shared life-worlds, as Delanty notes, it becomes focused on opposition to an Other: "We" is defined not by reference to a framework of shared experiences, common goals and a collective horizon, but by the negation of the Other.[540] In the Other Serbian case, "We" is merely defined by the negation of nationalism. Delanty notes that this issue boils down to the question of diversity or division: self-identity can be formed by the recognition of otherness or by the negation of otherness, by solidarity or exclusion.[541] I find that identification in the Other Serbia discourse takes place through the imposition of Othernesss in the formation of a binary typology of "Us" and "Them.

---

[537] Cathleen Kantner, "Collective Identity as Shared Ethical Self-Understanding: The Case of the Emerging European Identity," *European Journal of Social Theory*, 9, no. 4, (2006), p. 501–524 at 501.

[538] Ibid., p. 501.

[539] Sander L. Gilman, *Difference and Pathology: Stereotypes of Sexuality, Race, and Madness* (Ithaca, NY and London: Cornell University Press, 1985), p. 44.

[540] Gerald Delanty, *Inventing Europe: Idea, Identity, Reality* (Palgrave Macmillan, 1995), p. 5.

[541] Gerard Delanty, *Rethinking Europe: Social Theory and the Implications of Europeanization* (London: Routledge, 2005), p. 34.

Chapter 5:
Mapping the Debates: "Point of Departure" and "Missionary Intelligentsia"

The primary aim of this chapter is to focus on the two public debates which are commonly known as "Point of Departure" [542] and "Missionary Intelligentsia." The secondary aim is to analyze how Other Serbia actors are referred to linguistically, and to identify the traits, characteristics, qualities and features that are attributed to Other-Serbians, in "First" Serbia texts. Therefore, the intention of this chapter is to consider how much merit there is to the claim that the "Othering" of Other-Serbians and Europe is a deliberate strategy in the discursive construction of collective Serbian identity in First Serbia discourses, and consider the reasons for it. Closer scrutiny is directed to the ways in which First Serbia constructs Other Serbia and, in turn, Other Serbia interprets First Serbia. This structural analysis is particularly useful as it allows us to identify the basic discourse of First Serbia upon which the discourse of Other Serbia and the discourse on Europe and identity is built.

The post-2000 political elites in Serbia frequently refer, implicitly or explicitly, to the rearticulation of the concept of the nation, and this is done quite deliberately in order to legitimize their political and foreign policy decisions. At the same time, these debates are increasingly marked by a concern for rejuvenating a properly political sphere of action as such, after the period of authoritarianism under Milošević. I raise issues of identity politics, arguing that the Self or group forms an identi

---

[542] "Tačka Razlaza" (Point of Departure) was a debate which took place in *Vreme* magazine from August 1 to November 21, 2002 between "Other" Serbia actors. Dragović-Soso suggests that this debate exposed the existence of two alternative narratives of the Serb experience of the wars of the 1990s. See Jasna Dragović-Soso, "The Parting of Ways: Public Reckoning with the Recent Past in Post-Milošević Serbia," in Timothy Waters (ed.), *The Milošević Trial—An Autopsy,* (Oxford: Oxford University Press, 2014), p. 1.

ty that is in fact defined by its radical opposition to an Other. I explore, in empirical terms, the ways in which the Serbian subject forms an identity that is defined by its exclusion of Europe. The construction of Serbian identity is accomplished primarily through discursive formation of in-groups and out-groups, for example the demarcation of the Self and Other, the European and non-European, and the Serbian and anti-Serbian.

From a methodological perspective, I follow Hansen's understanding of identity as a product of processes of linking and differentiation and I identify the terms which indicate a clear construction of the Other, such as *evil, traitor, spy* and *infidel,* or of the Self, such as *good, moral, civilized* and *exclusive*. Identity construction, therefore, is not accomplished solely through the designation of one particular sign for the Other, such as Other Serbia or "Europe," but rather through the location of these signs within a larger *web of meaning* situated in the First Serbia discourse.[543] Fowler explains: "Ideology is already imprinted in the available discourse. A discourse provides a set of possible statements about a given area, and organizes and gives structure to the manner in which a particular topic, object, process is to be talked about, in that it provides descriptions, rules, permissions and prohibitions of social and individual actions.[544] In other words, discourse represents a complex of meanings that supports and reinforces ideology. In addition, the analysis touches upon the construction of Russia as the alternative to "Europe," and considers the main points which are put forward in that construction of difference from the European Other. This chapter follows directly from the discussion in Chapter 4 of the ways in which Europe is conceptualized in the First and Other Serbia discourses, and addresses the extent to which this contested image is significant in the way processes of Europeanization are perceived.

---

[543] Lene Hansen, *Security as Practice: Discourse Analysis and the Bosnian War* (London and New York: Routledge, 2006), p. 44.

[544] Roger Fowler, *Language in the News: Discourse and Ideology in the Press* (London: Routledge, 1991), p. 42.

Mapping debates

Methodologically, the next section builds upon the previous in turning to a discussion of how discourses can be seen to be organized within a field of debate. On the one hand, one could argue that every single text articulates a unique construction of identity and policy, and thereby constitutes a separate discourse.[545] But, on the other hand, I suggest that the Point of Departure and Missionary Intelligentsia political debates are united by their concern for a set of shared issues and one might therefore define a smaller number of basic themes that structure these debates. When analyzing how these debates unfold, it is useful to examine how facts are brought together to constitute events.[546] Mapping debates around key events offers a methodological technique for tracing the stability of the official discourse.[547] Following Hansen, I argue that while facts are dependent upon actors and discourses for their production, they do not carry with them automatic political responses; they need to be located inside a discourse, and must be read, if they are to have a particular effect on policy and/or the representation of identity.[548]

In the Missionary Intelligentsia debate emphasis was placed on an article of that name written by Slobodan Antonić and published in *Vreme* magazine in February 2003. This article prompted a three-month long public discussion in which actors sought to sustain the Eastern or Western leanings of Serbia. To this end, I argue that the Milošević regime's official state discourse on the imperial "West" metamorphosed after 2000 into the First Serbia discourse on Europe, having been overridden with themes of the relativization of war crimes. During the Missionary Intelligentsia debate, the basic identity narratives proclaimed by the Milošević elite were rearticulated and set in a new context. These narra-

---

[545] Lene Hansen, *Security as Practice. Discourse Analysis and the Bosnian War* (London and New York: Routledge, 2006), p. 82.
[546] The term *key events* refers to those situations where important facts manifest themselves on the political or media agenda and influence the official policy-identity constellation or force the official discourse to engage with the political opposition and media criticism. Ibid.
[547] Lene Hansen, *Security as Practice: Discourse Analysis and the Bosnian War* (London and New York: Routledge, 2006), p. 82.
[548] Ibid.

tives continued the "ideological and interpretative repertories"[549] which had dominated the public sphere in the 1990s yet, at the same time, Antonić and other public actors tried to differentiate themselves from the prevailing antediluvian nationalism. I believe that an exploration of continuities with, and differentiations from, the Milošević era elite discourses is crucial when investigating the political contestation of "Europe" and the Self–Other nexus in the post-Milošević public space. Therefore, this chapter traces the manner in which political and cultural identities arose from the Missionary Intelligentsia debate. The next section introduces the political and social context that existed prior to the 2003 Missionary Intelligentsia debate.

The background to the debate: "Coming to the terms with the past"

In the aftermath of October 5, 2000, the understandings which people held of their recent history, first the communist era and then the dissolution of Yugoslavia, were crucially important in shaping their responses toward processes of European integration. According to Dragović-Soso, the official state discourse during the Milošević regime was that Serbia was not at war with its neighbors, and that the conflicts in Croatia and Bosnia was a civil war pitting hostile secessionist states against the victimized Serb population that wished to remain in Yugoslavia.[550] In terms of reckoning with the past, the official state discourse of the Milošević period metamorphosed after 2000 into the "First" Serbia discourse, which was still overridden with themes of denial of crimes. Obradović-Wochnik notes that denial was evident in the public sphere, and was reflected in mainstream political discourse, while political parties such as the SRS incorporated denial of war crimes as a purportedly-acceptable and normative way of dealing with the legacy of Serbia's

---

[549] See Margaret Wetherell, "Positioning and Interpretative Repertoires: Conversation Analysis and Post-structuralism in Dialogue," in *Discourse and Society*, 9, no. 3, (1998), p. 387–412 at 388.

[550] Jasna Dragović-Soso, "Apologising for Srebrenica: The Declaration of the Serbian Parliament, the European Union and the Politics of Compromise," in *East European Politics* 28, no. 2, (2012), p. 163–179.

involvement in the wars.⁵⁵¹ Even within Belgrade's anti-war and anti-Milošević liberal intelligentsia circles, doubts about the wisdom of Milošević's "extradition" to stand trial at the ICTY, and about the proper way to confront the past, started to create divisions. Dragović-Soso finds that the Point of Departure debate further exposed two distinct approaches to the question of responsibility for the crimes committed in those wars and two deeply opposed visions of the role played by the West in Serbia's democratic transition.⁵⁵² In terms of external pressure from the US and various European states for Serbia to cooperate with ICTY, the debate exposed a narrative which mimicked the political conflict between PM Djindjić and President Koštunica,⁵⁵³ in which the former endorsed rapprochement with the West, while the latter advocated a more neutral position toward the ICTY. These circumstances, discussed in detail in Chapter 4, set the context for the 2002 Point of Departure and 2003 Missionary Intelligentsia debates.

Point of Departure: Serbian guilt

The debate started with the text *De-helsinkisation Mrs Biserko*, written by the chief editor of *Vreme*, Dragoljub Žarković. The crux of the discussion was the question of whether it was true that the Serbian elite used independent media such as *Vreme* and B92 in order to relativize and de-

---

[551] Jelena Obradović-Wochnik, "Strategies of denial: resistance to ICTY cooperation in Serbia," in Judy Batt and Jelena Obradović-Wochnik (eds.), *War Crimes, Conditionality and EU Integration in the Western Balkans*, (Challiots Papers, Institute for Security Studies, Paris, 2009), p. 34.

[552] See Jasna Dragović-Soso, "The Parting of Ways: Public Reckoning with the Recent Past in Post-Milošević Serbia," in Timothy Waters (ed.), *The Milošević Trial — An Autopsy*, (Oxford: Oxford University Press, 2013), p. 1.

[553] Djindjić advocated the position that Serbia had to accept such demands in order to receive the foreign aid which was conditional thereon and thereby have a better hope of achieving economic recovery, as well as a rapprochement with the West. Koštunica argued that cooperation with the ICTY should not be a priority and should be undertaken only within a framework of legal change. Koštunica felt a sense among the population, however, that Serbia simply had no choice but to give in to what was perceived as Western blackmail. Dragović suggested that this perception was reinforced by Đinđić himself, who justified Milošević's handover as a purely financial transaction, without engaging in any discussion of the moral imperatives of trying Milošević for crimes committed in Kosovo, Croatia and Bosnia. See Ibid. p. 4/5.

ethnify war crimes.[554] Very quickly and very clearly two options emerged. One, supported by the governmental elite (in the form of the weekly journal *Vreme* and its supporters), presented the argument that their reporting on crimes was objective and that the crimes needed to be de-ethnified as their ethnification pointed to the "collective guilt of a whole nation."[555] Žarković noted that "Biserko called for the de-Nazification of Serbia during the NATO bombing," and argued that "Biserko was actually endorsing the extreme nationalists' slogan, that the Serbian nation as a whole was on trial along with Milošević in The Hague."[556] The dominant themes used by the group defending *Vreme* were about who the victims and perpetrators were, as summed up by Stojan Cerović:[557]

> When it comes to genocide it is the ethnicity of the victim that is relevant, not that of the perpetrator (they can have the same nationality as the victim), whereas claiming the opposite represents a stubborn selective presentation of facts and refusal to discuss anything else other than Serbian guilt. It does not matter what happened before or after, or what the others have done. According to that theory, it was only the Serbs that did things, whereas the others are irrelevant, and that includes the great powers. All this is of course just the reverse of the story about the 'heavenly people.'[558] As far as I am concerned, I absolutely do not care about any stories where the Serbs are presented as the best or the worst people. I leave it to the patriots and anti-patriots to resolve this [but] there is a sort of investigative hysteria in Serbia, almost as if the country is brimming with war criminals. Serbia is still walled-in as a sort of quarantine, so irritation is caused exclusively by voices that talk about guilt, the moral fall and pact with nationalists.[559]

---

[554] See Olivera Milosavljević, *Tačka (The Moment of Parting Ways): povodom polemike vodjenje na stranicama Vreme*, in Helsinške Sveske, No. 16. (Izdavac: Helsinški odbor za ljudska prava u Srbiji, 2003), p. 5.

[555] Jasna Dragović-Soso, "The Parting of Ways: Public Reckoning with the Recent Past in Post-Milošević Serbia," in Timothy Waters (ed.), *The Milošević Trial—An Autopsy*, (Oxford: Oxford University Press, forthcoming, 2013), p. 8.

[556] Ibid.

[557] Stojan Cerović was a well-known Serbian journalist. He made a name for himself as an uncompromising political critic for the independent weekly magazine *Vreme*.

[558] The idea of the Serbs as a "heavenly people" is in fact the idea of the Serbs as eternal victims, of a Heavenly Serbia, of a fear of vanishing. As Anzulović argues, this idea is fresh in the minds of the Serbs. It would later be the cause of much death and destruction in the Balkan Wars of the 1990s when Yugoslavia fell apart into chaos. See Branislav Anzulović, *Heavenly Serbia: From Myth to Genocide* (London: Hurst, 1999), p. 12.

[559] Stojan Cerović, 'Tvrdoglava selektivnost' (Stubborn Selectivity) in *Vreme*, no. 610, (September 12, 2002) p. 33.

Cerović points out that Serbs react negatively to such discriminatory statements because they also suffered and, consequently, the voices calling for atonement will fall on deaf ears.[560] Cerović also addressed questions which were very important to him, such as the issue of "purification and collective exorcism":

> No acts of ritual purification trying to wash off sins, and no collective exorcism will make you immune to history, wars, crimes and suffering. That is the key (and clearly mystical) religious thought of these people ['Other' Serbian hard liberals] who are generally left-wing and have almost no interest in the church. The fact that they consider themselves experts in issues of morality does not mean that this group of lay spiritual healers that shout: 'Repent' as they threaten everybody with Last Judgment is all that Serbia needs on its road to Europe.[561]

There are different forms of guilt and responsibility, political guilt, moral guilt and according to Jaspers even metaphysical guilt;[562] undeniably guilt and responsibility cut deeply into the nation's Self. Since Cerović draws a distinction between "them" who ask for "collective exorcism" and "us" who do not, it is clear that such differentiation in respect of responses to issues of collective responsibility and Serbian guilt created fissures within the Other Serbia echelons. Cerović, who was always normatively and practically against Milošević and his politics, here articulates a disparity of attitude with his Other Serbia fellows. However, ordinary citizens of Serbia universally opposed the 1999 NATO intervention actions largely based on the false perception that, if they do not oppose it, they would admit the responsibility for the wars. As a result, the Point of Departure debate has contributed to the ongoing construc-

---

[560] Ibid. In the same text, Cerović reflects on Milošević and his legacy: "I used to think that Milošević was our great problem, and that at the time we did not have to ask ourselves who is helping us or why in order to get rid of him. It now turns out that nothing was resolved, that Serbia itself is the problem (and that includes each one of us), and that now the real work has to start. Well my friends, I do not intend to wage a war against my own ID card. It is what it is."

[561] Ibid.

[562] Karl Jaspers, *The Question of German Guilt* (Fordham University Press, New York, 2000).

tion of in-groups and out-groups, as Ramet puts it, in terms of soft liberals and hard-liners or hard liberals.[563]

Hard-line liberals: Responsibility for war crimes

An opposing opinion was presented by the hard-line Other Serbia, which maintained that *Vreme* was in fact relativizing crimes—as it is impossible to "de-ethnify" ethnic cleansing. It also argued that it was not the "collective guilt of a whole nation" which was implied, but the moral responsibility of society. Srdja Popović, the human rights lawyer, suggested that:

> The image of this country in the world, and its international identity, were shaped in the years of Milošević's wars almost exclusively through the images of Sarajevo, Vukovar, Dubrovnik, Srebrenica. Until then the world knew little about us. When Milošević fell we had the opportunity to change this image, to show the world that Milošević was falsely hiding behind the 'nation' and that we do not accept the crimes he committed as ours and justified in the name of the 'Serb nation' and that we have no reason to deny them. It is our national interest to make that clear.[564]

In terms of framing the possible meaning of Serbian identity in relation to the processes of victimization, the hard liberals suggested that "crime is a heavy burden for Serbia, and the point of view on 'de-ethnification' of crime reduces Serbian identity to an ideology of an organic nation."[565] In the end, the discussion revolved around questions such as: why the war in Yugoslavia happened; who the victims and the perpetrators were; and who has the moral right to take part in this type of discussion on collective guilt and responsibility for violence.[566] In this respect, Milosavljević and the Other Serbia hard liberals argued that "accepting the correction of memory would mean becoming an accomplice to crimes that have already been committed; the 'incidents' that the other side

---

[563] Ola Listhaing, Kristen Ringdal and Albert Simkus, "Serbian Civic Values in a European Context," in Sabrina Ramet (eds.), *Civic and Uncivic Values: Serbia in the Post-Milošević Era* (Budapest: Central University Press, 2011), p. 4.

[564] Srdja Popović, "A šta su drugi radili?" (And what did the other do?) in *Vreme*, no. 609. (September 19, 2002).

[565] Latinka Perović, "Žive Mete" (Live Targets) in *Vreme*, no. 606. (August 15, 2002).

[566] Olivera Milosavljević, "Tačka razlaza: povodom polemike vodjenje na stranicama Vreme," Helsinške Sveske, No. 16. (Izdavac: Helsinški odbor za ljudska prava u Srbiji, 2003), p. 7.

[First Serbia and the soft liberal faction of Other Serbia] refers to are crimes against innocent people; they show indifference toward the victims and understanding for crimes; what we have is basically general amnesty in action."[567] The Point of Departure debate is particularly useful for this research, as it is interested in clearly identifying the hard-line discourse of Other Serbia upon which the discourse of the soft liberal faction of Other Serbia is generated and built.

Departure on issue of gender

Gordy suggests that the principal targets of attacks were NGOs and advocates of human rights in general, but that three women in particular, namely Biserko, Kandić and Vučo, were targeted. They were, and remain, considered by many to be anti-Serbian traitors and representatives of a domestic fifth column which stands for foreign interests. [568] Unsurprisingly, given that most of the prominent NGO activists were women, the issue of gender has played a meaningful role in the discourse of the attackers. As a result, the discussion has touched upon the gender issue in the anti-war and anti-Milošević movement. In terms of gender, Cerović, the defender of *Vreme*, argues that:

> Ultimately, is someone who does not completely share these [NGO activists] points of view a misogynist and aggressively patriarchal? That is what Nataša Kandić would claim, as she considers any response to accusations made by Sonja Biserko a brutal attack against all women. And I was almost prepared to swear that the 'women's question' was about equality and not about recognizing that they are right by default.[569]

The opposition to *Vreme* had a different perspective on the subject of gender in the debate. Lazar Stojanović defended Other Serbia's hard-line arguments stating that "these hated women" are requesting a public discussion and want to establish the level of responsibility of the perpetrators as well as the instigators of crimes that turned Serbia into a "shel-

---

[567] Ibid.
[568] Eric Gordy, *Guilt, Responsibility and Denial: The Past at Stake in Post-Milošević Serbia* (University of Pennsylvania Press, 2013).
[569] Stojan Cerović, "Tuzilačka revnost" (Prosecutor's Zeal) in *Vreme*, no. 608. (August 29, 2002).

ter for murderers and a grave for their victims."[570] Stojanović contended that "their patient and persistent engagement on re-establishment of the values of democratic society in Serbia and Montenegro has caused anger and consternation among the authors of various sinister articles as well as shouts calling for 'the witches to be burned.' "[571] I draw from Dragović-Soso's article[572] the claim that the main factors that split the liberal intelligentsia (i.e. "Other" Serbia) into hard liberals and their opposition soft liberals[573] were the questions of reckoning with the past, the subject of gender in the anti-war movement, the image of the "nation" and the 1999 NATO intervention.[574]

The Orthodox Church: Changing the cultural model

The *Vreme* initiative was backed by influential quarters of Serbian society, including the Serbian Orthodox Church. In the course of the Point of Departure debate, the SOC published its own views on the matter in question: "The Serbian Orthodox Church yesterday rejected the accusations from a group of intellectuals who ... declare a conspiracy by the Church, the Academy of Sciences and Arts, the army and some politicians against their own people; they accuse their own people of extreme nationalism and Nazism."[575]

---

[570] Lazar Stojanović, "Otrovna značenja" (Poisonous Meanings) in *Vreme*, no. 609. (September 5, 2002).
[571] Ibid.
[572] Dragović-Soso, Jasna, "The Parting of Ways: Public Reckoning with the Recent Past in Post-Milošević Serbia," in Timothy Waters (ed.), *The Milošević Trial — An Autopsy*, (Oxford: Oxford University Press, forthcoming, 2013).
[573] Sabrina Ramet (eds.), *Civic and Uncivic Values: Serbia in the Post-Milošević Era* (Budapest: Central University Press, 2011), p. 5.
[574] The rift can be traced to the 1999 April petition against NATO intervention signed by twenty-seven prominent members of the liberal intelligentsia, such as Stojan Cerović, Vojin Dimitrijević, Sonja Liht, Veran Matić, Borka Pavičević, Ivan Vejvoda, etc. Those who decided to refuse to sign it, such as Nataša Kandić, Filip David, Ivan Čolović, clearly did so because, in their view, Milošević alone was responsible for the bombing campaign. See Nataša Kandić, "Neprijatelj u Srbiji—otvorenost, snaga i integritet nekoliko žena," (Enemy in Serbia—Sincerity, Strength and the Integrity of a Few Women) in *Vreme*, (August 22, 2002).
[575] "The Orthodox Church: Changing the Cultural Model," in Tačka razlaza (The Moment of Parting Ways) in *Helsinške Sveske*, No. 16, (Izdavac: Helsinški odbor za ljudska prava u Srbiji, 2002), p. 123.

The SOC also stated, while all these intellectuals seek changes in the cultural model, they do not offer St. Sava, Mihailo Pupin, Stevan Mokranjac, Hajduk Veljko, Stefan Milenković or Dejan Bodiroga[576] as role-models.[577] Instead, "they offer themselves and those that they consider as the intellectual elite in Serbia."[578] The SOC added that "apart from changes to the economic and legal systems, Serbia needed changes to the cultural model that would stem from the orthodox Christian faith and all-encompassing popular knowledge. Only then will our state be ready to join the European union of nations as an equal and enrich Europe with Serbia's authentic values."[579] With regard to the political role of the Church, I draw a significant distinction between mere populism put forward by the Church and, in contrast, occasions when the Church exerts a degree of political control, or at least influence, over issues of identity politics.

Re-conceptualized "discourse of non-interference"

The sections above have addressed the manner in which the most significant themes of disagreement were framed by "Other" Serbia factions, and their discourse on the past, identity and Europe. The 2002 Point of Departure debate aroused themes including Serbian guilt, responsibility, victims and perpetrators, ethnonationalism, and gender in the anti-war movement. To this end, I have considered the discursive strategies deployed by *Vreme* journalists, especially Cerović, and by their opposition, the hardline liberals of Other Serbia and other actors, the aim of each group being to articulate a new political identity. This investigation is informed by the assumption that the political elites' construction of identity, "Europe" and the national interest depends upon their need to reformulate their own political identity in the aftermath of the change

---

[576] Pupin was a world-renowned scientist working at Columbia University in New York. Stevan Mokranjac was influential music composer, and Stefan Milenković was a child prodigy who at the moment works at the Juilliard School. Hajduk Veljko was a hero from First Serbian Uprising in 1804. Dejan Bodiroga is a famous basketball player who played for Panathinaikos and Barcelona, among other clubs.
[577] Ibid.
[578] Ibid.
[579] Ibid.

from an authoritarian to a democratic regime, and in light of their newly recalibrated political interests.

I suggest that when the defenders of *Vreme* proclaimed abandonment of the principles and ideology of their Other Serbia associates, their political identity was reconstructed during the period between 2000 and 2003, through rearticulation of some old elements of the anti-European discourse. I argue that this rearticulation was a consequence of the rearticulation of the "discourse of non-interference," especially "non-interference by foreign factors" in Serbian domestic affairs. A result of this was the recreation of groups of so-called sovereignists in both the "First" and "Other" Serbia groupings. This development is important, especially in light of the fact that more than seven years after Kosovo's declaration of independence that territory's sovereignty continues to remain hotly contested between Serbs and Albanians, which keeps the issue at the center of the political debate. Rossi suggested that this development has not only forced pro-Western parties in Serbia to retain narratives of national defense, but it has significantly aided illiberal democratic parties which have openly called for the cessation of further cooperation with the West until Serbia's territorial integrity is guaranteed.[580] The illiberal strata have re-conceptualized the "anti-imperialist" discourse from the Milošević era, however with the difference that it is now aimed not at the West in general but at Brussels in particular.

The Missionary Intelligentsia Article

The following section is divided into two parts: the first part closely analyzes the Missionary Intelligentsia article, and the related public responses which discussed the "nation," "First" and "Other" Serbs and "Europe." The section examines First Serbia's attempts to construct Other Serbia as the "enemy within," especially in connection with the construction of Europe as a foreign factor. In this way First Serbia attempts to create a new political identity for itself through the rearticulation of certain elements of the old Milošević discourse on the "nation," "Serbian

---

[580] Michael A. Rossi, "Resurrecting the Past: Democracy, National Identity and Historical Memory in Modern Serbia, PhD thesis Graduate School—New Brunswick Rutgers, (2009).

identity" and the "West." The second part of the section investigates the continuities and shifts in Other Serbia articulations of the nation and Europe against the backdrop of their political repertoire, which was largely formulated in the Point of Departure debate. My aim is to answer the following research questions: what are the traits, characteristic, qualities, and features which are attributed to Other-Serbians or to Serbia in First Serbia texts; and from what perspective or point of view are these referential/nomination strategies, positive or negative predications of the Self and the Other, and arguments for or against Europe expressed?

Other Serbia as the "enemy within"

The Missionary Intelligentsia article by Slobodan Antonić was published in *Vreme* in February 2003. The author expressed in the article his intention to start a discussion about the Serbian elites. A cutting exchange followed immediately highlighting the main lines of the debate which lasted for the next three months: first, the question of whether there is such thing as "missionaries" in Serbia; and second, what is the acceptable degree of patriotism? I suggest that this set of issues builds upon the themes discussed previously in the Point of Departure debate. The underlying themes evoked are various, but still the political spectrum of meaning gathers around the missionary intelligentsia, a group of people that consider themselves as "missionaries of the Atlanticist community and its values in Serbia."[581] In the article, Antonić contended that this community face "resistance from their surroundings" and rejection at the hands of "the people",[582] that is, of the "wider community."[583] In general, in the author's words, the missionary intelligentsia "despise

---

[581] Slobodan Antonić, "Misionarska inteligencija u današnjoj Srbiji" (Missionary intelligentsia in today's Serbia) in *Vreme*, no. 631, (February 5, 2003).
[582] "The people," (Serbian "narod") remains a significant word in the Milošević discourse, as it implies and comprises all the people of the Serbian nation.
[583] Slobodan Antonić, "Misionarska inteligencija u današnjoj Srbiji" (Missionary intelligentsia in today's Serbia) in *Vreme*, no. 631, (February 5, 2003).

society as a whole; and make attacks against their own people."[584] Antonić clearly sets out his view of the position promoted by the ideology of this "missionary intelligentsia":

> Of course there is no longer a single party that dictates policies as was the case before (in communism). What we have instead, pursuing the same aim and functions, are certain NGOs dealing with human rights or certain institutes for democracy based in Washington DC or Brussels. Using their annual funding programs for certain local media, NGOs and trade unions they set the priorities for various campaigns that are imposed on the Serbian public: facing Serbian crimes in Croatia, Bosnia and Kosovo; reconstruction of Serbia as a multi-ethnic and multi-cultural state; combating terrorism (only the one aimed against the US, that goes without saying); the rights of Roma, the gay community and children with special needs; humane treatment of animals, etc.[585]

In the first dimension of analysis, this discourse is examined with regard to its manifest content, the focus being on "what is apparently said or written."[586] It is clear that Antonić understands this particular liberal ideology as something Serbs should fight against. On the other hand, he argues that nationalism in Serbia had already lost its original strength by 1995 and for the next two years, he writes, Other-Serbians "continued to repeat their mantras of how the Serbian people and its elites are irreversibly corrupted by nationalism."[587] Antonić develops argumentative schemes which clearly delineate between the "outside" and the "inside" perspective by suggesting that Other Serbia understand Serbian society to be "democratically insufficient," and that certain intellectuals want to have "foreign rule" established.[588] Later in the same article, Antonić supports the illiberal front by arguing that "they" (Other-Serbians) are in combat against "us" in that their priorities continued to consist of the fight against greater-Serbian nationalism, conservatives, traditionalism (the Church and the Academy of Sciences and Arts), monarchism, the

---

[584] Ibid. This term has a pejorative meaning, and implies servitude to the "foreign forces." Not long after the article was published the term forced its way into widespread public use.

[585] Ibid.

[586] Rainer Hülsse, "Imagine the EU: The Metaphorical Construction of a Supranationalist Identity," in *Journal of International Relations and Development* 9, (2006) p. 396.

[587] Slobodan Antonić, "Misionarska inteligencija u današnjoj Srbiji" (Missionary intelligentsia in today's Serbia) in Vreme, no. 631, (February 5, 2003).

[588] Ibid.

Ravna Gora movement, bourgeois morality, aimless legalism, etc.[589] In addition to this, Antonić finds that "if liberalism is so much as mentioned *they* always follow this with a comment about how "true" liberalism in Serbia is only possible in the shape of anti-nationalism."[590]

Anti-liberal stance

Antonić advocates the establishment of a form of civilizational pluralism in which actors in Serbia would enjoy the freedom of expression to express liberal as well as illiberal positions. In this extract Antonić identifies the "ideological matrix of domestic missionary work":

> The people of Serbia are essentially primitive, anti-modern and anti-European. They offer the cure for Serbian nationalism in decisive measures of repression: banning books, banning public speaking, prison sentences, and generally repression of 'anti-civilizational pluralism'. All of these requests can be characterized as deeply anti-liberal and anti-democratic. A good example is Mihailo Ramač's call for Radovan Karadžić's book (the comedy 'Sitovacija') to be banned. It is based on an assumption that literary work should be banned based on who wrote it and not because of its content.[591]

Antonić suggests that calls for members of *Obraz*[592] to be put on trial are based on the misguided premise that the bare propagation of nationalist ideas ought to be criminalized, and therefore an organization ought to be banned just because it supports nationalist views.[593] Antonić asserts that, without evidence that members of Obraz committed a criminal offence, there can be no justification for punishing membership or banning this organization.[594] Antonić suggests that "otherwise we would once again find ourselves in a situation where a "verbal offence" is a crime and people are punished because of their views and opinions."[595]

---

[589] Ibid.
[590] Ibid.
[591] Ibid.
[592] The far-right organization Obraz is notorious for inciting violence against gays, and in particular for their 2001 attack on the first ever Belgrade Gay Pride parade which left several LGBT marchers and police officers injured. Obraz was banned by the Serbian Constitutional Court in June 2012.
[593] Slobodan Antonić, "Misionarska inteligencija u današnjoj Srbiji" (Missionary intelligentsia in today's Serbia) in *Vreme*, no. 631, (February 5, 2003).
[594] Ibid.
[595] The author draws a parallel with the socialist times, in which criticism of the Yugoslav communist party or Josip Broz Tito was often punished with imprisonment. Ibid.

In the name of civilizational pluralism, the author advances the argument that the right to engage in hate speech, or to express hostile or even fascist ideas which are in direct contrast with the human rights agenda of the establishment, is an integral part of any democratic system. What is certain is that most authors define ethno-nationalist structures as part of "uncivil society" mainly on the basis of distinctions between the ideals of the organizations involved. To this end, Kopecký and Mudde find that "uncivil" society is then defined by the myriad organizations with non-democratic or (right-wing) extremist ideas.[596] I contend that, by stressing that the extreme-nationalist voice need not be silenced, regulated or controlled, Antonić's critique becomes part of the anti-liberal discourse.

Other-Serbians, according to Antonić, claim that "nationalism is so entrenched in every nook and cranny of Serbian society that absolutely everyone is contaminated by it—except themselves of course."[597] Antonić goes on to posit that, even by firmly rejecting the ideology of Serbian nationalism, one does not automatically receive non-nationalist legitimacy.[598] Furthermore, writes Antonić, if one rejects some of the minor arguments put forward by the "missionaries," if one mentions elementary patriotism, one immediately qualifies as a "moderate nationalist."[599] This represents Antonić's attempt to carve a third road for himself and his fellows by highlighting the existence of "good" and "bad" nationalism in Serbian society.[600] Indeed, the question of how to treat discourses that appear to be illiberal, intolerant and anti-democratic is a vexed one indeed and represents a persistent bone of contention within the civil society literature.

---

[596] Petr Kopecký and Cas Mudde Cas (eds.), *Uncivil Society? Contentious Politics in Postcommunist Europe* (Routledge, 2003), p. 11.
[597] Slobodan Antonić, "Misionarska inteligencija u današnjoj Srbiji" (Missionary intelligentsia in today's Serbia) in Vreme, no. 631, (February 5, 2003).
[598] Ibid.
[599] Ibid.
[600] By making this distinction, Antonić makes an effort to carve a third way between strong nationalism and hard-line anti-nationalism, a road that will be called "Third Serbia."

"First" Serbia significant others

As is obvious from Antonić's line of argumentation, the core strategy in the "First" Serbia discourse on identity is the construction of in-groups and out-groups. Through these constructions, Antonić is involved in an ongoing process of identity formation. He positions the First Serbia discourse, and the perspective from which it views the political landscape, by employing various discursive strategies. In what follows, I will provide an analysis of the referential and nomination strategies which lie at the core of the discursive construction of "identity" in the public debate, before proceeding further into an analysis of how certain values are attributed to the in-groups and out-groups. Referential and nomination strategies serve to construct and represent social actors.[601] More specifically, I focus below on how the First Serbia actors construct the in-groups and out-groups and predicate certain values to the Serbian Self, and subsequently the European Other. Antonić proposed that "the first group [Other Serbians] wants to turn Serbian citizens into Europeans, whereas the other group [First Serbians] wants to let them live according to their valid customs that are no less European than any others; the first group talks about probity, rationality and wellbeing, the other talks about morality, feelings and postulates."[602]

It is significant to note that in Antonić's Missionary Intelligentsia article, Other-Serbians are constructed as not part of the Serbian Self, but part of the European Other. They are constructed as "home-grown missionaries," who have been "rejected by the wider community," and who consider that society is "far too broken for a meaningful democratic transformation."[603] They are "domestic tyrants" who wish to serve, please, flatter, and pretend, while there is also this other wish for "freedom, dignity and authenticity."[604] Thus, the missionary intelligentsia is a

---

[601] Ruth Wodak, *The Discourse of Politics in Action: Politics as Usual* (Basingstoke: Palgrave, 2009).

[602] Slobodan Antonić, "Odgovor Popovu I Dereti" (Answer to Popov and Dereta) in *Vreme*, no. 632. (February 5, 2003).

[603] All these constructs can be found in Slobodan Antonić, "Misionarska inteligencija u današnjoj Srbiji" (Missionary intelligentsia in today's Serbia) in Vreme, no. 631, (February 5, 2003).

[604] Ibid.

group of people who consider themselves to be missionaries of the Atlanticist community and its values in Serbia. First Serbia understands Other-Serbians to hold the view that "[the] primitive people of Serbia are essentially anti-modern and anti-European and as such are collectively diseased by nationalism."[605] As presented above, various strategies of differentiation are used more or less implicitly to construct the difference between Other and First Serbia, between "Us" and "Them." The argumentation strategies employed in this article emphasize the difference between the values of "servitude" and values of "freedom" and at the same time seek to obscure any similarities between the two ideological matrices. In this common strategy of perspectivation, Other Serbia is constructed as not only threatening the "real, authentic, genuine Serbian identity" in overall terms, but also as a danger to "their own people" as they might send an "open invitation to 'civilized foreigners' to come and occupy the country."[606] In this negative identification, the First Serbia discourse continually compares the Other-Serbians with the European aggressor and finds them to be identified with everything that is different, strange, aggressive and threatening, and most of all, with Europe.

Following Delanty, I submit that identities are always relational; however, what matters is not the representation of the Other as such, but the nature of the difference which is constructed.[607] Thus, I find that the difference attributed to Other-Serbians in Antonić's texts is almost natural and essential, and deeply rooted in history, religion, culture and civilization. In this sense, the Serbian Self not only remains outside the European Self, incapable by its very nature of assimilating itself, but also willingly decides to remain outside of, and "free" from, that European hypocrisy that Other-Serbians not only embrace but are an active part of. Such in-group bias is a very common example of "ideologically-based strategies" of positive Self and negative Other presentation.[608] However, the essence of the difference constructed by Antonić in the Missionary

---

[605] Ibid.
[606] Ibid.
[607] Gerald Delanty, *Inventing Europe: Idea, Identity, Reality* (Palgrave Macmillan), p. 5.
[608] Ruth Wodak and Teun A. van Dijk, (eds.) *Racism at the Top: Parliamentary Discourses on Ethnic Issues in Six European States* (Klagenfurt: Drava Verlag, 2000), p. 45.

Intelligentsia article is civilizational, as Other-Serbians are constructed not as part of the Serbian Self, but as part of the European Other.

The construction of Serbian identity in the Missionary Intelligentsia debate

The civilizational difference

In what follows, I will provide an analysis of the referential and nomination strategies which lie at the core of the discursive construction of Serbian identity in the public debate on Missionary Intelligentsia. More particularly, I will seek to ascertain from what perspective these referential/nominational strategies, positive or negative predications of the Self and the Other, and arguments for or against certain value systems, are expressed. And how is the negative discourse, the discourse of othering Other Serbia, mitigated and intensified? Referential strategies, according to Wodak and Reisigl, are employed in discourse to construct and represent social actors in a given context.[609] The construction of in-groups and out-groups is achieved linguistically through membership categorization, lexicalization, and the selective use of possessive pronouns.[610] One dominant referential strategy in First Serbia discourse is to equate Other Serbia with traitors and themselves with patriots. This can be seen where the First Serbia discourse criticizes the "missionaries" for proposing that Serbia be denied its right to identity "in the name of peace in the Balkans, interests of other nations, and other internationally recognized requirements."[611]

In successive texts, Other Serbia members are described as "nothing more than Tito's former troopers, quasi-dissidents hidden in caves and

---

[609] See Ruth Wodak and Martin Reisigl, *Discourse and Discrimination: Rhetorics of Racism and Anti-Semitism* (London: Routledge, 2001), p. 45.

[610] Paul Chilton, and Christina Schäffner, "Introduction: Themes and Principles in the Analysis of Political Discourse," in Paul Chilton and Christina Schäffner, (eds.), *Politics as Text and Talk: Analytic Approaches to Political Discourse* (Amsterdam: John Benjamins, 2002).

[611] Dragan Milosavljević, "Povratak 'Otpisanih'" (The return of 'Otpisanih') in *Vreme* (May 6, 2003).

exponents of state-run institutes, former members of 'Praxis,'[612] gathered together in order to execute one mission, namely 'to speak badly about their own country.' "[613] In First Serbia writings, the "missionaries" are presented as establishing "a front against fascism in their own country, in order to de-nazify the Serbian people."[614] Slobodan Samardžić[615] believes that nationalists are equated to criminals in Other Serbia's terminology. In his view, any punishment of nationalists and attempts to re-educate the people would lean too far in the direction of totalitarian policies of the kind employed by Pol Pot.[616] Samardžić sees "the nation," that is the majority of the population of Serbia, as having been under the control of an internal self–condemnation for a long time.[617] This section identifies the constructions in which Serbian discursive actors are involved by analyzing the core discursive strategies in political discourses about Serbian identity. The next section tackles the meaning of "new nationalism" in the Serbian public sphere.

The concept of "good" and "bad" nationalism

A prominent theme which emerges in First Serbia texts is concerned with the existence of good and bad nationalism. Divjak argues that there

---

[612] The Praxis school was a Marxist humanist philosophical movement. It originated in Zagreb and Belgrade in the SFR Yugoslavia, during the 1960s. Prominent figures among the school's founders include Gajo Petrović and Milan Kangrga of Zagreb and Mihailo Marković of Belgrade. They organized a summer school on the island of Korčula in Croatia which was a meeting place for philosophers and social critics from across the world. Some of the prominent participants included Ernst Bloch, Eugen Fink, Erich Fromm, Herbert Marcuse, Jürgen Habermas, Henri Lefebvre, Richard J. Bernstein and Shlomo Avineri, to name but a few. See Mihailo Marković and Robert S. Cohen, *Yugoslavia: The Rise and Fall of Socialist Humanism: A History of the Praxis Group* (Nottingham, Spokesman Books, 1975).

[613] Dragan Milosavljević, "Povratak 'Otpisanih' " (The return of 'Otpisanih') in *Vreme* (May 6, 2003).

[614] Ibid.

[615] Samardžić is professor at the Faculty of Political Science in the department of European Studies. He became well known for his hardline euroskeptic stance, as he is an expert in the area and is a constantly present voice in the media. He is also a member of Koštunica's DSS party.

[616] Slobodan Samardžić, "Od mrzovolje do zla" (From grumpiness to evil) in *Vreme*, no. 638 (March 27, 2003).

[617] Ibid.

are two significantly different types of nationalism. While the first is ethnic (chauvinist) and is anti-liberal, as it completely precludes the creation of a liberal or ethnically-neutral state, the second is not set against the principles of a liberal state.[618] Divjak sets out the concept of "liberal nationalism" which is basically an "acceptable degree of patriotism" without which even liberal states can barely function.[619] Samardžić, on the other hand, points to Other Serbia's radical criticism of nationalism as going too far and throwing the baby out with the bathwater, as it were:

> Therefore, nationalism equals crime, automatically and for all of us. It is presented as some sort of an a priori social fact which is necessarily practically materialized in the actions not only of direct perpetrators of crimes but also [many] of those which give it spiritual, i.e. ideological support. After a diagnosis is given, there follows a therapy. A people imbued with nationalism must first face a collective catharsis, and in parallel a somewhat less far-reaching punishment. Hidden behind the equation of nationalism and crime is the thesis of collective guilt, which assumes subsequent punishment not only for alleged mass support for mass-crime but also for the entire historical and spiritual preparation for the crime. Nationalists should be physically isolated and the people (what is left) should be re-educated.[620]

Samardžić offers the concept of equality between nation and nationalism which is a quite common perspectivation strategy in the First Serbia discourse. I put forward that contemporary nationalism in the First Serbia discourse has become more and more preoccupied with the preservation of national values, mostly as a result of a particular cultural-essentialist understanding of the Self. From the sections presented above, it is obvious that the selective use of the first person plural pronoun "we," and third person plural pronoun "they" provides the speaker with an opportunity to perspectivate their discourse. By the reference to "these home-grown missionaries" who wish to speak badly about their own country, Other Serbia is understood to be disapproving and critical of nationalism, or even to reject it altogether. Consequently, Other Serbia is understood not to be the true, authentic Serbia.

---

[618] Slobodan Divjak, "Kontradikcije Nenada Dakovića" (The contradictions of Nenad Daković) in *Vreme*, no. 639, (April 3, 2003).
[619] Ibid.
[620] Slobodan Samardžić, "Od mrzovolje do zla" (From grumpiness to evil) in *Vreme*, no. 638 (March 27, 2003).

Manufacturing nationalists

Some other "First" Serbia actors argue that there is an ongoing process of "manufacturing nationalists" which is the only activity that can be profitable for Other-Serbians in today's Serbia.[621] Vasović sets out the idea that the nationalists themselves are the essence and cause of "Other" Serbia's existence: "The fight against nationalists brought out of anonymity all of the former privileged shirkers: former civil servants, union leaders, apparatchiks, educated apologists, untalented culture workers, civil security officials, and typical socialist intellectuals— 'general experts'."[622] Vasović asked what they would eat if it weren't for foreign scholarships, and NGO funding, arguing that Other Serbia have built their careers on the "nationalists" and thus created a name for themselves.[623] One can suggest that a major referential strategy performed in the debates for equating Other Serbia with the home-grown missionaries is the construction of first, "inside outsiders" and second, in-group homogeneity. The First Serbia discourse not only equates Other Serbia actors as "serving the enemy," it also constructs them as a highly homogenous entity. In the discursive construction of in-group homogeneity, no matter how diverse the Other Serbia spectrum of NGO groups, scholars, politicians, journalists and others, the Other Serbia is always constructed as a homogenous entity. Construction of in-group homogeneity and sameness is well documented to be a major semantic strategy which is instrumental in the discursive formation of collective identity.[624] What is remarkable in the building of in-group sameness in the First Serbian discourse on identity is that differences within the Other Serbia group are most often de-emphasized or denied. Antonić and his supporters, when discussing Other Serbia actors' connections to Serbia, seldom mention the cultural or political differences between many liberal institutions within the governmental, non-governmental and cultural

---

[621] Mirjana Vasović, "Proizvodnja nacionalista" (Manufacturing nationalists) in *Vreme*, no. 634, (February 27, 2003).
[622] Ibid.
[623] Ibid.
[624] Ruth Wodak, *The Discourse of Politics in Action: Politics as Usual* (Basingstoke: Palgrave. 2009), p. 124.

political bodies. The perception of a homogenous Other Serbia adapts almost automatically to the changes in the in-group over time. Considered over the complete span of the analysis undertaken in this field, the discourse of homogenous Other Serbia appears to be responsive to the needs of the First Serbia discourse for finding an "inner enemy" or "enemy within" or nemesis, in opposition to which the nationalist discourse can flourish.

The cultural war in Serbia

In the long aftermath of this discussion, in 2008 Antonić published *The Cultural War in Serbia: Essays on the Culture of 'Other' Serbia* in which he continues to use the same rhetoric: Other-Serbians are just local copies of their American and European instigators.[625] Antonić defines the concept of cultural war as a war led by a segment of the cultural elite against certain values. In his view, the content of such a war is the denial or slighting of certain cultural values and its main form is humiliation, ridicule and cynicism directed against the principal symbols and their bearers.[626] Antonić goes on to summarize the aim of Other-Serbians as the desire to change the cultural and political identity of the Serbs by separating them from the Cyrillic script and from a basic understanding of the national interest.[627] He analyzes the cultural values that have been imposed on the Serbs such as political correctness, the extension of marriage to homosexuals, as well as the radio talk show *Peščanik* (*Hourglass*) as a guillotine of the civic "Bloody Thermidor" in the media. The following section, paraphrasing Churchill, clearly outlines what Antonić believes should be First Serbia's response to the redefinition of ideological power in Serbia:

---

[625] Antonić, Slobodan, "Kulturni rat u Srbiji: eseji o kulturi 'Druge' Srbije: of Marka Vidojkovića do Radomira Konstantinovića," (The cultural war in Serbia: Essays on Culture of 'Other' Serbia: from Marko Vidojković to Radomir Konstantinović) (Belgrade: Zavod za udžbenike, 2008), p. 10.
[626] Ibid., p. 12.
[627] Ibid.

We will fight! We will no longer sit and quietly observe how you are taking over institution after institution, step by step, until you occupy the entire society .... We will fight in the newspapers, we will fight on web sites, we will fight in public debates, we will fight in books, we will fight in theatres, we will fight in galleries .... Never shall we surrender! We will show you that our values are better than yours! And we are sure that in the end, this country and this culture will triumph![628]

Antonić belongs to the First Serbia discourse that understands Serbia to be "always on the right side," and which makes little or no reference to regional enmities of the recent past, the Yugoslav wars or responsibility for the war crimes committed in those wars. The in-group bias in this particular sub-type of predication often leads to the assertion of the superiority of its own culture, without fear of isolation. In this type of in-group favoritism, Serbia is constructed as the home to genuine culture, and has the strength to stand alone.

The "Other" Serbia response

As part of the "Other" Serbia response, Vojin Dimitrijević[629] rejects both of the propositions stated in Antonić's Missionary Intelligentsia text: that the author of an article cannot be judged based upon the quality of the journal he publishes in; and that a man should not be judged based upon who he gets his salary from.[630] Popov,[631] on the other hand, criticizes Antonić's claim that "certain groups of authors" write about the Serbs in a derogatory way, stating that "hundreds of texts were published in *Republika* in the last fourteen years (informative, analytical and research articles) about ideas of freedom, relevant actors and actions of certain individuals, groups, parties, NGOs, and movements that fought for

---

[628] Ibid., p. 37–38.
[629] Vojin Dimitrijević was a distinguished human rights activist and international law expert. He was the founder and head of the Belgrade Centre for Human Rights—an organization opposed to the government of Slobodan Milošević. A former graduate, then professor at the University of Belgrade Faculty of Law, he was dismissed from his position in 1998, and went on to oppose the involvement of Serbia in various conflicts in the region. He served as an ad hoc judge on the International Court of Justice from 2001 to 2003, and was reinstated as an honorary law professor in 2005.
[630] Vojin Dimitrijević, "Tvrdnja i Celina," (Allegations and the Whole) and "Urednik zabranio" (The editor forbids) in *Vreme,* no. 642–643, (April 23, 2003).
[631] Nebojša Popov is a professor of sociology, anti-war activist, founder and chief editor of Belgrade newspaper Republic.

democratic change in Serbia."[632] Still, the response by Other Serbia actors to Antonić's article was not immediate, as was the case in respect of the 2002 Point of Departure public debate. However, as Odalović notes, Antonić was the first person to make a "list of undesirable public personalities," which cemented the first serious "academic" split in Serbian society in post-October 2000 Serbia.[633] Antonić's list and the ensuing debate caused the most significant media event of the time until the tragic event of Djindjić's assassination on March 12, 2003 swept it aside. Despite this event, Vučelj[634] has tried to position the article in the political and historical context of the present moment and argued that Antonić is attempting to create a "black list of journalists," followed by foreign mercenaries, i.e. NGOs which promote some form of anti-racist, anti-nationalist and/or anti-homophobic ideas:

> Torov, Pančić, Biserko, Odalović, Popov. I and Mr. Antonić are perfectly aware of the profile of these people. Vesna Pešić, Vojin Dimitrijević, and Nataša Kandić can also be added to the list. I am sure that he has a strong aversion toward them as well. On the other hand, it is absolutely clear what the political and intellectual profile of Slobodan Antonić is. It is the position shared by the Serbian Academy of Sciences and Arts, the Serbian Association of Writers at Francuska 7, the DSS and members and sympathizers of this party who joined after October 5, 2000. In short, Slobodan Antonić is a Serbian nationalist par excellence.[635]

Among the proponents of the similar view, Pištalo[636] elaborated most clearly that the true division among Serbian intellectuals has nothing to do with missionaries or aborigines.[637] Pištalo argues that this is a division between "professional worshipers of people in power and critical

---

[632] Nebojša Popov, "Poražavajuća kik-nauka, odgovor Antoniću" (Defeating kik-science, response to Antonić) in *Vreme*, no. 638, (March 27, 2003).

[633] Nataša Odalović, "Spiskovi nekad i sad," (Lists, then and now) in *Danas*, (October 2, 2008).

[634] Nermin Vučelj is professor of French language and literature at the University of Niš.

[635] Nermin Vučelj, "Bela knjiga," (White Book) in *Vreme*, no. 638, (March 27, 2003).

[636] Vladimir Pištalo is a Serbian writer, most notably winning the 2008 NIN Prize for best novel. He graduated from the University of Belgrade's Law School and earned his doctorate at the University of New Hampshire writing on the theme of the identity of Serbian immigrants. He now works at Becker College in Brewster, Massachusetts where he teaches World and US history.

[637] Vladimir Pištalo, "Ples duhova i dalje o 'misionarskim intelektualcima' " (The dance of the ghosts and more about "missionary intellectuals") in *Vreme*, no. 644. (May 8, 2003).

intellectuals," and adds that Antonić's attitudes correspond to the statement "Let it be our way, even if it makes us worse off."[638] Pištalo put forward that the intellectuals with a propensity to criticize were labelled *foreign mercenaries*.[639] On the theme of patriotism, Pištalo had something to add:

> Those who spent ten years smelling the flowers in Mira Marković's hair while having fun in Bambilend[640]... were upset by the discovery that there is no such concept as patriotism or a mystical concept of 'legality' that murderers could hide behind. They are worried by the fact that criminals are being arrested all over the place, people with blood on their hands who did so many evil things to us and—do not forget—to others.[641]

Similar to Pištalo's perspective, Kazimir[642] suggested that this societal phenomenon concerning "facing the past, the position of Roma and other minorities, homosexuals and cats and dogs, people are interested in of their own free will and because of their sense of conscience and compassion and not because they were instructed to do so by Washington or Brussels."[643] Kazimir argues that in Antonić's text certain people are singled out for criticism because of their lack of love and understanding for their own people.[644] Daković[645] purports that Antonić is disqualifying the so-called missionaries in the same way as the graffiti *Get out of Serbia* that can be read in a corridor of the building in which the Helsinki Committee for Human Rights in Serbia is based.[646]

Daković goes on to argue that there is an internal bond between nationalism and crime.[647] This is why nationalism, in his view, is not just an

---

[638] Ibid.
[639] Ibid.
[640] Bambilend is an entertainment park in Milošević's home city of Požarevac built by his son Marko Milošević.
[641] Ibid. Ultimately, Pištalo poses the question of whether the late Prime Minister Zoran Djindjić was a missionary intellectual.
[642] Kazimir is a journalist and a founder of the media archive Ebart.
[643] Velimir Ćurgus Kazimir, "Radikalski pamphlet" (A Radical Pamphlet) in *Vreme* no. 631, (February 5, 2003).
[644] Ibid.
[645] Nenad Daković is well-known Serbian philosopher.
[646] Nenad Daković, "Tacka Razlaza" (Point of Departure) in *Vreme*, no. 636, (March 13, 2003).
[646] Ibid.
[647] Ibid.

ideology of banality but an elementary evil, a momentary evil, meaning that, in Daković's words, after all that has happened, being a nationalist in Serbia today means to be an open or opportunistic accomplice in a voluntary crime.[648] Other Serbia's vocabulary frequently employs and references the horrifying concept that nationalism is "the anthropological experience which indicates that mass-murder can be based on *culture, a sense of honor*, and even *a quest for holiness*.[649] The Missionary Intelligentsia public debate indicates that nationalism was not the only key point of disagreement between "First" and "Other" Serbia political elites, another such divergence having arisen in respect of the charge of crimes against humanity. Daković finds that the words *everything that happened* has a normative meaning which Samardžić cannot understand. In this sense, Daković adds: "That is why I say: I refuse! I refuse crimes!"[650] Daković views Samardžić as an advisor, a "thinker of continuity" and a potential "ideologist of the Red Berets"[651] as a part of their public criminal activity these "national workers" could not, and did not want any distance of thought.[652] Daković, on the other hand, does not think nationalism and crime are one interconnected thing, since he himself finds this mantra of collective guilt repulsive.[653] Daković adds that since "unlike Samardžić who always speaks in the name of the people — I believe that the *people* does not exist, I speak from an existentialist perspective and in my own name and I am unable to do otherwise."[654] He continues that there is no such thing as collective guilt but there is such a

---

[648] Ibid.
[649] Ibid.
[650] Nenad Daković, "Etikete i argumenti: odgovor Slobodanu Samardžiću" (The labels and arguments: the response to Slobodanu Samardžiću) in *Vreme*, no. 639, (April 3, 2003).
[651] The Red Berets, or "Frenki's boys," as they came to be known, helped invent the 1990s version of "ethnic cleansing" and went on to become the most feared paramilitary unit of the Balkan wars. Without such units, politicians like Milošević and Radovan Karadžić would never have had the means to carry out their radical ethnic policies. The Bloody Red Beret, in *Time Magazine*, (March 11, 2001).
[652] Nenad Daković, "Etikete i argumenti: odgovor Slobodanu Samardžiću" (The labels and arguments: The response to Slobodanu Samardžiću) in *Vreme*, no. 639, (April 3, 2003).
[653] Ibid.
[654] Ibid.

thing as political responsibility for crimes: "I imagine I am politically as responsible as Samardžić, unless perhaps he thinks he is innocent."[655] Similarly, Vesna Rakić Vodinelić[656] claims that "Serbian society is (not) ready to tackle the past…as one of the segments of such a process would be lustration of bearers of public functions."[657] Rakić Vodinelić puts forward that there is no consensus among the political parties when it comes to dealing with the past. In her words, "even though the public administration of this country is often seen as reformist, it is difficult to argue that it is serious when it comes to dealing with the past."[658] In the same vein, Stanisavljević addresses the Hague Tribunal:

> The Hague Tribunal is currently our largest landfill, where we dispose of our rubbish. However, it only accepts the largest items of rubbish. Where should we put hundreds and thousands of little Šešeljs? For example those that spat and threw stones at those poor people that were kidnapped from a train in Sjeverin. Or those proud citizens of Šamac who freely entered the local prison on a daily basis and exercised their patriotism by beating up the captured 'Turks' with impunity.[659]

Nebojša Popov writes that a large number of texts have indeed been published in *Republika* on the topic of the obstacles that actors mentioned earlier had to negotiate, namely "the deluge of fear, hatred, and violence" that has been wreaking havoc across "these parts."[660] But they, Popov strongly claims, do not contain any statements that connect an entire nation to violence, crimes, theft and other crimes.[661] Popov finds that in *Republika* the comments addressed individual, rather than collective, responsibility for the crimes.[662]

---

[655] Ibid.
[656] Vesna Rakić Vodinelić is a professor at the Faculty of Law in Belgrade.
[657] Taken from Marinko M. Vučinić, "Da li je nacionalizam naša sudbina?" (Is nationalism our destiny?) in *Vreme*, no. 635. (March 6, 2003).
[658] Ibid.
[659] Miodrag Stanisavljević, "Klovnovi i kriminalci" (Clowns and criminals) *Republika*, no. 304/305, (March 7, 2003).
[660] Nebojsa Popov, "Poražavajuća kik-nauka, odgovor Antoniću" (Defeating kik-science, response to Antonić) in *Vreme*, no. 638, (March 27, 2003).
[661] Ibid.
[662] Ibid.

Let us be human, even if we are Serbs

The final issue is the one which attracted the most attention, namely, Professor Samardžić's assertion that "since the Serbs in Serbia are politically irrelevant, it is acceptable for B92 to send them a public message: 'Let us be human, even if we are Serbs'[663] several times per day with no public condemnation whatsoever."[664] Samardžić suggests that it fits almost perfectly the "Other" Serbia actors' story about collective crimes against humanity (equated with nationalism) "whose mass executioners do not deserve to be considered a part of humanity."[665] Samardžić closes by saying, "unless, of course, they submit themselves to de-nazification followed by re-education."[666] In the aftermath of Samardžić's text, Veran Matić claimed that the supposed recording of Patriarch Pavle's words was made during the first massive student protest in front of the Terazije fountain in 1991 and that it was an authentic statement. Nevertheless, a section of the public was convinced that it was an invention.[667] On the other side, Samardžić wrote that he resented these somber words spoken by the Patriarch Pavle, and considered them to be an "idiotic joke," because he feels that the Patriarch implied that the Serbs are "inhumane."[668] Daković sees this statement as a moral warning and not a predicative sentence.[669] Matić claims that this statement was not an "idiotic joke with racist content" and was made by a "wise man who knows how to remove himself from phantasmagorical constructions about the heavenly people by using irony."[670] Consequently, among the prominent

---

[663] Serbian Orthodox Church Patriarch Pavle's famous sentence from the 1991 anti-regime street protests.
[664] Slobodan Samardžić: "Od mrzovolje do zla" (From Grouch to Evil), in *Vreme*, no. 638, (March 27, 2003).
[665] Ibid.
[666] Ibid.
[667] Veran Matić, "Nije montaža" (It is not a montage), in *Vreme*, no. 638, (March 27, 2003).
[668] Slobodan Samardžić, "Od mrzovolje do zla," (From Grouch to Evil), in *Vreme*, no. 638, (March 27, 2003).
[669] Nenad Daković, "Etikete i argumenti: odgovor Slobodanu Samardžiću" (The labels and arguments: the response to Slobodanu Samardžić), in *Vreme*, no. 639, (April 3, 2003).
[670] Veran Matić, "Nije montaža," (It is not a montage), in *Vrem*e, no. 638, (March 27, 2003).

themes in both First and Other Serbia discourses are the subjects of *serbophobia*, an anti-Serb sentiment, or "un-serbness," and self-hating Serbs who consider they are not Serbian enough. Stanisavljević mentioned how the philosopher Ljuba Tadić,[671] in a state of righteous anger, pointed out to patriots the level of his "un-Serbness" and serbophobia. In Stanisavljević's words, "Serbness and patriotism were an elixir of youth for Tadić and many people of his age."[672]

Image of the Serbs as brutal and violent

Another practice in the liberal intelligentsia discourse is to construct the "First" Serbia supporters as religiously fanatical. I consider this to be a stereotypical construction, in which "Serbs" emerge as Orthodox fundamentalists who without European or Western supervision would certainly defy the existing liberal values such as secularism, equal rights to men and women, the rights of Roma, the gay community and children with special needs, and humane treatment of animals, among others. The prevalence of this particular image attached to the First Serbia can be found especially in the visual discourse of Koraks's caricatures[673] published in daily newspaper *Danas*. "The Serbs" are typically pictured as wearing a traditional peasant suit, traditional *opanci* shoes, and in some cases wearing the traditional Serbian hat. The image created is always presented in a stereotypical way. It could be said that the First Serbian Other is seen to be uniquely religiously reckless and threatening. The First Serbian Other appears in the discourse of liberal intelligentsia and liberal hard-liners to have almost a natural inclination for intolerance and even violence, especially against the weaker members of society, such as religious or ethnic minorities, women, gays, Roma and animals. This particular image is constructed by frequent use of adjectives

---

[671] Ljubomir Tadić is a member of the Serbian Academy of Sciences and Arts, as well as being one of the founding members of the Democratic Party. He is the father of former president of Serbia Boris Tadić.

[672] Miodrag Stanisavljević, "Klovnovi I Kriminalci," (Clowns and criminals) in *Republika*, no. 304/305, (March 7, 2003).

[673] Koraks is a well-known political caricaturist that depicts everyday political life in Serbia. He is particularly famous for his depiction of Slobodan Milošević and his wife Mira Marković.

such as *brutal, aggressive, militaristic, nationalist* etc. All of these negative features which are commonly attributed to the First Serbian Other are also either implicitly or explicitly linked to Milošević's wars and/or to the Orthodox Church.

"First-Serbian" as a radical Other to being European

To sum up, it can be said that within the Other Serbia discourses, the First Serbian Other is attributed a highly derogatory difference from the European and Other-Serbians, and is even demonized. Older stereotypical images are still being overtly produced, in the same unmitigated manner as before 2000. Negative identification is almost strong enough to make "First" Serbia the "ultimate Other" to being "European" in Serbia. Amidst this negativity, the nationalistic "Other" emerges as a subordinate term, a would-be internal source of destabilization, existing within the identity of the dominant term, that is a European/civilized identity. This is how the Serbian candidacy for EU membership is initially perceived by many, including Srdja Popović, as "proof of possible reformation."[674] The mere existence of First Serbia, the nationalist Other, today in Serbia, disturbs the "civilizational order" simply by being Other and/or by being there. The narrativization of the Serbian Self constructed in this particular way implies an emphasis on the existence of a binary dilemma. The constant focus of First and Other Serbia groups, on self-display and self-recognition on the national level, demonstrates their logic of self-presentation which solely reproduces their alternatives. As a result, such a civilizational hierarchy can only produce endless counter-hierarchies and counter-publics. I draw one significant conclusion from this analysis: the principal themes of identity, nationalism, crimes, auto-chauvinism and patriotism were framed by the Serbian elites primarily in terms of the activity of finding the official historical narrative. The Point of Departure and Missionary Intelligentsia debates reflected the equal strength of two opposing sides, as there was no direct denial of the war crimes, but certainly there was still a need to claim victimhood for the Serbs along the lines of the Serbian nationalist narra-

---

[674] Srdja Popović, "Čas anatomije" (The Class of Anatomy), in *Peščanik Series*, (June 1, 2007).

tives propagated since the mid-1980s. As has been seen, these two phenomena were inextricably linked.

Chapter 6:
Serbian "Auto-chauvinism" or "Identification with the Aggressor"

Although attributing positive values to the Self, and negative values to the Other, are two strategies that are known to play important roles in identity formation, such positioning need not be put in radical terms. I have shown that both activities are widespread and are crucial for the construction of identity in the "First" and "Other" Serbia debate on Europe and Serbian identity. This chapter explores the phenomenon of auto-chauvinism[675] in the First Serbia texts which relate to the political contestation of Europe, and the Self-Other nexus, in post-Milošević public space.[676] The phenomenon of auto-chauvinism is frequently depicted as auto-racism. But these two concepts do not overlap. The term auto-racism was coined by the Slovene sociologist and activist Primož Krašovec. It aims to qualify the disdain of Eastern European elites toward their own *peoples* which they consider as inferior, lazy, incompetent, and unable to fulfill the norms and standards of Western liberal democracies and European culture.[677] On the other hand, in the specific Serbian context, the term auto-chauvinism stems directly from the right-wing nationalist discourse, and its origins lie in Mile Lompar's theses on "the spirit of self-denial" which is particularly and solely a characteristic

---

[675] Auto-chauvinism implies conscious or unconscious hate and disgust for one's own people

[676] "Serbian auto-chauvinism or identification with the aggressor" was published in the April 2012 issue of *New Serbian Political Thought,* a political theory and social research periodical as a series of interviews conducted by Rade Ivković with distinguished writers and historians such as Vladimir Kecmanović, Predrag Marković, Radoslav Pavlović and Siniša Kovačević.

[677] See Primož Krašovec, *Racism as an Ideology and Auto-racism,* (November 26, 2014). http://maz.hr/index.php/ tekstovi/clanci/42-primoz-krasovec-rasizam-kao-ideologija-i-autorasizam

of the Serbs.[678] Lompar puts forward that Serbian public consciousness had become a combination of a range of different cultural politics, none of which was truly Serbian.[679] Lompar found himself in circumstances where he felt that the Serbs were under "colonial occupation."[680] Current "non-Serbian cultural politics" is in fact auto-chauvinist, and has a spirit of national self-denial. It also has a tendency to encourage Serbians not to attach to their own people, and not to integrate with the cultural existence of the "Serbian spirit," but instead with the enemy and his state of mind.[681] Themes such as *auto-chauvinism*, the *perverted system of values*, the legacy of communism, the "external" donations, "foreign mercenaries" and the perceptions of Serbian statehood are all confronted in this section, which explores the practices employed within the First Serbia texts in constructing the national identity in post-Milošević Serbia.

Here, I focus on the April 2012 text "Serbian auto-chauvinism or identification with the aggressor" published in the magazine *New Serbian Political Thought*. The text is envisioned as a series of interviews which tackles the subject of the Serbian nation, identity and history. Serbia is presented as a "land of bad miracles," that is, a country incomprehensible not only for foreigners but to Serbs as well.[682] Ivković[683] commences the debate on the issue of Other Serbia and statehood:

> Since the 1990s, a section of our intellectual, artistic and political elite has used every opportunity to unfairly criticize its own people while offering a legitimate political criticism. Members of this section of the intelligentsia—fortunately not very numerous—have no issues with making some of the hardest accusations against the Serbian people, in particular attacking anything that could form the basis of its identity and statehood.[684]

---

[678] See Milo Lompar, *Duh samoporicanja. Prilog kritici srpske kulturne politike* (Novi Sad: Orpheus, 2011).

[679] Ibid., p. 472.

[680] Ibid., p. 472.

[681] Ibid., p. 472.

[682] "Serbian auto-chauvinism or identification with the aggressor," article published in *New Serbian Political Thought*, (April 2012).

[683] Rade Ivković is, among other things, a journalist of the *New Serbian Political Thought*.

[684] Rade Ivković, "Serbian auto-chauvinism or identification with the aggressor," in *New Serbian Political Thought*, (April 2012).

Thus, the Other Serbia intelligentsia is systematically criticizing the Serbian people, very unfairly, the consequence of which is that Serbian identity and statehood is threatened. It can be put forward here that the strength of negative predication indicates that the othering of the Other Serbia actors has been an important part of self-construction of First Serbia in general terms, as the only "real and genuine" identity. Such practices are not infrequent, as even Therborn argues that identity "is operative only dialectically, i.e. in connection with the opposite, otherness … there is primacy of otherness over sameness in the making of identity."[685] However, what is noteworthy is the radicalization of Otherness, whereby Other Serbia is seen as menacing, as a threat to be feared. Remarkably, the First Serbia negative predication strategy is still the dominant strategy in that discourse, even such a long time after the change of regime. What can be deduced from the claims of Ivković and the other interviewees that First Serbia are building the position that the Other Serbia elite should be considered as the "the enemy within?"

Program-based destruction of national culture

Further in the text, Kecmanović[686] suggests that the phenomenon of auto-chauvinism, in which Other Serbia is involved, is a sort of "pathology similar to cases of rape victims who start to blame themselves for their ordeal."[687] Kecmanović is not certain about the motivation behind such

---

[685] Göran Therborn, *European Modernity and Beyond: The Trajectory of European Societies, 1945–2000* (London: Sage, 1995), p. 229.

[686] Kecmanović is a novelist of the younger generation.

[687] Indeed, the metaphor of rape in not unusual within the "First" Serbia discourse. In a text titled "One day" published in his regular column in *Politika* in 2007 Antonić wrote: "Someone has already compared the abduction of Kosovo to a scene of rape. Bully rapists are big and strong and the unfortunate girl could get beaten if she resists too much, and perhaps it is better for her not to resist …. But what can be said about those people who, while all of this is happening, tell the girl that: "she is too conservative and that these guys are simply doing her a favor, that she should be modern and enjoy sex, particularly when the main bully lies on top of her, then she should groan and shout – Yes!, Yes!, More!, More!" Yes. The main bully likes to think that he is a great lover. But my dear Serbia, you do not have to act like you are happy because of him. Feel free to cry. And, more importantly, remember them all. Both those that took turns on top of you, and those that cheered them on. For one day… Yes, yes, one day… " Antonić, Slobodan, Jednoga Dana! (One Day!) in *Politika*, (April 15, 2007).

actions, as he argues there can be two different varieties: "One a true or spontaneous auto-chauvinism and the other a program-based destruction of national culture."[688] Of course, Kecmanović adds, "a true auto-chauvinist will never say that his goal is the defeat of the Serbian national tradition, but will claim that the cultural tradition of every nation is contentious by definition."[689] Kecmanović argues within the lines of national determinism, suggesting that it is not possible to destroy the "spiritual tradition of the Serbian nation," but suggesting that the damage has already been done (by Other Serbia).[690]

The Communists

Continuing the debate, Predrag Marković[691] defines the phenomenon of auto-chauvinism as *hatred toward one's own people*: "Our auto-chauvinists—i.e. the people who despise the Serbian identity—are often prisoners of the past. They only recognize the Yugoslav identity, which actually makes them bigger hegemonists than the Serbian nationalists."[692] Moreover, Marković suggests that the Other Serbia members are on the left of the political spectrum because "there was no authentic auto-chauvinism in Serbia until the appearance of communism … as there are in fact no other auto-chauvinists except communists and neo-communists."[693] Marković argues that auto-chauvinism is an ideological leftover of communism: "Their closeness to communists can be seen through—for example—their adoration of a foreign power. For old-style communists this power used to be Moscow, for today's ones it is Brussels and Washington, but either way, they are ready to subjugate national interests to those of some global ideological centre."[694] Playwright

---

[688] Vladimir Kecmanović, "Serbian Auto-chauvinism or Identification with the Aggressor," in *New Serbian Political Thought*, (April 2012).
[689] Ibid.
[690] Ibid.
[691] Marković is a well-known historian of the younger generation.
[692] Predrag Marković, "Serbian auto-chauvinism or identification with the aggressor," in *New Serbian Political Thought* (April 2012).
[693] Ibid.
[694] Ibid.

Radoslav Pavlović[695] adds that "communism is re-emerging in the shape of some political parties such as the LDP and SPS, and to a great extent the Democratic Party." One can notice here how the term Other-Serbians in First Serbia discourse is applied to communism and is used in a highly derogatory sense. Kovačević, a well-known writer of the older generation, understands that it is very problematic that "the people who belong to this circle of auto-chauvinists today are in fact biological and political extensions of the Serbian communists."[696] One can observe this phenomenon, which is, according to Delanty and O'Mahony, a process of defining characteristics of in-groups;[697] still, I suggest that the emphasis is not on what members of the in-group have in common but, rather, on what separates them from other groups. Therefore, this process of definition of in-group characteristics is performed throughout a form of self-referencing, which Delanty and O'Mahony called "the purity and stability of 'We,'" and is guaranteed first in the naming, then in the demonization of Otherness.[698] By way of illustration, Kecmanović suggests there are two different types of the average Serbian auto-chauvinist. A small proportion of them are "truly and honestly convinced of their messianic role."[699] However, a much large portion of them belong to the "type whose critical anti-Serbian zeal is fired up through foreign donations."[700]

Identification with aggressors

Pavlović notes that the phenomenon of auto-chauvinism is not new: "phases in the history of Balkan peoples also contain their identification with various aggressors. This applies to long periods of our history

---

[695] The writer is currently the closest advisor to the new president of Serbia, Tomislav Nikolić.
[696] Siniša Kovačević, "Serbian Auto-chauvinism or Identification with the Aggressor," in *New Serbian Political Thought* (April 2012).
[697] Gerard Delanty and Patrick O'Mahony, *Nationalism and Social Theory: Modernity and the Recalcitrance of the Nation*, (London: Sage, 2002), p. 59.
[698] Ibid.
[699] Vladimir Kecmanović, "Serbian Auto-chauvinism or Identification with the Aggressor," in *New Serbian Political Thought*, (April 2012).
[700] Ibid.

when some foreign power would take over and would execute, shoot, impale, pillage, bomb and occupy our region."⁷⁰¹

At this level of discourse, negative lexicalization occupies a central place in predicating the "Other" Serbia out-group in relation to the Other/Aggressor. In describing aggression against Serbia, the speakers make selective use of negative lexicals to better accentuate the negative traits attributed to the Other/Aggressor. In this way, these actions and actors are often referred to using terms such as *murders* and *occupiers*. In a discourse created in this way, words with emotional weight, according to Kolstø, are regularly repeated in order to provoke a grave sentiment of disgust, hate and anger.⁷⁰² In "First" Serbia thought, Pavlović suggests, it is implied that "everything that ever happened, and everything that happens, to the Serbs is their own fault":

> There are no aggressors, no causes, no questions about who pacified the Serbs by killing 6000 people in a single morning, no questions about who pacified the Serbs by sending them to Gradiška and Sajmište concentration camps, or by throwing cluster bombs on Niš. If any Serbs were killed in Jasenovac it happened only because some other Serbs behaved badly. Jasenovac is a logical and understandable consequence of the behavior of Serbs that were in power between the two world wars. If Belgrade was bombed on April 6, 1941, it only happened because of the anti-German demonstrations on March 27, 1941. If Belgrade was bombed once again on March 24, 1999, it was not the fault of the Americans and an alliance of 19 nations, it was Milošević's fault. That is auto-chauvinism. It wants to blame those that hurt themselves by excluding the causes and focusing purely on the premise of self-injury.⁷⁰³

By juxtaposing the events of the Second World War, the bombing of Belgrade in 1941 and the 1999 NATO intervention, Pavlović connects them and implies that they are equivalent, and then presents them as a part of one continuously hostile "European" and "Western" policy toward Serbia. In the First Serbia texts, the Western and European Other is quite often constructed as *arrogant, brutal* and *aggressive*, which is, in general, a typically recognized stereotypical image of the Other. The "topos of abuse" by Western powers is common in the First Serbia dis-

---

⁷⁰¹ Radoslav Pavlović, "Serbian auto-Chauvinism or Identification with the Aggressor," in *New Serbian Political Thought*, (April 2012).

⁷⁰² See Pål Kolstø, ed., *Media Discourse and the Yugoslav Conflicts: Representation of the Self and Other* (Farnham, UK: Ashgate, 2009), p. 21.

⁷⁰³ Radoslav Pavlović, "Serbian auto-Chauvinism or Identification with the Aggressor," in *New Serbian Political Thought*, (April 2012).

course, with different layers of abuse such as political, ideological, and financial. The continuously constructed image of Europeans abusing the "proud, naïve and genuine" Serbs shows us the power and persistence of the idealized and idyllic peasant narrative which includes anti-European and anti-colonial narratives. Furthermore, Pavlović adds that the world has changed since the end of the Cold War but that "the mission of the Serbian communists has remained the same: to make the Serbs humble and subservient, to keep pointing out the weaknesses and faults of the Serbian people and make an auto-chauvinist imprint on the collective psyche so that the people would blame themselves for all of their problems."[704] According to the First Serbia narrative, the cause of all Serbian problems is to be found outside Serbia. Others, including the Western powers as well as regional neighbors, never wished Serbia well, and always wanted to see Serbia suffer and perish.

Loyalty to foreign masters

One can argue that referring to "Other" Serbia interchangeably with *traitors* and *missionaries* underlines first and foremost the importance of the political, rather than cultural, dimensions of our perceptions. This way, Other Serbia is constructed discursively as a socio-political entity with well-defined, bounded membership, rather than as primarily a group of loosely-associated intellectuals. Based on this finding, it can thus be argued that in the "First" Serbia discourse, the identity of Other Serbia is conceptualized more on the grounds of socio-political belonging (political unity, or unity of values, traditions, norms, etc.) to foreign masters than as affiliation to a particular organized group with its own values and rules. The theme of "external" donations and financing dominates the First Serbia discourse on the NGO and civil society sector:

---

[704] Ibid.

> The non-governmental sector was very powerful in the 1990s and was able to buy almost anyone for very little money. At the time the NGOs that were particularly active were financed by foreign governments. In fact, the majority of NGOs in our country are financed by foreign governments even today. An average Serb is basically cheap to buy. Due to poverty and lack of principles many people succumbed to temptations and have accepted donations. As if by inertia, the auto-chauvinists behave as if we are still living in the 1990s when it was very lucrative to disparage one's own people and country.[705]

This way of representing Other Serbia as "loyal to foreigners" turns the issue of European perspective and EU accession automatically into a question of "merchandising Serbia," "selling out for profit" and "giving in to the Great powers and great business." The arguably more pertinent questions of Serbian Europeanness and of the practical benefits of EU integration policies are left behind. When discussing Serbian "national values" and Other Serbia's hatred toward them, Siniša Kovačević, suggests that there is "a perverted system of values, particularly with the Serbs, who consider anything national as highly undesirable."[706] In this light, Vukadinović writes:

> I have a friend who still keeps in his room a small American flag that he intended to wave as the US troops were entering Belgrade in 1999 …. However, what requires some thinking about is the fact that an unusually high percentage of the educated population in Serbia with an age between twenty and forty-five has very similar views and nurtures an almost pathological hatred of their own country and anything that can be deemed Serbian.[707]

Marković believes these auto-chauvinists do not have full state support and do not represent the ideology of the ruling coalition (the DS and SPS at the time); yet, in his view, the auto-chauvinists represent a powerful threat as an interest group.[708] In order to illustrate the auto-chauvinist phenomenon, that, according to auto-chauvinists themselves, can be present within culture, shows, art and paintings, they often put forward the evidence of Serbian modern cinematography. Marković cites Srdjan

---

[705] Predrag Marković, "Serbian Auto-chauvinism or Identification with the Aggressor," in *New Serbian Political Thought*, (April 2012).

[706] Siniša Kovačević, "Serbian Auto-chauvinism or Identification with the Aggressor," in *New Serbian Political Thought*, (April 2012).

[707] This excerpt is from a text entitled "Cute little occupation," in *Politika*, (February 13, 2007) which subsequently caused a heated debate.

[708] Predrag Marković, "Serbian Auto-chauvinism or Identification with the Aggressor," in *New Serbian Political Thought*, (April 2012).

Dragojević's film "St. George Slays the Dragon"[709] as an example of the harm that can be caused by auto-chauvinist cinema. The film represented Serbian soldiers as freaks, and the Serbian people as immoral scum.[710] Art should be descriptive and prescriptive, not anti-Serbian, Kecmanović opines. In this respect, Kecmanović suggests that "when someone constantly insists on demystifying and destroying myths, he engages in something that is intellectually shallow: a myth cannot be destroyed by reality, as no one has a true image of reality; a myth can only be destroyed by imposing a different type of myth."[711] Following the same line of thought, Pavlović put forward the idea that "the auto-chauvinists attack everything that the people view as sacred and as part of their historic-mythological tradition."[712] What is interesting here is that Serbian culture is taken to be a static, historically determined and non-evolving phenomenon throughout the First Serbia texts. Those who oppose the process of Europeanization and Serbia's accession to the EU on cultural and historical grounds base their arguments on the objective of preserving or protecting Serbian culture against something that is presented to be very different, confrontational and threatening.

Patriotism, national self-image and Kosovo

The extracts presented above are just a relevant sample of the ways in which culture, history and tradition have been instrumentalized simultaneously in assessing Serbia's position toward Europe and the West, but more importantly, in assessing the views on identity held by its inner elite structures. In relation to the question of Kosovo, in the "First" Serbia texts, *auto-chauvinism* is presented as self-injury and self-negation

---

[709] "St. George Slays the Dragon," is a 2009 Srdjan Dragojević film about the First World War in Serbia. The film stirred considerable controversy as it depicted veterans and invalids, as well as all able-bodied men in the village being recruited for combat. The film received a huge budget from the Republic of Serbia and Republika Srpska.

[710] Predrag Marković, "Serbian Auto-chauvinism or Identification with the Aggressor," in *New Serbian Political Thought*, (April 2012).

[711] Vladimir Kecmanović, "Serbian Auto-chauvinism or Identification with the Aggressor," in *New Serbian Political Thought*, (April 2012).

[712] Radoslav Pavlović, "Serbian Auto-chauvinism or Identification with the Aggressor," in *New Serbian Political Thought*, (April 2012).

because, in Kovačević's words, Kosovo is "the place where a nation was created." Questioning Kosovo is a self-defeating phenomenon.[713] The essential causal connection between the subject of Kosovo and the construction of "patriotism" in the First Serbia writings is evident from the texts. The last section of this chapter is dedicated to a detailed analysis of the political themes of Kosovo which are employed in the "First" and "Other" Serbia texts. Kosovo, in these writings, is treated as an idea, a concept and a phenomenon, it is an imagined place in the discourse on identity in which First Serbia continuously reproduces the narrative of patriotism. In a similar key, Kovačević finds that:

> A claim is often made that the Serbian public is divided with regard to Kosovo. An artificial dilemma is constructed on whether a "U-turn"[714] is needed or we need to defend the emotional and statesmanlike approach based on the premise that Kosovo is where we all come from, that we are not orphans, and that our nicest poems and our nicest churches were created out of the bones of our ancestors. Kosovo shows us the direction in which we should take our offspring.[715]

As is obvious from the above, the imagined "Kosovo" provides a valuable example of the symbolic battleground. Whichever images of Kosovo one concentrates on, in the First Serbia texts, one locates the national trajectory and each argument is about the "true identity of the nation," which is the essentialist stronghold. Thus, the highly embedded symbolism of Kosovo is often instrumentalized to suggest the circular rhetoric of patriotism. Moreover, themes of the fear of losing identity with Kosovo's independence, the perceived loss of control of the European integration process and as a consequence rising skepticism toward Europe, the inability of the Serbian model to deal with cultural diversity within its own society, and the return of the extreme right to the political scene, were all found to cast a shadow on the First Serbia texts.

---

[713] Siniša Kovačević, "Serbian Auto-chauvinism or Identification with the Aggressor," in *New Serbian Political Thought,* (April 2012).

[714] "U-Turn" or "Turnover" (Serbian: Preokret) was a political coalition in Serbia, headed by Čedomir Jovanović from the Liberal Democratic Party. The coalition participated in the 2012 Serbian parliamentary election, receiving 6.52% of the popular vote.

[715] Siniša Kovačević, "Serbian Auto-chauvinism or Identification with the Aggressor," in *New Serbian Political Thought,* (April 2012).

Conclusion

This chapter has explored the concept of "auto-chauvinism," principally through an examination of the text "Serbian Auto-chauvinism or Identification with the Aggressor" published in *New Serbian Political Thought* in 2012. Identity necessarily concerns a relation between Self and Other; "Othering" is, as Beyza notes, an important activity in the construction of collective identities.[716] Given this assumption, this study also explores whether "Othering" Europe, and each other, is a continuous strategy in the discursive construction of collective Serbian identity. If othering is a significant discursive strategy, this chapter addressed what characteristics and nature of this Otherness are attributed to, first each other, and then "Europe," in First and Other Serbia discourses. Othering very often involves the ascription of varying degrees of negativity to out-groups. However, in this study of the Serbian debate on identity in post-Milošević Serbia, I have shown that negative predication of Other Serbia is a salient feature of the First Serbia oppositional discourse on Europe. Simultaneously, First Serbia is a defining feature of the Other Serbia discourse on Serbian identity. In this negative identification, the First Serbia discourse continually uses comparisons of the Other Serbia with the European "aggressor" and finds it to be self-identified with that which is different, strange, aggressive and threatening, that is, with Europe. In this process of narrativization of the Serbian Self, the questions of what First and Other Serbia discursive actors mean by nationalist, patriot or traitor has been addressed through analysis of their public debates. "Nation," "national ideology" and "nationalism" are all rearticulated as equivalent to "national interests" in the First Serbia discourse, while at the same time, these terms are asserted to be the principal difficulty associated with facing the past in the Other Serbia discourse. Thus, the meanings of each of these individual notions remain deeply contested, unstable and unfixed. The way they are constructed in these opposing discourses means that these terms obtain their meaning only in strict relation to what they are not. In the First Serbia discourse,

---

[716] Tekin C. Beyza, *Representations and Othering in the Discourse: The Construction of Turkey in the EU Context* (Amsterdam: John Benjamins, 2010), p. 34.

"the past" is strictly constructed as the traditional Serbian trajectory, the story of the historical losses, the Kosovo cycles, the Byzantine narratives, with an emphasis on Orthodox geopolitical belongings. The "past" as an issue is not circulated within the public simply because it serves as an arousing set of stories and narratives. The past is debated to arouse public sentiment to support certain political policies. As Davis argues, nationalist movements tend to lean on the restorative function, which actively seeks to re-establish society's links to a glorified past that has been ruptured by "inauthentic" groups such as unpatriotic elites, external occupiers, treacherous minorities, and political dissidents.[717] Not so long ago, the success of the Milošević regime was achieved primarily by utilizing the framework of a glorified past to ensure loyalty and support from nationalist social strata. Finally, I draw a conclusion from this analysis: that the framing of the "Serbs" and "Europe" in post-Milošević political discourses is inextricably linked to nationalist and anti-nationalist political interests.

---

[717] Eric Davis, *Memories of State: Politics, History, and Collective Identity in Modern Iraq* (Berkley, CA: University of California Press, 2005), p. 58.

Conclusion

Is the past over yet?
The evolution of Serbian national identities

In October 2015 the British ambassador to Serbia, Denis Keefe, demonstratively left the Sava Centre in Belgrade, where the Progressives (SNS) were celebrating the seventh anniversary of the founding of their party, seemingly in response to a speech given by famous Serbian film director Emir Kusturica. Kusturica said:

> Kosovo represents the largest instance of political plunder in the recent history of Europe. There has not been anything like it since the amputation of the Sudetenland from Czechoslovakia. Kosovo marks the beginning of a new imperialism, whereby the old-style vassals that used to sit in tents were moved to Hyatt and Regency hotels and were sat in front of microphones to relate that it is better to be a slave than a pharaoh. It was the English that always led the way with these sorts of ideas. Therefore, my dear Aleksandar Vučić, it is no coincidence that it was the English foreign minister that brought you the news that joining Europe means recognizing Kosovo's independence. It was written in books that a long time ago, during the Ottoman Empire, the English lords sent reports from Istanbul to the Queen Mother that described the Serbs as little Russians of Europe.[718]

One can see how, in the complex game of identity politics, all sides use history for political ends. The film director confirms that the question that is continually being repeated concerns the constant presence of the two world superpowers, the USA and Russia, and the ongoing imaginary Cold War that continues within the Serbian mind-set. The definition of Serbian national identity has been central to much of Serbian foreign policy and public debate over more than two decades. Serbia has, since 1945, been a divided nation of fervent partisans and scattered monarchists, continuously preoccupied with bitter debates over its own history and identity, to an extent that scarcely has parallels elsewhere. I

---

[718] After the intervention of members of SNS, Keefe returned to the celebrations. However, the Russian ambassador, Aleksandar Čepurin, got the biggest ovation. See "SNS's Celebration: The Ambassador of Great Britain to Serbia Denis Keefe Demonstratively left the Belgrade's Sava Centre" in *Blic* (October 17, 2015). http://www.blic.rs/Vesti/Politika/599162/PROSLAVA-SNSa-Ambasador-Britanije-napustio-salu-dok-je-govorio-Kusturica.

have asked what kind of national pride, established patriotism or civic nationalism could be acceptable after Srebrenica and the massacres of the Yugoslav wars. I have sought to set these debates into broader perspective, locating the unique case of the fractured Serbian identities within the wider context of national identity formation.

Milošević left behind two Serbias. "First" and "Other" Serbia identity narratives have been conceptualized as two different responses to the idea of the modern political and national community. One Serbia, partisan, Yugoslav, with the legacy of modernization, internationalism and unresolved crimes. The other, victimized, mostly nationalist and monarchist, with many fervent members in the diaspora and with mass support from the rural nationalists and the Orthodox clergy. Both, in different ways, claimed to be the "better Serbia": the keeper of the true values of the past and the future. For this reason, this book has taken the First and Other Serbia public debates and their construction of "Europe" as two case studies. This has been done by exploring the First and Other Serbia actors' discursive strategies of differentiation with regard to the nation, Europe and the interrelationships that exist between them. In the existing literature, political and cultural elites' construction of the nation, and the intelligentsia's narratives of Europe and Serbian identity, have been largely neglected in the analysis of post-Milošević Serbian politics. Likewise, little attention is paid to the interplay between the different constructions of Europe and Serbian identity on the one hand, and the interests and identities of the two main political factions on the other. This study fills this gap in the literature. Of course, Serbian national identity could have been approached from a different angle, with chapters organized and written differently, or with examples drawn from other sources. It is my hope that this book, at least, clarified the ways of approaching this intrinsically complex issue.

Since the fall of Milošević, the public sphere in Serbia has demonstrated the essential characteristic whereby its main actors are engaged in rethinking their political identities and renegotiating their meanings. Even as the writing of this book was coming to an end, the Serbian public sphere continued to be largely characterized by an unstable combination of the two main discourses: First Serbia's anti-West narratives, in part similar to those of the Milošević era, and Other Serbia's ambiguous, but consistent, narrative bemoaning the lack of inherent Serbian European identity. I have asked whether the past in the Balkans will ever be allowed to rest. Or will it find a new voice in newer generations, inspired by the new dominant political conservatism? When the Progressives won power in May 2012, many from the older generation felt relief at the more nationalist drift of Vučić's conservatism. The new generation of politicians expressed the idea that it might be time to reappropriate the past, and to feel fully proud once more to be Serbian. It was this popular chord that the political center right struck with such resonance as to expand their support. Yet few could have predicted that the Progressives would embrace so wholeheartedly such fierce and aggressive pro-EU politics, discard their previous isolationist and nationalistic inclinations and take the advantage on European integration. Did Aleksandar Vučić take the Other Serbia political program? One thing is certain—his politics are not supported either by the majority of First or Other Serbia. For a few months after the Progressives won the elections in 2012, and the unconditional turn in domestic and foreign policy toward the EU, it appeared that there was a chance for the past to finally become history. That, of course, did not happen. The Progressives in Serbia do not really support Europe's ideological human rights project, instead EU membership is construed as offering a response to a sense of economic crisis. The new historical realities with the Progressives in power have put forward new identity constructs. Vučić's discourse on Europe employs one principal strategy: he presents the lack of attachment to Europe as a viable threat to Serbian national interests. This idea, of course, can be found in some parts of Other Serbia, as well as in the newly-reformed grouping of pro-European First Serbians. Their message is that with its prospective EU membership, Serbia could be economically stable, distinguished and even a leader in the region. In such a discourse, Serbia is seen as undeniably European and expresses characteristics and values in common with its EU neighbors, and the EU is seen as a forum within which Serbian interests can be exercised. As a result, Europe creates an environment where a number of Serbian national identity characteristics can be strengthened: openness, creativity and innovation, to name but a few. Vučić has stressed many times that, "Serbia's place is in Europe, and Serbia has to reject the ideological approach to progress ... because in Europe there is space for the right and for the left and for the centre politics but not for "us" and "them," nor for haters, or hate.[719] Vučić's stance on Europe includes national identity, together with a sense of pragmatism and rationalism—in stark contrast to the myth-laden anxieties and emotionalism of old First Serbia. Since the Progressives pledged the platform of the aggressive Europeanism, the interrelations between states are increasingly regarded in the light of the pragmatic necessity. Subsequently, the main jargon of idealistic nationalism is replaced by a rational realism. Serbia's relationship toward the EU is now seen as a matter-of-fact reality which will advance national interests in the future. Europe will always be our neighbor. In Croatia, Bulgaria, Greece and Serbia, identity was always shaped by its presence. Such a very commonsense approach is not the dominant view among either left-wingers or right-wingers of First or Other Serbia, but it recognizes the inevitability of accession to the EU. Such a position always stands in contrast to the scare-mongering and hysteria of First Serbia anti-Europeans. Accordingly, this book puts forward that although the Serbian government's official stance is normatively pro-European at the moment, the empirical findings suggest that difference, discontinuity and disruption have, more often than not, punctuated the discourses of First and Other Serbia. Regarding the Progressive's politics of global influence, one can see friendships reaching as far as the Middle East, the Indian subcontinent and China which help to position Serbia in a more worldwide context. It has to be said that new Progressive 'First' Serbia does not want to be inward-looking any longer, instead it wants a greater influence outside of the sphere of Europe, and to function as a global player once more as did Yugoslavia back in the days of the polarized, Cold War world. Still, this foreign policy inclination is not always constructed as a threat to Serbia's European path, but as a means to forge

---

[719] In December 2015, Serbia opened the first chapters in the negotiations with the EU. See "Vučić: Najrevolucionarniji dan u novijoj srpskoj istoriji," CDM News, (December 14, 2015). http://www.cdm.me/svijet/region/vucic-najrevolucionarniji-dan-u-novijoj-srpskoj-istoriji

greater connections worldwide. Here, I would argue that two further readings on Serbia arise from such a position. The first is Serbia as a international initiative. The influence which Serbia has via the Non-Aligned Movement has proved to be a thing of relevance in the present and not a mere relic of the past. The ability for these relationships to retain any significant influence is very much attached to the configuration of new Progressive Serbia as an emerging global nation that can connect the Far East and the West. Secondly, once again as was the case during the Cold War, Serbia can be a kind of world power. This is an evolving and fresh concept but it will become more evident with time in the way Serbia, in new 'First' Serbia Progressive discourse, is being configured as a more domineering and ambitious entity. Such transnationalism builds upon the legacy of Yugoslav foreign policy and is presented as a challenge to European supremacy. For instance, Vuk Jeremić's politics[720] in the aftermath of Kosovo's independence aligns with such transnational policymaking.[721] It is a risky strategy as it further enfranchises the government in Serbia by providing it with the tools with which they can exercise economic or cultural power beyond the grip of the West. This may lead Serbia into unexplored territory. This new narrative finds its voice within the echelons of First Serbia that belong to the relative new Progressive influences, however, the stronger voices within the elites themselves have a nationalist and isolationist orientation. These are largely made up of factions from old DSS circles who demand that Serbia must depend on its own economic neutrality and independent sovereignty. It is clear, nevertheless, that such a demand hides the economic interest of further rapprochement with the Russian Federation and possible closer economic cooperation with other countries of the East. The Progressive's political platform reveals the shifting nature of

---

[720] Jeremić was the Minister of Foreign Affairs at the time, and his lobbying included traveling to countries such as Brazil, Argentina, Chile, Peru, Egypt, South Africa, Ghana, Nigeria, Mexico, Indonesia, Singapore, Philippines, Pakistan, Iran and Oman, to name but a few.

[721] Serbia forged a new partnership with China that doesn't stop at economic co-operation but also includes close political partnership. In 2014 alone, Belgrade signed 13 agreements and memoranda with Beijing regarding finance, infrastructure, telecommunications and transport. See "Don't leave Serbia to Russia and China, *EuObserver*, Berlin (March 27, 2015) https://euobserver.com/opinion/128157

political actors in the Serbian public sphere. Strangely enough, the Progressive's positive platform on Europe has so far been coupled with social conservatism, media privatizations, and occasional panic around a non-existent coup-d'etat. This can be viewed as comparable with some of the choices made in Milošević's Serbia, which in turn raises the question of whether the repertoires of difference and otherness have changed, or if traces of earlier representations remain intact in contemporary Serbian society.

My research time frame, unfortunately, did not allow me to include a detailed consideration of development of certain type of liberal nationalism by Progressive Serbia. This book has explored whether there is genuine discursive continuity with the pre-2000 public sphere Milošević-era narratives in First Serbia as well as in Other Serbia discourses on identity and "Europe." Here, discursive methodology has been used as it is appropriate for a study interested in how "facts" about Europe are reproduced by the liberal and nationalist intelligentsia. This is due to the fact that discursive methodology can account for continuities and shifts of articulations of ever-changing national identity. This work has found that the essence of dispute between the main actors of First and Other Serbia can be traced first to the issues of victimization of Serbia and Serbian responsibility/guilt for the Yugoslav wars. Here the Serbs are interchangeably seen as both the main "victims" and as the main "perpetrators." Second, the essence of dispute can be traced to diverging, almost ambivalent attitudes toward Europe, or the West, which are seen either as a "friend," comparable to the Serbian Self, or as an "enemy," i.e. a radical and significant Other. Although the main affiliates of First and Other Serbia are presented as opposing each other, I put forward that the symbiosis of their relationship is clear: they help create each other's political identities and justify each other's political concepts.

Results of research

Writing this book on the Serbian national identity felt, in many ways as one imagines one would feel participating in the pursuit of the Holy Grail. The topic is never-ending, peculiar, irregular and non-conforming. I have shown that national identity in the aftermath of a decade of the

Milošević regime appears not to have an unchanging essence, and I have displayed the processes and the factors that contributed to its continual and intense fluctuation. It is evident that the elites and the new governments, in order to recreate the fresh collective entity, engaged extensively with both the collective past, in this case the Yugoslav conflicts, and some vision of a common future within the EU. The noise and the quarrel left after the disagreements between First and Other Serbia suggested that binding elements of their common legacy and destiny are not easily identifiable. I shall briefly review the peculiarities of the Serbian case in light of these broader reflections. My research has suggested that the failure of Other Serbia civil actors to appropriate an integrated model of political community, which would link Serbian national identity with the European system of values, has been an impediment to achieving democratic maturity and European integration. Instead, images of Europe have become those of self-imposed exclusion. In this sense, unlike most empirical studies of discourse analysis, this book has been concerned with contestation in which both parties characterize each other and themselves in their texts. As noted in Chapter 1, I put forward the idea that construction of national identity is only possible through simultaneous delineation of something which is different or "Other," an idea which is central to my research. In this respect, the greater emphasis has been on the ways in which "First" Serbia constructs "Other" Serbia and "Other" Serbia interprets "First" Serbia. In Chapters 3, 4, 5 and 6 my goal was to examine whether patterns of self-exclusion have changed, or indeed if the Other Serbia discourse follows the same established patterns of Self-othering in the post-2000 public sphere as in the pre-2000 period. In this sense, the purpose of this work has been, by applying a discursive approach, to reveal the structures of the dominant discourse, in this instance the First Serbia discourse, which act both as constraints or enablers in respect of all political actors/discursive agents. This method is particularly useful for the Serbian case, and this book was interested in clearly identifying the basic discourse of First Serbia upon which the discourse of Other Serbia, and the discourse on "Europe" and identity, are built.

"First" Serbia's return to national symbols during transition

The general issues are clear. 2014 brought the centenary of the outbreak of the First World War, which was marked by the unveiling of a commemorative plaque in Niš. Current Labor Minister Aleksandar Vulin, said that Serbia never caused any wars, but that it was often dragged into wars started by "insatiable kings and empires" against its own will. He added "Serbia was always on the side of light and freedom and was never on the wrong side." Both Vulin's and Vučić's speeches seemed to be often indulging in the narrative of victimization"[722] Of course, such interpretations of history raise additional questions about Gavrilo Princip, Bosnian Serb assassin of Archduke Franz Ferdinand in Sarajevo in 1914, who for some is a hero and for others in the former Yugoslav region is a terrorist. Thus, the discursive practices of First Serbia narratives throughout the 1990s internalized the heroic victim, and externalized the more powerful enemy, be it the Turks, the West or Europe. This main narrative was established in the early 1990s, and has now been reshaped and re-interpreted, but remains the key framework within which is presented Serbia's impalpable past. Such constant recollection of the past is so profound in the 'First' Serbia discourse that these essentialist arguments about patriotism and faith have often been instrumentalized in such discourses to play a significant part in the story of 'who Serbs ought to be'. Thus, Progressive 'First' Serbia offers the exclusivist narrative of nationhood. However, additionally, when the nation's elite splits into First and Other Serbia, and each opposes and abhors the other, how can Serbs distinctively reclaim and reinterpret a common heritage? I have argued that First Serbia's discursive continuity with Milošević-era narratives has manifested itself in two distinct ways. First, it is evident that the discourse on "victims and perpetrators" continued to function in the same historical framework. Second, as the images and perceptions of Europe were persistently challenged and contested this resulted in the development of what Heuser and Buffet have called a myth of special

---

[722] Marija Ristić, "Serbia Marks "Heroic" WWI Centenary," in *Balkan Insight* (July 28, 2014). http://www.balkaninsight.com/en/article/serbia-marks-start-of-ww1

relationships, in this case with Russia.[723] In the case of First Serbia, this is evident in the political orientation, which leans openly toward Russia. This observation also supports my finding that Orthodox Christianity appears to be a major constitutive element of Serbian identity as seen through the prism of the more conservative First Serbia discourse. In this respect, it is clear that religious differences contribute greatly to the Otherness of Europe in First Serbia texts. Since 2000, the power of national populist parties has continued to rely on First Serbia's social support for their agendas and their opposition to international integration. The strength of such populists has remained in their ability to continue to monopolize the framework of national identity as a force of resistance to international influence and European integration. The delayed transition and EU integration processes have been an important development, particularly in view of the fact that more than seven years after Kosovo's declaration of independence, the territory's sovereignty continues to remain contested between Serbs and Albanians, keeping the issue determinedly at the center of the political debate in both Priština and Belgrade. Following Dragović-Soso's analysis of how the intellectual opposition came to define the "Kosovo question" in the 1980s, consequently turning it away from its liberal, universalist aspirations toward a more narrow nationalist agenda,[724] this research concurs with that view and notes that the Kosovo question looks set to cause a similar outcome yet again. What is new here is this study's demonstration of the fact that Kosovo is the contextual background for the post-2000 Serbian discourses on Europe. I have suggested that the Serbian idea of Europe, of domestic political agendas, of recent transformations, and of the national crisis in 2008 caused by Kosovo's declaration of independence, were all echoed in the First and Other Serbia discourses on prospective EU accession. The fear of conceivable identity loss due to Kosovo's independence, rising Euroskepticism and the inability of the Serbian state model to deal with the cultural diversity in society, were all found to cast a

---

[723] For myths of special relationships see: Beatrice Heuser, and Cyril Buffet, *Haunted by History: Myths in International Relations* (Oxford: Berghahn, 1998), p. 260.

[724] Jasna Dragović-Soso, *"Saviours of the Nation": Serbia's Intellectual Opposition and the Revival of Nationalism* (London, Hurst and Montreal: McGill-Queen's University Press, 2002), p. 32.

shadow on the First Serbia discourse. Accordingly, this work has thoroughly analyzed these elements as its contextual background. In this respect, this book has demonstrated that First Serbia texts exemplify the construction of the European Other as having divergent values in respect of issues including the Yugoslav dissolution and Kosovo's independence. First Serbia affiliates constructed Europe as a supranational political body that continually wants to take something away from Serbia. What is presented here is a complex history of dissonance and dissent. Modern Serbs were led to believe that they had collectively been the innocent victims of history when in fact they have been active participants. Serbs lost the wars, were bombed by NATO, witnessed the exodus of the young educated people of their nation, and all of that was accompanied by surviving nationalism. Yet, for most of the population, the simultaneous processes of understanding the genuine, factual past and the reinterpretation of that past by the nationalists, was overly complicated by the process of surviving the political present. From this distance, it seems that many of those who lived through the 1990s want to forget it, and new generations do not come to maturity with a desire to explore this mantra of victimhood toward the past. Some of First Serbia's myths are self-defeating: once supported by the regime, now these myths, such as the myth of innocence and that all the villains were (and are) in the West, are failing to fully resonate with the Serbian population. When the visa liberalization came in 2008 alongside the agreement with the Schengen countries, Serbian citizens could travel, allowing them to see the striking dissonances between the official views, on the one hand, and the real first-hand experiences of Europe on the other. Still, most young people do not travel and many believe it is necessary, due to the myth of innocence, to be tremendously proud to be Serbian. They are exhausted with having Srebrenica apparently "shoved down their throats" all the time; most of them simply want to be allowed to be normal, freed from the demanding legacies of Serbian history and its recent past.

"Other" Serbia:
Sustaining the anti-nationalist orientation

Quite contrarily, the "Other" Serbia associates came to believe that it is quite impossible, indeed impermissible, to be proud to be Serbian. Theirs is the view that the history of Serbia should not be "normalized" until one acknowledges the confessions of responsibility and the guilt for the wars in the 1990s. Other Serbia associates see themselves as responsible for keeping these memories alive. Yet the sheer scale of Other Serbia insistence on this may well have been counterproductive, as many became more and more fed up with the insistence on the heavy burdens of responsibility for the recent past. Other Serbia took a very different direction than First Serbia toward a more cosmopolitan, competitive, but at the same time often overtly moralistic orientation, involved in a constant defense of the pillars of the newly-founded democracy. Former member of LDP and a prominent public Other Serbia figure, Nenad Prokić, tried to explain the current phenomenon of national identity:

> A single national policy needs to be set based on national interests, not changed on a daily basis. After the collapse of Yugoslavia, toothless petty thieves and gangsters were declared heroes. Currently we are not sure if Mladić was a hero or a war criminal, and since we did not make a decision about it at a state level everyone has the right to think what they like. But once that decision is made at a state level, then we will know how to behave and what sort of history textbooks to print. Still, we seem to be far from resolving this issue. Currently we are not able to say exactly who we are, where we are, where our borders lay, and we cannot even fix a simple trajectory of where we want to go. Say we decide to go toward the West: if that is our choice, then we will have to do certain things which we do not particularly want to do to get there. If, however, we choose Russia, we will still have to do some other things we do not want to do. You cannot have it both ways, both apples and oranges. The main consequence of this lack of clarity in our state policies is the lack of clarity in our minds. Another consequence is the fact that there is a great deal of disorganization in our society.[725]

What relationship is proposed between Serbia and Europe? The European idea in Serbia was never completely developed into a coherent narrative and European values never fully internalized and thus Serbs always

---

[725] Nenad Prokić, "Yugoslavia has Fallen Apart so We Can all Buy Stuff at Lidl," (July 23, 2015). http://www.bastabalkana.com/2015/06/zasto-se-jugoslavija-raspala-nenad-prokic/

remained rather reluctant Europeans. Secondly, this work has analyzed the way in which the regime change of 2000 brought about the consequence of Other Serbia's and the democratic intelligentsia's acceptance of responsibility for the acts of the Milošević state apparatus during the 1990s. More importantly, post-2000 disagreements about the Hague Tribunal and the legacy of the 1999 NATO intervention further contributed to the Other Serbia differences of opinion on joining the EU. I have put forward that the perceived harshness of the EU's conditions resulted in Other Serbia elites questioning whether the pro-European parties and coalitions intend to tap into already existing pro-European public sentiment. Their appeal to follow the "European road" was sidelined by the democratic elites' decision to build their political programs and manifestos along the lines of the split in Other Serbia. This division was also apparent in the party politics of the democratic bloc. The soft liberal narrative about the past is best represented politically by the Democratic Party of Boris Tadić, whereas the hard-line position is best represented by the Liberal Democratic Party of Čedomir Jovanović. In terms of Kosovo, soft liberal elites have chosen Tadić's dual track objective of "Kosovo in Serbia and Serbia in Europe,"[726] which was touched upon in Chapter 4. The end result is that parties on the liberal end of the democratic spectrum have yet to validate a narrative on Europe and Serbian identity that diverges in any tangible way from that appropriated by the nationalist parties. The continued use by the Democratic Party of similar narratives on Kosovo shows that they must have adhered to these principles in order to gather electoral support. This book strongly advocates that until a favorable European narrative is constructed that is appropriated by the Other Serbia intelligentsia as well as by the wider population, the ethnocentric narratives of the Milošević era will continue to dominate the Serbian public sphere, albeit in a slightly differing format. Joining the European Union has been the official national preference and was at the top of the civil society agenda in the aftermath of the 2000 elections. But, on the other hand, the European idea was never completely developed and fully internalized. Subotić rightly suggests that this came about as a consequence of Other Serbia's inner disagreements

---

[726] Tadić, Boris, *Entering Europe with our identity*, B92 News, (December 12, 2009).

about the role played by the EU and the West in Serbia's overall democratic transition.[727] The post-Milošević political and cultural elites of Other Serbia have attached various meanings to Europe as well as to the Self (the Serbian state), in which the new political discourses are rearticulations of those of the 1990s. In Other Serbia texts, the Serbian state (Self) is represented as not European (civilized), and the favorable link between Europe and Serbia is lacking. This position concurs with the assumed hierarchy in which the West or Europe is superior to the East or the Balkans as in the Western *Balkanist* discourses. As argued in Chapter 5, these particular identity narratives originate from the Other Serbia discourse which was constituted during the Milošević years. In fact, I have established that much of Other Serbia's identity since the 1990s has derived from the fact that the Serbian post-communist intellectuals, amidst war and Milošević's authoritarianism, have searched for the particular meaning to give their group a common or collective identity. In fact, Pešić defines what others have failed to notice: that Other Serbia gathers around the "doubt that it is Serbia at all."[728] In this respect, I have argued that Other Serbia actors produce and construct their discourses, but at the same time these actors are themselves products of the values, norms and social exclusion that exist in those discourses. In this way, Other Serbia political and societal affiliates helped construct and further strengthen the normative framework in which they operate. As shown in Chapter 4, the anti-First Serbia identity constituted the behavior of these actors in the 1990s, but at the same time the existence of such a strong anti-nationalist platform simultaneously constrained it. However, after 2000, the legitimacy of "being European" has not been measured against the criteria of whether individuals advocated human rights or European values, but against fulfilling the EU conditions for candidacy and membership. The narrative on Europe is still incomplete and is being written. Other Serbia figure, Nenad Prokić, contends that for the, "failure of the October 5, 2000 revolution, the citizens of Serbia

---

[727] Jelena Subotić, "Europe is a State of Mind: Identity and Europeanization in the Balkans," *International Studies Quarterly*, 55, (2011), p. 309–330.

[728] Vesna Pešić, "Istorijski i društveni akteri" (Historical and Social Actors), in *Druga Srbija deset godina posle: 1992–2002 (Other Serbia Ten Years Later: 1992–2002)*, edited by Aljoša Mimica, (Helsinški odbor za ljudska prava, 2002), p. 59.

need to thank the Democratic politicians as they turned out to be mere thieves, a bunch of corrupt hoodlums who damaged the country and destroyed all that was good about the ideas of October 5. It was the Democratic Party that did it. They have stolen anything that could be stolen. They have ruined a good cause. We thought that Milošević was our enemy and that they were on our side. They pilfered, they did nothing, they were incompetent, they employed friends and family in state-run companies and institutions, they did all the bad things that one can think of. Therefore, we have to ask ourselves: if the revolution of October 5, 2000 did nothing to improve its protagonists, how could it improve the society as a whole? That is why October 5, 2000 remains but an imaginary date in Serbian history. It actually never happened."[729] It is taken for granted in identity studies, that shared historical memories form integral elements in the construction of a strong sense of national identity. From Prokić's statement it is clear that most Serbians cannot agree what October 5 means to them. Are there any other days that have more symbolic meaning than that day? What are the main commemorations that are regularly re-enacted that help to form powerful common bonds across society? What is more emotionally significant— June 28 or March 9, 11, 12, or 24?[730] Every March, Serbians go through a minefield of exploding sensitivities, in which no simple or widely-accepted story about the nation's recent history is endorsed. These days in March, the days of atonement and possible reconciliation, days of sadness, reveal a lot about values and emotions supported by at least those who organize the ceremonies of remembrance. However, the construction of the perceptions and attitudes toward the recent past always serves the interests of a particular version of identity. March 9 remembrance is organized by Vuk Drašković, March 12 by hardline actors of Other Serbia and March 11 and 24 is organized by First Serbia affiliates. As a consequence, the

---

[729] Nenad Prokić, "Yugoslavia has Fallen Apart so We Can all Buy Stuff at Lidl," (July 23, 2015). http://www.bastabalkana.com/2015/06/zasto-se-jugoslavija-raspala-nenad-prokic/

[730] On March 9, 1991, there were unsuccessful demonstrations against the media control of the Milošević regime. On March 11, 2006, Slobodan Milošević died. On March 12, 2003, Prime Minister Zoran Djindjić was killed, and on March 24, 1999, the NATO intervention started.

political as well as emotional power here is transformed into symbolic power, power that has an ability to alter how we see the past. In that way political elites constantly reinterpret and rearticulate elements of identity narratives in new political contexts and in ways which strengthen First and Other Serbia ideological positions within the discursive/political field.

Disparate visions of "Europe" in the Serbian elites: change and continuity

Does this never-ending soul-searching offer any hope for eventual resolution? There are many possible avenues through which these questions could be approached. In the chapters above, I have chosen selected examples from "First" and "Other" Serbia debates, selected for their vocabulary of different forms of historical belonging and different public representations of the past. It is these fractured identities that prevented the Serbs from accepting any single narrative about their past, and which also contributed to the fact that they cannot agree to simply forget about it. The ambition of this work was: first, to present the constructivist scholarship on identity formation and difference; second, to outline the discourse analytical methodology which accompanies it; and, finally, to bring the two together in a textual analysis of the First and Other Serbia debate on "Europe." Furthermore, one further objective of this work was to explore the representations that First and Other Serbia elites' hold with regard to the nation, the EU and Europe as well as the interrelationships that exist between them. To this end, as Kaldor notes, for many people the term "Europe" has had an almost mythical significance; it was considered synonymous with civilized behavior and emblematic of an alternative "civic" outlook to which those who opposed nationalism aspired.[731] However, in contrast to this habitual idea of Europe, I argue that the available scholarship cannot fully account for the diversity in the cases of various states on the EU's periphery, such as Serbia. Thus, the available constructivist or culturalist studies cannot entirely account for the Serbian case, as scholars have failed to develop a

---

[731] Mary Kaldor, *New and Old Wars*, (Cambridge: Polity, 2006), p. 13.

theoretical account that can explain how and why these different modes of differentiation coexist in the context of the EU periphery. In this sense, Wilkinson notes that there is a presumption that European understandings of society and the state are universal.[732] Therefore, the Serbian case illustration forms an empirical critique which highlights how theoretical shortcomings result from a simplified and Westernized description of the situation that does not take into account the specific local sociopolitical context. This is why I have addressed the diverse argumentation schemes of discursive actors in which they try to justify and legitimize their decisions to support or oppose Serbia's European perspective, portraying "Europe" as a source of friendship or enmity. Also, this work has explored the practices of differentiation implicated in the confrontation between Self and Other, and their different modes of figuration. Does today's Serbia replicate the Milošević-era discourses in terms of externalizing difference and legitimizing a violent relationship with its Other/s or has it succeeded in constructing a political community where Self/Other distinctions are unclear not only within the community but also in relation to its outside, i.e. Europe? This book has put forward the notion that in Serbia the constitutive role of Otherness is most often perceived as emerging from radical difference or a particular relation of negativity. However, demonizing the Other, and perceiving it as a radically negative entity, as Rumelili rightly notes, is a choice made by the perceiver rather than an inherent necessity.[733] Bearing this remark in mind, this book has broken with the general application found in the literature, and has argued that a constitutive role does not necessarily arise from radical difference alone.

To summarize, I have argued that the First Serbia discourse on Europe and identity is the dominant discourse in the Serbian public sphere. Its discursive formation of "nation, Church, God" is, in my view, political, because the processes of framing "different Europe" is political, and because the decisions for or against effecting undesired European inte-

---

[732] Claire Wilkinson, "The Copenhagen School on Tour in Kyrgyzstan: Is Securitization Theory Useable Outside Europe?" *Security Dialogue,* 38, no. 1, (March 2007), p. 6.

[733] Bahar Rumelili, "Constructing Identity and Relating to Difference: Understanding the EU's mode of differentiation," *Review of International Studies*, 30, no.1, (January 2004), p. 35.

gration, are political decisions. It could be said that the First Serbian Self is constituted through its difference to the European Other and Other Serbians, constructed as being genuine, categorical and even undisputable. By juxtaposing the events of the Second World War , the bombing of Belgrade in 1941 and the 1999 NATO intervention, First Serbia actors connect them and imply that they are equivalent, presenting them as part of one continuous "European" and "Western" policy toward Serbia. In the right-wing discourse, the Western and European Other is quite often constructed as *arrogant, brutal* and *aggressive*, which is a recognized stereotypical image of the Other. The image of "Europeans" abusing the "proud, naïve and genuine" Serbs shows the power and persistence of an idealized and idyllic rural narrative that includes anti-European and anti-colonial themes. Serbian identity and culture are taken as static, historically determined and non-evolving phenomena throughout the First Serbia discourse. Those who oppose the process of Europeanization and Serbia's accession to the EU on cultural and historical grounds base their arguments on the objective of preserving or protecting this culture against something which is, in their view, very different and confrontational, that is, Europe.

To sum up the findings of Chapter 4, it can be said that the First Serbian Other is constituted through its difference to Europe and Other-Serbians, and is much maligned, and even demonized in the Other Serbia texts. Older stereotypical images are still being reproduced overtly, in the same uncompromising manner as in the 1990s. Negative identification is very strong, to the extent that it almost makes First Serbia look like the "ultimate Other" to being "European" in Serbia. The nationalistic Other emerges as a would-be internal source of destabilization, existing within the identity of the dominant term, that is European/civilized identity. This is the way in which the Serbian candidacy for EU membership was initially perceived by many, including Srdja Popović as a "proof of possible reformation."[734] The mere existence of First Serbia, the nationalist Other in Serbia today, disturbs the "civilizational order" by simply being Other/there. The narrativization of the Serbian

---

[734] Srdja Popović, "Čas anatomije" (the Class of Anatomy) in *Peščanik Series* (June 1, 2007).

Self constructed in this particular way implies an emphasis on the existence of the obstinate binary dilemma. Also, it is interesting that Progressive First Serbia portrayals of "Europe" end up varying significantly from newspaper to newspaper and from journal to journal. Hence, I have suggested that their construction of Europe in the Serbian public space differs according to the intended audience. This is potentially problematic as these different constructions may cause different conceptions and expectations of Europe which may constitute a serious impediment to the progress of the European project in Serbia. "Europe" as an image and representation has always been in motion, but the fact is that the European Other has consistently served as a mirror for delineating particular elements of Serbianness. My research shows that in the late 1990s, and especially after 2000, the Serbs engaged with these images of the European Other (as well as the Turkish, American and Russian Other) in order to define their proper Selves, and to delineate what is Serbian and what is not. I argue that the recent debates on identity and Europe are a continuation of the Serbian tradition of geopolitical deliberation. The issue of Europe is instrumentalized in order to discuss domestic political issues, serving merely as a vehicle to defend and elaborate on the particularities of Serbian identity itself. In these ongoing constructions in First and Other Serbia discourses, I have identified the fact that the continuation of past images, historical explanations and representations, that existed before 2000, is widespread and rampant. In fact, historical events are not identical in the discourses of both the opponents and supporters of EU accession.

Direction for further research

This research project opens a number of options for further research. Future research could be developed in two main directions. The first possibility is to look further at the methodology and include a variety of different sources. In this respect, it would be interesting to include new media types, including film, but also particularly the internet, as the limitations of this research did not allow much scope for this. The motivation for including films and documentaries into potential new research is that they have become the measure of thrust and credibility, and thus play a significant role in the production and reproduction of societal identities and in the affirmation or contestation of perceptions and attitudes.[735] As Reisigl notes, analysis of the visual semiotics and visual narratives of films and their orientation contributes to an understanding of the representational meaning of the images.[736] By including these new types of analysis, future research would be able to detect alternative discourses to those of "First," "Other" and "Third" Serbia. The question is what possible alternative discourses there are to those that already exist. Can these alternative Third and Fourth Serbias remain unassimilated by the hegemonic discourses of First and Other Serbia while remaining compatible with the democratic identity of the Serbian state?

The second interrelated domain would look into the Self/Other nexus. It would be interesting to explore further the manner in which liberal and illiberal values are constituted and whether some additional discourses on "Europe" would allow for the positive articulation of difference between Self and Other/s. However, given that identity is constructed upon difference, the next conflict may be expected to be "simulated" outside official state institutions by peripheral political actors. For this reason, I have not presented these constitutive dimensions of First and Other Serbias as an exhaustive list, nor have I claimed to have provided a list which captures all possible variations of the self/other relationship which can ever be drawn in any case study. In this respect, the process of differentiation is not finite in the sense that it is a closed process. For example, the images of "Serb" or "European" accumulate meanings, or play their meanings off against one another across a variety of texts and media.

Finally, I find that First and Other Serbia's choice on "Europe" is somewhat absurd. As Radomir Konstantintinović notes in his *Philosophy of Parochialism* back in 1969, the Balkans spirit of 'parochialism' antithetical to modern subjectivity.[737] Bjelić notes Konstantinović's *palanka* (small

---

[735] See Martin Reisigl, "Analyzing Political Rhetoric," in Ruth Wodak and Michal Krzyzanowski, eds., *Qualitative Discourse Analysis in the Social Sciences* (Basingstoke: Palgrave Macmillan, 2008), p. 77.

[736] Ibid., p. 90.

[737] Radomir Konstantintinović, *Philosophy of Parochialism,* (Nolit, Belgrade, 1969).

town) is a "reactionary placenta of tribal habits, traditions and self-enclosure, and it is also a cognitive error as it rejects rationality or anything beyond the sensual experience".[738] Therefore, the choice between First and Other Serbia is a false choice. It is a choice between absorption of modernity presented as alien by Other Serbia, and return to the simulated authenticity of (ethnic or religious) origins as seen by First Serbia. This is indeed an intolerable position, and it is crucial to investigate what further possibilities exist for transcending this unfeasible choice. This work intends to be part of those developments which have the potential to destabilize and deconstruct this dualist logic between First and Other Serbia. This book has both engaged the conceptual vocabulary to theorize this unfeasible interplay and hopefully provided a model which captures it empirically. Thus, while the subject of this book concerns history and national identity in Serbia in the aftermath of Milošević, a complementary goal is to raise wider questions about these issues in principle, with relevance to other countries and other nations in the region. Ongoing acerbic debates over national identity and the political misuse of history are of course not a peculiarly Serbian phenomenon.

---

[738] Dušan I. Bjelić, *Normalizing the Balkans: Geopolitics of Psychoanalysis and Psychiatry* (Ashgate, 2011), p. 104.

Bibliography

PRIMARY SOURCES

Antonić, Slobodan. "Misionarska inteligencija u današnjoj Srbiji" (Missionary Intelligentsia in Today's Serbia). *Vreme*, no. 631, February 5, 2003.

Glišić, Vladan, "Questions of Serbian Identity." February 2006, Belgrade. *Srpski Sabor Dveri*. Accessed February 10, 2006. http://www.dverisrpske.com/sr-CS/index.php.

Druga Srbija, edited by A. Mimica. (Beogradski Krug, Beograd. 1992).

Druga Srbija—deset godina posle: 1992–2002 (Other Serbia: Ten Years Later: 1992–2002). Helsinski odbor za ljudska prava, 2002.

Kostunica, Vojislav. *Political Manifesto of Democratic Party of Serbia* (DSS). Accessed January 19, 2012. http://dss.rs/category/govori-i-analize/.

Mihailović, Kosta and Vasilije Krestić. *Memorandum: Odgovori na Kritike* (*Memorandum: The Answer to Criticism*). Beograd: SANU, 1995, 99–149.

Milosavljevic, Olivera. *Tačka Razlaza* (*Point of Departure*). Helsinske Sveske, Br.16. from 2003.

"Serbian auto-chauvinism or identification with the aggressor." Series of interviews published in *New Serbian Political Thought*, April 2012.

ARTICLES

Aliu, Fatmir. "Serbia and Kosovo to Resume Talks Soon." *Balkan Insight*, February 17, 2012.

Allcock, John B. "Rural-urban Differences and the Break-up of Yugoslavia." *Balkanologie 6*, no. 1–2, (2002): 101–134.

Anastasakis, Othon. "The Europeanization of the Balkans." *Brown Journal of World Affairs*, 7, no. 1, (2005): 77–88.

Anastasakis, Othon and Dimitar Bechev. *EU Conditionality in South East Europe: Bringing Commitment to the Process*. Post-conference paper published by South East European Studies Programme, European Studies Centre, St. Antony's College, University of Oxford (2003).

Antonić, Slobodan. "Izvorna i projektovana Srbija" (Genuine and projected Serbia). *Pečat*, March 2, 2010. http://www.pecat.co.rs/2010/03/slobodan-antonic-izvorna-i-projektovana-druga-srbija-i/.

Antonić, Slobodan. "Misionarska inteligencija u današnjoj Srbiji" (The missionary intelligentsia in Contemporary Serbia). *Vreme*, No. 631, February 5, 2003.

Antonić, Slobodan. "Odgovor Popovu i Dereti" (An answer to Popov and Dereta). *Vreme*, No. 640, April 10, 2003.

Arsenijević, Vladimir and Andrea Pisac. "An Accidental Serb." *Index of Censorship*, no. 38 (2009): 140. http://ioc.sagepub.com/cgi/content/abstract/38/3/140.

Baer, J. "Imagining Membership: The Conception of Europe in the Political Thought of T.G. Masaryk and Vaclav Havel." *Studies in East European Thought* 52, no. 3, (2000): 203–226.

Banac, Ivo. "What Happened in the Balkans (or Rather ex-Yugoslavia)?" *East European Politics and Societies*, no. 23, (2009).

Bakić-Hayden, Milica and Robert M. Hayden. "Orientalist Variations on the Theme 'Balkans': Symbolic Geography in Recent Yugoslav Cultural Politics." *Slavic Review* 51, no. 1 (1992).

Batić, Vladan. "Ljudi i vreme: izjava nedelje" (People and Time: Week Review). *Vreme*, No. 587, April 4, 2002.

Bećković, Matija. "Kosovo je najskuplja srpska reč" (Kosovo is the most expensive Serbian word). *Glas Crkve: časopis za hrišćansku kulturu i crkveni život* (Voice of the Church: Magazine for Christian Culture and Church Life), (1989): 19–28.

Benchev, Dimitar. "Constructing South East Europe: The Politics of Regional Identity in the Balkans." *Ramses Working Papers*, No. 1/06, March 2006. http://www.sant.ox.ac.uk /esc/ramses/bechev.pdf.

Bieber, Florian. "Nationalist Mobilization and Stories of Serb Suffering: The Kosovo Myth from 600th Anniversary to the Present" *Rethinking History* 6, no. 1 (2002): 95–110.

Bieber, Florian. "The Serbian Opposition and Civil Society: Roots of the Delayed Transition in Serbia." *International Journal of Politics, Culture and Society* 16, (2003): 73–90.

Birch, S. "The 2000 Elections in Yugoslavia: the 'Bulldozer *Revolution*' " in *Electoral Studies: an International Journal* 21, no. 3 (2002): 499–511.

Blagojević, Mirko. "Desecularization of Contemporary Serbian Society." *Religion in Eastern Europe* 28, no. 1 (2008): 37–50.

Bougarel, Xavier. "Yugoslav Wars: The 'Revenge of the Countryside' between Sociological Reality and Nationalist Myth." *East European Quarterly* 32, no. 2 (1999): 157–175.

Bowles, S. and H. Gintis. "Persistent Parochialism: Trust and Exclusion in Ethnic Networks." *Journal of Economic Behavior and Organization* 55, no. 1 (2004): 1–23.

Brubaker, R. and F. Cooper. "Beyond 'identity'." *Theory and Society* 29, no. 1 (2000): 1–47.

Budding, A. H. "Yugoslavs into Serbs: Serbian National Identity, 1961–1971." *Nationalities Papers* 25, no. 3 (1997): 407–426.

Debeljak, Aleš. "Cosmopolitanism and National Tradition: The Case of Slovenia." *International Journal of Politics, Culture, and Society* 17, no. 1 (2003).

Đelić, Božidar. "We Won't be Blackmailed into Giving up National Interests." *B92 News, Kosovo Status*, 30, October 2011.

Dević, Ana. "Anti-War Initiatives and the Un-Making of Civic Identities in the Former Yugoslav Republic." *Journal of Historical Sociology* 10, no. 2 (1997).

Diez, T. " 'Speaking Europe': The Politics of Integration Discourse." *Journal of European Public Policy* 6, no. 4 (1999): 598–613.

Diez, T. 2001. "Europe as a Discursive Battleground: Discourse Analysis and European Integration." *Cooperation and Conflict* 36, no. 1 (2001): 5–38.

Dijk, Teun A. van. "Principles of Critical Discourse Analysis." *Discourse and Society* 4, no. 2 (1993): 249–283.

Dijk, Teun A. van, ed., "The Study of Discourse: An Introduction." *Discourse Studies* 5, (2007): xix-xlii.

Dorian, Jano. "From 'Balkanization' to 'Europeanization': The Stages of Western Balkans Complex Transformations." *L'Europe en formation*, No. 349–350, (2008).

Doty, R. L. "Aporia: A Critical Exploration of the Structure-Agent Problematique in International Relations Theory." *European Journal of International Relations* 3, no. 3 (1997): 365–392.

Doty, R. L. "Foreign Policy as Social Construction: A Post-Positivist Analysis of US Counterinsurgency Policy in the Philippines." *International Studies Quarterly* 37, no. 3 (1993): 297–320.

Dragović-Soso, Jasna. "Apologising for Srebrenica: The Declaration of the Serbian Parliament, the European Union and the Politics of Compromise." *East European Politics* 28, no. 2 (2012): 163–179.

Dragović-Soso, Jasna. "Rethinking Yugoslavia: Serbian Intellectuals and the 'National Question' in Historical Perspective." *Contemporary European History* 13, no. 2 (2004): 170–84.

Dutu, Alexandru. "National Identity and Tensional Factors in South Eastern Europe." *East European Quarterly* 31, no. 2 (1997): 195.

Edmunds, Timothy. "Adapting to Democracy: Reflections on 'Transition' in Serbia and the Western Balkans." *Western Balkan Security Observer*, No. 7/8, October 2007.

Edmunds, T. "Illiberal Resilience in Serbia." *Journal of Democracy* 20, no. 1 (2009): 128–142.

Ejdus, Filip. "Security, Strategic Culture and Identity in Serbia, in Western Balkans." *Security Observer*, No. 7, October-December 2008.

Emerson, Michael. "Russia and the West." *ESF Working Papers (Closed)*, 2004.

Erjavec, K. and Z. Volčić. "The Kosovo Battle: Media's Recontextualisation of the Serbian Nationalistic Discourses." *Harvard International Journal of Press/Politics* 12, no. 3 (2007): 67–86.

Erjavec, K. and Z. Volčić. "We Defend Western Civilization—Serbian Representations of a Cartoon Conflict" in *ICMR/Islam and Christian-Muslim Relations* 19, no. 3 (2008): 305–321.

Fleming, K. E. "Orientalism, the Balkans, and Balkan Historiography." *The American Historical Review* 105, no. 4 (2000): 1218–1233.

Fraser, Nancy. "Rethinking the Public Sphere: A Contribution to the Critique of Actually Existing Democracy" in *Social Text*, no. 25/26 (1990): 56–80.

Freyburg, Tina and Solveig Richter. "National Identity Matters: The Limited Impact of EU Political Conditionality in the Western Balkans" *Journal of European Public Policy* 17, no. 2 (2010): 262–280.

Friedner, M. "Identity Formation and Transnational Discourses: Thinking Beyond Identity Politics." *Indian Journal of Gender Studies* 15, no. 2 (2008): 365–385.

Gil-White, Francisco J. "How thick is blood? The plot thickens . . .: If Ethnic Actors are Primordialists, What Remains of the Circumstantialist/Primordialist Controversy?" *Ethnic and Racial Studies* 22, no. 5 (1999): 789–820.

Glenny, Misha. "Stojan Cerovic: Brave Serbian Journalist Unafraid of Milošević." *The Guardian*, Saturday March 26, 2005.

Greenhill, B. "Recognition and Collective Identity Formation in International Politics." *European Journal of International Relations* 14, no. 2 (2008): 343–368.

Guillaume, X. "Foreign Policy and the Politics of Alterity: A Dialogical Understanding of International Relations." *Millennium* 31, no. 1 (2002): 1–26.

Guzina, Dejan. "Socialist Serbia's Narratives: From Yugoslavia to a Greater Serbia." *International Journal of Politics, Culture and Society* 17, no. 1 (2003): 91–111.

Guzzini, S. "A Reconstruction of Constructivism in International Relations." *European Journal of International Relations* 6, no. 2 (2000): 147–182.

Haenens, L. "Euro-Vision: The Portrayal of Europe in the Quality Press." *Gazette* 67, no. 5 (2005): 419–440.

Halikiopoulou, D., K. Nanou, and S. Vaslopoulou. "The Paradox of Nationalism: The Common Denominator of Radical Right and Radical Left Euroscepticism." *European Journal of Political Research* 51, no. 4 (2012): 504–539.

Hammond, Andrew. "Balkanism in Political Context: From the Ottoman Empire to the EU." *Westminster Papers in Communication & Culture* 3, no. 3 (2006): 6–26.

Hansen, L. and M. Williams. "The Myths of Europe: Legitimacy, Community and the 'Crisis' of the EU." *Journal of Common Market Studies* 37, no. 2 (1999): 133–149.

Harmsen, Robert and Thomas M. Wilson. "Introduction: Approaches to Europeanization." *Yearbook of European Studies*, no. 14 (2000): 13–26.

Hauser, Gerard. "Vernacular Dialogue and the Rhetoricality of Public Opinion." *Communication Monographs* 65, no. 2 (1998): 83–107.

Hristić, Zoran. "Provociranje građanskog rata: Moć, pretnje" (Provoking a Civil War: Power, Threats) in *NIN*, December 27, 1996.

Hülsse, Rainer. "Imagine the EU: The Metaphorical Construction of a Supra-nationalist Identity." *Journal of International Relations and Development* 9, no. 4 (2006): 396.

Hyder Patterson, Patrick. "On the Edge of Reason: The Boundaries of Balkanism in Slovenian, Austrian, and Italian Discourse." *Slavic Review* 62, no. 1 (2003): 110–141.

Iveković, I. "Nationalism and the Political Use and Abuse of Religion: The Politicization of Orthodoxy, Catholicism and Islam in Yugoslav Successor States." *Social Compass* 49, no. 4 (2002): 523–536.

Jackson, Thomas. "Demonization and Defence of the Serbs: Balkanist Discourses During the Break-up of Yugoslavia." *Slovo* 16, no. 2 (2004): 107–124.

Jansen, S. "National Numbers in Context: Maps and Stats in Representations of the Post-Yugoslav wars." *Identities: Global Studies in Culture and Power* 12, no. 1 (2005): 45–68.

Jansen, S. "Victims, Underdogs and Rebels: Discursive Practices of Resistance in Serbian Protest." *Critique of Anthropology* 20, no. 4 (2000): 393–420.

Jeremić, Vuk. "Ovation, Then Apology, for Serbian Song." *New York Times*, January 17, 2013.

Jeremić, Vuk. "Kosovo is our Jerusalem." *Nova Srpska Politička Misao* (New Serbian Political Thought), March 17, 2011.

Judah, Tim. "At Last, Good News from the Balkans" in *The New York Review of Books*, March 11, 2010.

Kandić, Nataša. "Losing ground." *Guardian*, May 9, 2007. http://www.theguardian.com/commentisfree/2007/may/09/natashakandic

Kandić, Nataša. "Neprijatelj u Srbiji—otvorenost, snaga i integritet nekoliko žena" (Enemies in Serbia—openness, strength and integrity of a handful of women) in *Vreme*, No. 607, August 22, 2002.

Kantner, C. "Collective Identity as Shared Ethical Self-Understanding: The Case of the Emerging European Identity." *European Journal of Social Theory* 9, no. 4 (2006): 501–524.

Kitromilides, P.M. 1989. " 'Imagined Communities' and the Origins of the National Question in the Balkans." *European History Quarterly* 19, no. 2 (1989): 49–192.

Kostovičova, Denisa and Vesna Bojičić-Dželilović. "Europeanizing the Balkans: Rethinking the Post-Communist and Post-Conflict Transition." *Ethnopolitics* 5, no. 3 (2006): 223–241.

Krašovec, Primož. "Rasizam kao ideologija i autorasizam" (Racism as an Ideology and Auto-racism). *Mreža antifašistkinja Zagreba (Network Anti-facist Zagreb)*, 26 November, 2014. http://maz.hr/index.php/%20tekstovi/clanci/42-primoz-krasovec-rasizam-kao-ideologija-i-autorasizam

Kubik, Jan and Amy Linch. "The Original Sin of Poland's Third Republic: Discounting 'Solidarity' and its Consequences for Political Reconciliation." in *Polish Sociological Review*, 153, no. 1 (2006).

Melčić, D. "Communication and National Identity: Croatian and Serbian Patterns." *Praxis International: A Philosophical Journal* 13, no. 4 (1994): 354.

Meunier, Sophie. "Globalization and Europeanization: A Challenge to French Politics." *French Politics* 22, no. 2 (2004): 125–150.

Mijatović, Boško. "Nije lako biti za Evropu" (It is not easy to be in favor of Europe). *Politika*, September 17, 2008: 32.

Milanovic, Branko. "Glas protiv pregovora sa EU" (A voice against negotiations with the EU). *Politika*, April 17, 2008.

Miller, Nicholas J. "Children of Cain: Dobrica Ćosić's Serbia." *East European Politics and Societies* 14, no. 2 (2000): 268–187.

Miller, Nick. "Postwar Serbian Nationalism and the Limits of Invention." *Contemporary European History* 13, no. 2 (2004): 151–169.

Milosavljević, Dragan. "Povratak 'Otpisanih' " (The Return of "Otpisani") in *Nova Srpska Politička Misao (New Serbian Political Thought)*, May 6, 2003.

Milosavljević, Olivera. "Antibirokratska revolucija 1987–1989. Godine" in *Dijalog povjesničara/istoričara* 8 (Zagreb: Friedrich Naumann Stiftung, 2004).

Milosavljević, Olivera. "Tačka Razlaza: povodom polemike vođene na stranicama Vremena" (The Moment of Parting Ways: With Regards to the Debate in Vreme) in *Helsinške Sveske*, no. 16, (2003) Helšinski odbor za ljudska prava u Srbiji.

Morus, Christina. "The SANU Memorandum: Intellectual Authority and the Constitution of an Exclusive Serbian 'People'." *Communication and Critical/Cultural Studies* 4, no. 2 (2007): 142–165.

Mylonas, C. "Serbian Orthodox Fundamentals: The Quest for an Eternal Identity." *The American Historical Review* 109, no. 3 (2004): 1001–1002.

Naumović, S. "On 'Us' and 'Them': Understanding the Historical Bases and Political Uses of Popular Narratives on Serbian Disunity." *CAS Sofia Working Paper Series*, Issue 1, (2007): 13.

Naumović, Slobodan. 2005. "The social origins and political uses of popular narratives on Serbian disunity." *Filozofija i društvo (Philosophy and Society)* 26, (2005): 65–104.

Neumann, Iver B. "European identity, EU expansion, and the integration/exclusion nexus." *Alternatives: Global, Local, Political* 23, no. 3 (1998): 397–416.

Neumann, Iver B. and Jennifer M. Welsh. "The Other in European Self-Definition: An Addendum to the Literature on International Society." *Review of International Studies* 17, no. 4, (1991): 327–348.

O'Brennan, John. "The EU in the Western Balkans: Enlargement as Empire? A Response to David Chandler." *Global Society* 22, no. 4 (2008): 507–518.

Patterson, Patrick Hyder. "On the Edge of Reason: The Boundaries of Balkanism in Slovenian, Austrian, and Italian Discourse." *Slavic Review* 62, no. 1 (2003): 110–141.

Pešić, Vesna. "Serbian Nationalism and the Origins of the Yugoslav Crisis." *USIP Peaceworks* no. 8 (1996): n.p.

Purcell, Darren and Janet E. Kodras. "Redrawing the Balkan Image of Slovenia." *Information, Communication & Society* 4, no. 3 (2001): 341–369.

Radaelli, Claudio. "Whither Europeanization? Concept stretching and substantive change." *European Integration Online Papers* 4, no. 8 (2000): n.p. http://eiop.or.at/eiop/texte/2000-008.htm.

Ramet, Sabrina P. "The Denial Syndrome and Its Consequences: Serbian Political Culture since 2000." *Communist and Post-Communist Studies* 40, no. 1 (2007): 41–58.

Ristić, Irena. "Serbian Identity and the Concept of Europeanness." *Panoeconomicus* 54, no. 2 (2007): 185–195.

Roudometof, V. "Invented Traditions, Symbolic Boundaries, and National Identity in Southeastern Europe: Greece and Serbia in Comparative Historical Perspective (1830–1880)." *East European Quarterly* 32, no. 4 (1998): 429–468.

Rumelili, Bahar. "Constructing Identity and Relating to Difference: Understanding the EU's Mode of Differentiation." *Review of International Studies* 30, no. 1 (2004): 27–47.

Sakwa, R. "The Problem of 'The International' in Russian Identity Formation." *International Politics* 49, no. 4 (2012): 449–465.

Schmidt, V. H. "Oversocialised Epistemology: A Critical Appraisal of Constructivism." *Sociology* 35, no. 1 (2001): 135–158.

Sekulić, D., G. Massey, and R. Hodson. "Who Were the Yugoslavs? Failed Sources of a Common Identity in the Former Yugoslavia." *American Sociological Review* 59, no. 1 (1994): 83–97.

Shigeno, Rei. "Nationalism and Serbian Intellectuals." *Perspectives on European Politics and Society* 5, no. 1 (2004): 135–159.

Štiks, Igor. " 'The Berlin Wall Crumbled Down upon Our Heads!': 1989 and Violence in the Former Socialist Multinational Federations." *Global Society* 24, no. 1, (2010): 91–110.

Štiks, Igor. "From Disintegration to European Integration: Nationality and Citizenship in the Former Yugoslavia." *Southeast European and Black Sea Studies* 6, no. 4 (2006): 483–500.

Stojanović, Dubravka. "An Explosive Device with a Delayed Effect." *Peščanik*, April 18, 2011. www.pescanik.net.

Stojić, Marko. "Between Europhobia and Europhilia: Party and Popular Attitudes Towards Membership of the European Union in Serbia and Croatia." *Perspectives on European Poitics and Society* 7, no. 3 (2006): 312–335.

Subotić, J. "Europe is a State of Mind: Identity and Europeanization in the Balkans." *International Studies Quarterly* 55, no. 2 (2011): 309–330.

Sverdrup, Ulf, and Stephan Kux. "Fuzzy Borders and Adaptive Outsiders: Norway, Switzerland, and the EU." *Journal of European Integration* 22, no. 3 (2000): 237–270.

Triandafyllidou, A. "Popular Perceptions of Europe and the Nation: The Case of Italy." *Nations and Nationalism* 14, no. 2 (2008): 261–282.

Triandafyllidou, A. "The Political Discourse on Immigration in Southern Europe: A Critical Analysis." *Journal of Community & Applied Social Psychology* 10, no. 5 (2000): 373–390.

Velikonja, Mitja. "In Hoc Signo Vinces: Religious Symbolism in the Balkan Wars 1991–1995." *International Journal of Politics, Culture, and Society* 17, no. 1 (2003): 25–40.

Vetta, Theodora "Revived Nationalism Versus European Democracy: Class and 'Identity Dilemmas' in Contemporary Serbia." *Focaal*, no. 55, (2009): 74–89.

Volčić, Z. "Belgrade vs. Serbia: Spatial Re-configurations of Belonging." *Journal of Ethnic and Migration Studies (JEMS)* 31, no. 4 (2005): 639–658.

Volčić, Z. "Blaming the Media: Serbian Narratives of National(ist) Identity." *Continuum: Journal of Media & Cultural Studies* 20, no. 3 (2006): 313–330.

Volčić, Z. "The Notion of 'The West' in the Serbian National Imaginary." *European Journal of Cultural Studies* 8, no. 2 (2005): 155–175.

Wendt, Alexander. "Anarchy is What States Make of it: The Social Construction of Power Politics." *International Organization* 46, no. 2, (1992): 391–425.

Wendt, Alexander. "Collective Identity Formation and the International State." *The American Political Science Review* 88, no. 2, (1994): 384–396.

Wetherell, M. "Positioning and Interpretative Repertoires: Conversation Analysis and Poststructuralism in Dialogue." *Discourse and Society* 9, no. 3 (1998): 387–412.

Wilkinson, Claire. "The Copenhagen School on Tour in Kyrgyzstan: Is Securitization Theory Useable Outside Europe?" *Security Dialogue*, 38, no. 1 (2007): 5–25.

Wilson, D. "Defending our Decadent West: The Meaning of Contemporary Atlanticism." *The European Journal: The Journal of the European Foundation* 4, no. 3 (1996): 22–23.

Woodward, Susan L. "Milošević Who? Origins of the New Balkans." In *The Hellenic Observatory, Discussion Paper No. 5*, 2001. The European Institute, London School of Economics & Political Science. http://eprints.lse.ac.uk/3328/1/Milošević_Who.pdf.

Žarković, Dragoljub. "Glava u Peščaniku, drugi put." *Vreme*, No. 782–783, December 29, 2005.

Žarković, Dragoljub. "Osam tačaka o slučaju Koraks." *Vreme*, No. 782–783, December 29, 2005.

Žitnik, Janja. "Statistical Facts are Human Fates: Unequal Citizens in Slovenia." *Journal of Ethnic and Migration Studies* 34, no.1 (2008): 77–94.

CHAPTERS

Altmann, Franz-Lothar. "Serbia's EU Membership and the Kosovo Issue." In *Serbia Matters: Domestic Reforms and European Integration*, edited by Wolfgang Petritsch, Goran Svilanović, and Christophe Solioz, 73–76. Paris, Vienna, Geneva: Nomos, 2009.

Bieber, Florian. "Territory, Identity and the Challenge of Serbia's EU Integration." In *Serbia Matters: Domestic Reforms and European Integration*, edited by Wolfgang Petritsch, Goran Svilanović, and Christophe Solioz, 65–72. Paris, Vienna, Geneva: Nomos, 2009.

Bieber, Florian. "The Other Civil Society in Serbia: Non-Governmental Nationalism." In *Uncivil Society? Contentious Politics in Post-Communist Europe*, edited by Petr Kopecky and Cas Mudde, 19–36. London: Routledge, 2003.

Biserko, Sonja. "Serbia's European Potential Crumbles." In *Serbia Matters: Domestic Reforms and European Integration*, edited by Wolfgang Petritsch, Goran Svilanović, and Christophe Solioz, 77–84. Paris, Vienna, Geneva: Nomos, 2009.

Bogdanović, Bogdan. "Ritualno ubijanje gradova" (The Ritual Killing of Cities). In *Druga Srbija*, edited by A. Mimica, Belgrade: Beogradski Krug, Plato, Borba, 1992.

Bowman, Glen. "Xenophobia, Fantasy and the Nation: The Logic of Ethnic Violence in Former Yugoslavia." In *Anthropology of Europe: Identity and Boundaries in Conflict*, edited by V. Goddard, J. Llober, and C. Shore, 143–171. London: Berg, 2004.

Carras, C. "Greek identity: A long view." In *Balkan Identities: Nation and Memory*, edited by M. Todorova, 294–326. London: Hurst, 2004.

Chilton, Paul and Christina Schaffner. "Introduction: Themes and Principles in the Analysis of Political Discourse." In *Politics as Text and Talk: Analytic Approaches to Political Discourse*, edited by Paul Chilton and Christina Schaffner, Amsterdam and Philadelphia: John Benjamins, 2002.

Citrin, J. and Sides, J. "More than Nationals: How Identity Choice Matters in the New Europe." In *Transnational Identities: Becoming European in the EU*, edited by R. Herrmann, M. Brewer, and T. Risse, 161–185. Lanham, MD: Rowman and Littlefield, 2004.

Ćosić, Dobrica. "1978 Inaugural Speech to the Serbian Academy of Sciences and Arts (SANU)" quoted in Dejan Jović, *Yugoslavia: the State that Withered Away*. Budapest: Central European Press, 2008.

Cyrus, Norbert. "Changing Rhetoric and Narratives: German Trade Unions and Polish Migrant Workers." In *Europeanization, National Identities and Migration, Changes in Boundary Constructions between Western and Eastern Europe*, edited by Willfried Spohn and Anna Triandafyllidou, London: Routledge, 2003.

David, Fillip. "Biti izdajnik" (To be a traitor). In *Druga Srbija*, edited by A. Mimica, Belgrade: Beogradski Krug, Plato, Borba, 1992.

Day, Dennis. "Being Ascribed, and Resisting, Membership of an Ethic Group." In *Identities in Talk*, edited by Charles Antaki and Sue Widdicombe, 151–170. London: Sage, 1998.

Đerić, Gordana. "Svakodnevne diskurzivne prakse o osobinama naroda i važnosti nacionalnog identiteta" (Daily discursive practices on national qualities and the importance of national identity). In *Politika i svakodnevni život: Srbija 1999–2002 (Politics and daily life: Serbia 1999–2002)*, edited by Zagorka Golubović, Ivana Spasić, and Đorđe Pavićević, 175–210. Belgrade: Institut za filozofiju i društvenu teoriju, 2003.

Dimitrijević, Nenad. "Srbija kao nedovršena država" (Serbia as an unfinished state). In *Između autoritarizma i demokratije: Srbija, Crna Gora i Hrvatska, Vol. II: Civilno društvo i politička kultura*, edited by D. Vujadinović, 57–73. Beograd: CEDET, 2004.

Dimitrijević, Nenad. "Words and Death: Serbian Nationalist Intellectuals." In *Intellectuals and Politics in Central Europe*, edited by Andras Bozoki, Budapest: Central European University Press, 1999.

Dimitrijević, Vojin. "Trouble Defining Serbia's National Interests." In *Serbia Matters: Domestic Reforms and European Integration*, edited by Wolfgang Petritsch, Goran Svilanović, and Christophe Solioz, 143–150. Paris, Vienna, Geneva: Nomos, 2009.

Dragović-Soso, Jasna. "Collective Responsibility, International Justice and Public Reckoning with the Recent Past: Reflections on a Debate in Serbia." In *The Milošević Trial—An Autopsy*, edited by Timothy Waters, Oxford: Oxford University Press, 2011.

Eder, Klaus. "Remembering National Memories Together: The Formation of a Transnational Identity in Europe." In *Collective Memory and European Identity: The Effects of Integration and Enlargement*, edited by Klaus Eder and Willfried Spohn, 197–220. Basingstoke, UK: Ashgate, 2005.

Fairclough, N., M. Reisigl, and R. Wodak. "Discourse and Racism: An Issue for Critical Discourse Analysis." In *The semiotics of racism: A Critical Discourse-Historical Analysis*, edited by R. Wodak, Vienna: Passagen 1998.

Gojković, Drinka. "The Birth of Nationalism from the Spirit of Democracy: The Association of Writers of Serbia and the War." In *The Road to War in Serbia*, edited by Nebojša Popov, Budapest: Central European University Press, 2000.

Gordy, Eric D. "Postwar Guilt and Responsibility in Serbia: The Effort to Confront It and the Effort to Avoid It." In *Serbia Since 1989: Politics and Society Under Milošević and After*, edited by Sabrina Ramet and Vjeran Pavlaković, 184–185. Seattle: University of Washington Press, 2005.

Grad, H., and L. M. Rojo. "Identities in Discourse: An Integrative View." In *Analyzing Identities in Discourse: Discourse Approaches to Politics, Society and Culture*, edited by R. Dolon, and J. Todoli, London: Routledge, 2009.

Habermas, Jürgen. "An Avantgardistic Instinct for Relevances: Intellectuals and their Public." In *Europe: The Faltering Project*, edited by Jürgen Habermas, Cambridge: Polity, 2009.

Hall, Stuart. "Ethnicity: Identity and Difference." In *Reframing Latin America: a cultural theory reading of the nineteenth and twentieth centuries*, edited by Erik Ching, Christina Buckley, and Angélica Lozano-Alonso, Austin, Texas: University of Texas Press, 2007.

Hamilton, Peter, "Heroes or Villains". In *Representation: Cultural Representations and Signifying Practices* edited by S. Hall, 223. Thousand Oaks, CA: Sage, 1997.

Hansen, Lene. "Introduction." In *European Integration and National Identity: The Challenge of the Nordic States,* edited by L. Hansen and O. Wæver, London and New York: Routledge, 2001.

Hudson, R. "Songs of Love and Hate: the Role of the Intelligentsia, Music and Poetry in Forging Serbian Ethnic National Identity." In *Why Europe?: Problems of Culture and Identity,* edited by Joe Andrew, Malcolm Crook, and Michael Waller, 167–181. Basingstoke: Palgrave Macmillan, 2000.

Jusić, Tarik. "Media Discourse and the Politics of Ethnic Conflict: the Case of Yugoslavia." In *Media Discourse and the Yugoslav Conflicts: Representation of the Self and Other,* edited by Pal Kolotø, London: Ashgate, 2009.

Kaelble, Hartmut. "European Self-Understanding in the Twentieth Century" in Eder, Klaus, and Willfried Spohn, eds. *Collective Memory and European Identity: The Effects of Integration and Enlargement* (Basingstoke, UK: Ashgate, 2005, 17–35).

Kesić, Obrad. "An Airplane with Eighteen Pilots: Serbia after Milošević." In Sabrina Ramet and Vjeran Pavlaković, eds., *Serbia Since 1989: Politics and Society Under Milošević and After.* 95–121. Seattle: University of Washington Press, 2005.

Kokosalakis, Nikos and Iordanis Psimmenos. "Modern Greece: A Profile of Identity and Nationalism." In State of the Art and Historical Reports—Representations of Europe and the Nation in Current and Prospective Member-States: Media, Elites and Civil Society, edited by Bo Strafh and Anna Triandafyllidou, Luxembourg: Office for the Official Publications of the European Communities, 2003.

Lazić, Mladen. "Od klasnog i nacionalnog monologa ka dijalogu" (From class and national monologue to dialogue). In *Druga Srbija,* edited by A. Mimica, Belgrade: Beogradski Krug, Plato, Borba, 1992.

Lazić, Mladen. "The Adaptive Reconstruction of Elites." In *Elites After State Socialism: Theories and Analysis,* edited by John Higley and György Lengyel, Boulder, CO: Rowman & Littlefield, 2000.

Listhaing, Ola, Kristen Ringdal, and Albert Simkus. "Serbian Civic Values in a European Context." In C*ivic and Uncivic Values: Serbia in the Post-Milošević Era,* edited by O. Listhaug, S. P. Ramet, and D. Dulić, Budapest: Central University Press, 2011.

Lyons, Carole. "The politics of alterity and Exclusion in the European Union." In *Europe's Others: European Law Between Modernity and Postmodernity,* edited by P. Fitzpatrick and J. H. Bergeron, Dartmouth: Dartmouth Publishing Company, 1998.

March, J. and Olsen, J. "The Logic of Appropriateness." In *The Oxford Handbook of Public Policy,* edited by M. Moran, M. Rein, and R. Goodin, 689–708. Oxford: Oxford University Press, 2006.

Matić, Jovanka. "The Media and Ethnic Mobilization: The Formula of Kosovo." In *Ethnicity in Postcommunism* Belgrade: Institute of Social Sciences, Forum for Ethnic Relations, 1996.

Mearsheimer, John, J. "Structural Realism." In *International Relations Theories: Discipline and Diversity*, edited by Tim Dunne, Milja Kurki, and Steve Smith, Oxford: Oxford University Press, 2006.

Milosavljević, Olivera. "The Abuse of the Authority of Science." In *The Road to War in Serbia*, edited by Nebojsa Popov, Budapest: Central European University Press, 2000.

Naumović, Slobodan. "Identity Creator in Identity Crisis: Reflections on the Politics of Serbian Ethnology." In *The Politics of Anthropology at Home*, edited by Christian Giordano, , Ina-Maria Greverus, and Regina Röhmhild, Münster: LIT Verlag, 2000.

Neumann, Iver B. "Russia and Europe." In *NUPI Conference Proceedings*, edited by J. Godzimirski, 1–26. March 4 1996.

Nikoliš, Gojko. "Koja je cena slobode?" (What is the price of freedom?) In *Druga Srbija*, edited by A. Mimica, Belgrade: Beogradski Krug, Plato, Borba, 1992.

Obradović-Wochnik, Jelena. "Revisionism, Denial and anti-ICTY Discourse in Serbia's Public Sphere: Beyond the 'Divided Society' Debate." In *Prosecuting War Crimes, Lessons and Legacies of the International Criminal Tribunal for the Former Yugoslavia*, edited by James Gow, Rachel Kerr, and Zoran Pajić, Abingdon, UK: Routledge, 2014.

Obradović–Wochnik, Jelena. "Strategies of Denial: Resistance to ICTY Cooperation in Serbia." In *War Crimes, Conditionality and EU Integration in the Western Balkans*, edited by Judy Batt and Jelena Obradović-Wochnik, Paris: Institute for Security Studies, 2009.

Perica, V. "The Sanctification of Enmity: Churches and the Construction of Founding Myths of Serbia and Croatia." In *Myths and Boundaries in South-Eastern Europe*, edited by P. Kolstø, 130–157. London: Hurst, 2005.

Perović, Latinka. "The Flights of Modernization." In *The Road to War in Serbia*, edited by Nebojša Popov, Budapest: Central European University Press. 2000)

Pešić, Vesna. "The War for Ethic States." In *The Road to War in Serbia* edited by Nebojša Popov, Budapest: Central European University Press, 2000.

Radić, R. "Serbian Orthodox Church and the War in Bosnia and Herzegovina." In *Religion and the War in Bosnia*, edited by P. Mojzes, 160–182. Atlanta, GA: Scholar Press, 1998.

Rajić, Ljubiša. "Srbija iz početka." (Serbia from the beginning). In *Druga Srbija*, edited by A. Mimica, Belgrade: Beogradski Krug, Plato, Borba, 1992.

Ramet, Sabrina P. "Serbia and Montenegro since 1989." In *Central and Southeast Euopean Politics since 1989*, edited by Sabrina P. Ramet Cambridge: Cambridge University Press, 2010.

Reisigl, Martin. "Analyzing Political Rhetoric." In *Qualitative Discourse Analysis in the Social Sciences*, edited by Ruth Wodak and Michal Krzyzanowski, 96–120. Basingstoke: Palgrave Macmillan, 2008.

Reus-Smith, C. "Constructivism." In *Theories of International Relations* edited by S. Burchill, Basingstoke: Palgrave, 1996.

Schimmelfennig, Frank and Ulrich Sedelmeier. "Introduction: Conceptualizing the Europeanization of Central and Eastern Europe." In *The Europeanization of Central and Eastern Europe*, edited by Frank Schimmelfennig and Ulrich Sedelmeier, 1–28. London: Cornell University Press, 2005.

Stavrakis, Yannis. "Passions of Identification: Discourse, Enjoyment, and European Identity." In *Discourse Theory in European Politics. Identity, Policy and Governance*, edited by David Howarth, and Jacob Torfing, 69–92. New York: Palgrave Macmillan, 2005.

Šušak, Bojana. "An Alternative to War." In *The Road to War in Serbia*, edited by Nebojša Popov, Budapest: Central European University Press, 2000.

Swoboda, Hannes. "Serbia and European Integration." In *Serbia Matters: Domestic Reforms and European Integration*, edited by Wolfgang Petritsch, Goran Svilanović, and Christophe Solioz, Paris, Vienna, Geneva: Nomos, 2009.

Tepavac, Mirko. "Da li je moguća Druga Srbija?" (Is Other Serbia even possible?). In *Druga Srbija*, edited by A. Mimica, Belgrade: Beogradski Krug, Plato, Borba, 1992.

Torfing, Jacob. "Discourse Theory: Achievements, Arguments, and Challenge." In *Discourse Theory in European Politics: Identity, Policy and Governance*, edited by David R. Howarth and Jacob Torfing, 1–31. Basingstoke: Palgrave Macmillan, 2005.

Vejvoda Ivan. "Civil Society versus Slobodan Milošević: Serbia 1991–2000." In *Civil Resistance and Power Politics: The Experience of Non-violent Action from Gandhi to the Present*, edited by Adam Roberts and Timothy Garton Ash, Oxford, New York: Oxford University Press, 2009.

Vejvoda, Ivan. "Logika konačnog rešenja." In *Druga Srbija*, edited by A. Mimica, Belgrade: Beogradski Krug, Plato, Borba, 1992.

Veličković, Vedrana. "Balkanisms Old and New: The Discourse of Balkanism and Self-othering in Vesna Goldsworthy's Chernobyl Strawberries and Inventing Ruritania." In *Facing the East in the West: Images of Eastern Europe in British Literature, Film and Culture*, edited by Barbara Korte, Eva Ulrike Pirker, and Sissy Helff, Amsterdam: Rodopi, 2010.

Velikonja, M. "Liberation Mythology: The Role of Mythology in Fanning War in the Balkans." In *Religion and the war in Bosnia*, edited by P. Mojzes, 20–42. Atlanta, Georgia: Scholar Press, 1998.

Vlahutin, Romana. "The European Union, the Western Balkans and Serbia: Can Things be Done Better?" In *Serbia Matters: Domestic Reforms and European Integration*, edited by Wolfgang Petritsch, Goran Svilanović, and Christophe Solioz, 55–64. Paris, Vienna, Geneva: Nomos, 2009.

Vuletić, Vladimir. "Serbia's Political Elite: Attitudes towards European Integration." In *Serbia Matters: Domestic Reforms and European Integration*, edited by Wolfgang Petritsch, Goran Svilanović, and Christophe Solioz, 85–92. Paris, Vienna, Geneva: Nomos, 2009.

Wæver, Ole. "European Integration and Security: Analyzing French and German Discourses on State, Nation, and Europe." In *Discourse Theory in European Politics: Identity, Policy and Governance*, edited by David R Howarth, and Jacob Torfing, 33–67. Basingstoke: Palgrave Macmillan, 2005.

Wæver, Ole. "Identity, Communities and Foreign Policy: Discourse Analysis as Foreign Policy Theory." In *European Integration and National Identity: The challenges of the Nordic States*, edited by L. Hansen, and O. Wæver, 20–47. London, New York: Routledge, 2001.

Wæver, Ole. "Security Analysis: Conceptual Apparatus." In *Security: A New Framework for Analysis*, edited by B. Buzan, O. Wæver, and J. de Wilde, 21–48. London: Lynne Rienner, 1998.

BOOKS

Aissaoui, Rabah. *Immigration and National Identity: North African Political Movements in Colonial and Postcolonial France*. London: Tauris Academic Studies, 2009.

Amanat, Abbas and Farzin Vejdani. *Iran Facing Others: Identity Boundaries in a Historical Perspective*. New York: Palgrave Macmillan, 2012.

Anderson, Benedict. *Imagined Communities: Reflections on the Origin and Spread of Nationalism*. London and New York: Verso, 1991.

Antonić, Slobodan. *Kulturni rat u Srbiji (The Cultural War in Serbia)*. Belgrade: Zavod za udžbenike, 2008.

Antonić, Slobodan. *Višijevska Srbija (The Vichy Serbia)*. Belgrade: Cigoja Štampa, 2011.

Anzulović, B. *Heavenly Serbia: From Myth to Genocide*. London: Hurst, 1999.

Arfi, Badredine. *Re-thinking International Relations Theory via Deconstruction*. London: Routledge, 2012.

Ashbrook, John. *Buying and Selling the Istrian Goat: Istrian Regionalism, Croatian Nationalism and EU Enlargement*. Brussels: Peter Lang, 2008.

Bakhtin, M. M. *The Dialogic Imagination: Four Essays*. Austin and London: University of Texas Press, 1981.

Barbullushi, Odeta. "The Politics of 'Euro-Atlantic Orientation': Political Identities Interests and Albanian Foreign Policy 1992–1997." PhD thesis, University of Birmingham, 2009.

Behnke, Andreas. *Re-Presenting the West: NATO's Security Discourse After the End of the Cold War*. Stockholm: Statsvetenskapliga institutionen, 2007.

Bhabha, Homi K. *Nation and Narration*. London: Routledge, 1990.

Bilić, Bojan. *We Were Gasping for Air: [Post-]Yugoslav Anti-War Activism and Its Legacy*. Baden Baden: Nomos, 2012.

Billig, Michael. *Banal Nationalism*. London and Thousand Oaks, CA: Sage, 1995.

Bjelić, Dušan and Obrad Savić, eds. *Balkan as Metaphor: Between Globalization and Fragmentation*. Cambridge: MIT Press, 2002.

Bloom, W. *Personal Identity, National Identity and International Relations*. Cambridge: Cambridge University Press, 1990.

Brisku, A. "Albanian and Georgian Discourses on Europe: From Berlin 1878 to Tbilisi 2008." PhD thesis, European University Institute, 2009.

Brisku, A. *Bittersweet Europe: Albanian and Georgian Discourses on Europe: from Berlin 1878 to Tbilisi 2008*. Oxford: Berghahn Books, 2013.

Brubaker, Rogers. *Nationalism Reframed: Nationhood and the National Question in the New Europe*. Cambridge: Cambridge University Press, 1996.

Buzan, Barry, Ole Wæver, and Jaap de Wilde. *Security: A New Framework for Analysis*. Boulder: Lynne Rienner, 1998.

Buzan, Barry and Ole Wæver. *Regions and Powers: The Structure of International Security*. Cambridge: Cambridge University Press 2003.

Byford, J. From "Traitor" to "Saint": Bishop Nikolaj Velimirović in Serbian Public Memory. Jerusalem: Hebrew University of Jerusalem, 2004.

Byford, J. Teorija zavere: Srbija protiv 'novog svetskog poretka' (Conspiracy Theory: Serbia vs. "The New World Order"). Belgrade: Beogradski centar za ljudska prava, 2006.

Campbell, David. National Deconstruction: Violence, Identity and Justice in Bosnia. Minneapolis, MN: University of Minnesota Press, 1998.

Campbell, David. Writing Security: United States Foreign Policy and the Politics of Identity. Minneapolis, MN and Manchester: University of Minnesota Press/Manchester University Press, 1998.

Campbell, David and Mort Schoolman, eds. The New Pluralism: William Connolly and the Contemporary Global Condition. Durham, NC: Duke University Press, 2008.

Calhoun, Craig. Nationalism as a Concept in Social Sciences. Buckingham, UK: Open University Press, 1997.

Calhoun, Craig. Nation Matters: Culture, History and the Cosmopolitan Dream. London: Routledge, 2007.

Castoriadis, Cornelius. World in Fragments: Writings on Politics, Society, Psychoanalysis, and the Imagination. Stanford: Stanford University Press, 1997.

Checkel, Jeffrey T. European Identity. New York, NY: Cambridge University Press, 2009.

Chilton, Paul. Analyzing Political Discourse: Theory and Practice. London: Routledge, 2004.

Chilton, Paul, and Christina Schäffner. Politics as Text and Talk: Analytic Approaches to Political Discourse (Amsterdam and Philadelphia: John Benjamins, 2002)

Cohen, Lenard J. Serpent in the Bosom: The Rise and Fall of Slobodan Milošević. Boulder, CO: Westview Press, 2001.

Cohen, Lenard J. and Jasna Dragović-Soso. State Collapse in South-Eastern Europe: New Perspectives on Yugoslavia's Disintegration. West Lafayette, Indiana: Purdue University Press, 2008.

Connolly, William. Identity/Difference: Democratic Negotiations of Political Paradox. Minneapolis, MN: University of Minnesota Press, 2002.

Clegg, S. R. Frameworks of Power. London, Thousand Oaks, CA and New Delhi: Sage Publications, 2002.

Čolović, Ivan. Bordel ratnika: folklor, politika i rat (The Warriors' Bordello: Folklore, Politics and War). Belgrade: Slovograf, 2000.

Čolović, Ivan. The Politics of Identity in Serbia. New York: NYU Press, 2002.

Davis, Eric. Memories of State: Politics, History, and Collective Identity in Modern Iraq. Berkley: University of California Press, 2005.

Dawson, James. Cultures of Democracy in Serbia and Bulgaria: How Ideas Shape Publics. London: Ashgate, 2014.

Delanty, Gerard. Inventing Europe: Idea, Identity, Reality. London: Macmillan Press, 1995.

Delanty, Gerard. Modernity and Postmodernity: Knowledge, Power, the Self. London: Sage, 2000.

Delanty, Gerard and Patrick O'Mahony. Nationalism and Social Theory: Modernity and the Recalcitrance of the Nation. London: Sage, 2002.

Delanty, Gerard, and Chris Rumford. *Rethinking Europe: Social Theory and the Implications of Europeanization.* London: Routledge, 2005.

Der Derian, J. and M. J. Shapiro, eds. *International/Intertextual Relations: Postmodern Readings of World Politics.* Lexington, Massachusetts: Lexington Books, 1989.

Derrida, Jacques. *Writing and Difference.* Chicago: University of Chicago Press, 1978.

Dijk, Teun A. van. *Discourse and Context: A Sociocognitive Approach.* Cambridge: Cambridge University Press, 2008.

Doty, Roxanne Lynn. *Imperial Encounters: The Politics of Representation in North-South Relations.* Minneapolis, London: University of Minnesota Press, 1996.

Dragojlović, N., ed. *Foreign Policy of Serbia: Strategies and Documents.* Belgrade: The European Movement, 2010.

Dragović-Soso, Jasna. *Saviours of the Nation: Serbia's Intellectual Opposition and the Revival of Nationalism.* London, Hurst and Montreal: McGill-Queen's University Press, 2002.

Duijzings, Gerlachus. *Religion and the Politics of Identity in Kosovo.* London: Hurst, 1999.

Dunne, Tim, Milja Kurki, and Steve Smith. *International Relations Theories: Discipline and Diversity.* Oxford: Oxford University Press, 2006.

Edmunds, Timothy. *Security Sector Reform in Transforming Societies: Croatia, Serbian and Montenegro.* Manchester: Manchester University Press, 2007.

Ejdus, Filip. *Democratic Security Sector Governance in Serbia.* Frankfurt am Main: Peace Research Institute Frankfurt, 2010.

Elias, Norbert. *The Established and the Outsiders: A Sociological Enquiry into Community Problems.* London: Sage, 1994.

Eriksen, Thomas Hylland. *Ethnicity And Nationalism.* London: Pluto Press, 2010.

Fairclough, Norman. *Critical Discourse Analysis.* Boston: Addison Wesley, 1992, 1995.

Fairclough, Norman. *Language and Power.* London: Longman, 2001.

Foucault, Michel. *The Archaeology of Knowledge.* London: Routledge, 1972.

Fowler, Roger. *Language in the News: Discourse and Ideology in the Press.* London: Routledge, 1991.

Fulbrook, Mary. *German National Identity after the Holocaust.* Cambridge: Polity, 2007.

Gibbins, Justin. *Britain, Europe and National Identity: Self and Other in International Relations.* Basingstoke: Palgrave Macmillan, 2014.

Gagnon, Valère Philip. *The Myth of Ethnic War: Serbia and Croatia in the 1990s.* Ithaca and London: Cornell University Press, 2004.

Galasińska, Aleksandra and Dariusz Galasiń. *The Post-communist Condition: Public and Private Discourses of Transformation.* Amsterdam and Philadelphia: John Benjamins, 2010.

Gellner, Ernest. *Nations and Nationalism.* Oxford: Blackwell, 1983.

Giddens, Anthony. *Modernity and Self-identity.* Cambridge: Polity, 1991.

Gilman, Sander L. *Difference and Pathology: Stereotypes of Sexuality, Race, and Madness.* Ithaca and London: Cornell University Press, 1985.

Goldstein, Judith and Robert O. Keohane, eds. *Ideas and Foreign Policy: Beliefs, Institutions, and Political Change*. Ithaca and London: Cornell University Press, 1993.

Goldsworthy, Vesna. *Inventing Ruritania: The Imperialism of the Imagination*. London: Yale University Press, 1998.

Gordy, Eric D. *The Culture of Power in Serbia: Nationalism and the Destruction of Alternatives*. University Park, Pennsylvania: Pennsylvania University Press, 1999.

Griffiths, Martin, ed. *International Relations Theory for the Twenty-First Century*. London: Routledge, 2012.

Hall, Brian. *The Impossible Country: A Journey Through the Last Days of Yugoslavia*. New York: Penguin Books, 1994.

Hall, S. *Representation: Cultural Representations and Signifying Practices*. Thousand Oaks, CA: Sage, 1996, 1997.

Hall, Stuart and Paul du Gay. *The Questions of Cultural Identity*. London: Sage Publications, 1996.

Hansen, Lene. *Security as Practice: Discourse Analysis and the Bosnian War*. London and New York: Routledge, 2006.

Heuser, Beatrice and Cyril Buffet. *Haunted by History: Myths in International Relations*. Oxford: Berghahn, 1998.

Hobsbawm, Eric and Terence Ranger, eds. *The Invention of Tradition*. Cambridge, New York: Cambridge University Press, 1983.

Holquist, Michael. *Dialogism: Bakhtin and His World*. London: Routledge, 2002.

Hopf, Ted. *Social Construction of International Politics: Identities and Foreign Policies*. Ithaca, London: Cornell University Press, 2002.

Hønneland, Geir. *Borderland Russians: Identity, Narrative, and International Relations*. Basingstoke: Palgrave Macmillan, 2010.

Honneth, Axel and Hans Joas, eds. *Communicative Action: Essays on Jürgen Habermas's The Theory of Communicative Action*. Cambridge: Polity, 1991.

Hosking, G. and G. Schöpflin, eds. *Myths and Nationhood*. London: Hurst, 1997.

Howarth, David R. and Jacob Torfing, eds. *Discourse Theory in European Politics: Identity, Policy and Governance*. Basingstoke: Palgrave Macmillan, 2005.

Hutchinson, John and Anthony D. Smith, eds. *Nationalism*. Oxford: Oxford University Press, 1994.

Ichijo, Atsuko. *The Balancing Act: National Identity and Sovereignty for Britain in Europe*. Exeter: Imprint Academic, 2008.

Inayatullah, Naeem and David Blaney. *International Relations and the Problem of Difference*. New York, London: Routledge, 2004.

Jakelić, Slavica. *Collectivistic Religions: Religion, Choice, and Identity in Late Modernity*. Farnham: Ashgate, 2010.

Jansen, S. *Antinacionalizam: etnografija otpora u Zagrebu i Beogradu (Anti-nationalism: The Ethnography of Resistance in Zagreb and Belgrade)*. Belgrade: Biblioteka XX Vek, 2005.

Jaspers, Karl. *The Question of German Guilt*. Fordham University press, New York, 2000.

Jenkins, Richard. *Social Identity*. London: Routledge, 2008.

Jović, Dejan. *Yugoslavia: the State that Withered Away*. Budapest: Central European Press, 2008.

Judah, T. *The Serbs: History, Myth and the Destruction of Yugoslavia*. New Haven, CT: Yale University Press, 2000.

Kaldor, Mary. *New and Old Wars*. Cambridge: Polity, 2006.

Kaplan, Robert D. *Balkan Ghosts: A Journey Through History*. London: Picador, 1993.

Kecmanović, Dušan. *Da li smo sišli s uma ili dokaži da si Srbin: o etnonacionalizmu i o nama (Are We Out of our Minds or Prove You are a Serb: On Ethnonationalism and Us)*. Sremski Karlovci: Izdavačka knjižarnica Zorana Stojanovića, 2006.

Kolarz, W. *Myths and Realities in Eastern Europe*. London: Lindsay Drummond, 1946.

Kolstø, P., ed. *Myths and Boundaries in South-Eastern Europe*. London: Hurst, 2005.

Kolstø, P., ed. *Media Discourse and the Yugoslav Conflicts: Representation of the Self and Other*. London: Ashgate, 2009.

Laclau, Ernesto, ed. *The Making of Political Identities*. London: Verso, 1994.

Lapid, Yosef, and Friedrich Kratochwil, eds. *The Return of Culture and Identity in IR Theory*. London: Rienner, 1995.

LeBor, Adam. *Milošević: A Biography*. London and New Haven: Yale University Press, 2004.

Lompar, Milo. *Duh samoporicanja. Prilog kritici srpske kulturne politike (The spirit of self-denial. Contribution to the Critique of Serbian cultural policy)*. Novi Sad: Orpheus, 2011.

MacDonald, D. B. *Balkan Holocausts? Serbian and Croatian Victim-centred Propaganda and the War in Yugoslavia*. Manchester: Manchester University Press, 2002.

Macey, David. *Dictionary of Critical Theory*. London: Penguin Books, 2000.

Mälksoo, Maria. *The Politics of Becoming European: A Study of Polish and Baltic post-Cold War Security Imaginaries*. London and New York: Routledge, 2013.

McCormick, John. *Europeanism*. Oxford: Oxford University Press, 2010.

Mertus, J. A. *Kosovo: How Myths and Truths Started a War*. Berkeley, CA: University of California Press, 1999.

Meštrović, Stjepan. *The Balkanization of the West*. London: Routledge, 1994.

Mihailović, Kosta and Vasilije Krestić. *Memorandum: odgovori na kritike (The Memorandum: Responses to Criticisms)*. Belgrade: SANU, 1995.

Miller, Nick. *The Nonconformists: Culture, Politics, and Nationalism in a Serbian Intellectual Circle, 1944–1991*. Budapest and New York: Central European University Press, 2007.

Milošević-Đorđević, Jasna. *Čovek o naciji: Shvatanje nacionalnog identiteta u Srbiji* (Man on Nation: Understanding the National Identity in Serbia). Belgrade: Institut za Političke Studije, 2008.

Milutinović, Zoran. *Getting Over Europe: The Construction of Europe in Serbian Culture*. Amsterdam and New York: Rodopi, 2011.

Mimica, A., ed. *Druga Srbija (Other Serbia)*. Belgrade: Beogradski Krug, Plato, Borba, 1992.

Mimica, Aljoša. *Druga Srbija—deset godina posle: 1992–2002 (Other Serbia—Ten Years Later: 1992–2002)*. Belgrade: Helsinški odbor za ljudska prava u Srbiji, 2002.

Mouffe, Chantal. *The Return of the Political*. London: Verso, 1993.

Mylonas, C. *Serbian Orthodox Fundamentals: The Quest for an Eternal Ientity*. Budapest and New York: Central European University Press, 2003.

Neumann, Iver B. *Russia and the Idea of Europe: A Study in Identity and International Relations*. London: Routledge, 1996.

Neumann, Iver B. *Uses of the Other: "The East" in European Identity Formation*. Manchester: Manchester University Press, 1999.

Obradović-Wochnik, J., J. Batt, V. Dimitrijević, F. Hartmann, D. Jović, and T. Memišević, eds. *War Crimes, Conditionality and EU Integration in the Western Balkans*. Paris: Institute for Security Studies, 2009.

Ostojić, Mladen. *International Judicial Intervention and Regime Change in Serbia 2000–2010*. PhD diss., University of London, 2011.

Ostojić, Mladen. *Between Justice and Stability: The Politics of War Crimes Prosecutions in Post-Milošević Serbia*. Farnham, UK and Burlington, VA: Ashgate, 2014.

Özkirimli, Umut. *Theories of Nationalism: A Critical Introduction*. Basingstoke: Palgrave Macmillan, 2010.

Passerni, Luisa. *Europe in Love, Love in Europe: Imagination and Politics in Britain Between the Wars*. London: Tauris, 1999.

Perica, V. *Balkan Idols: Religion and Nationalism in Yugoslav States*. Oxford and New York: Oxford University Press, 2002.

Petritsch, Wolfgang, Svilanović, Goran, and Solioz, Christophe (eds.), *Serbia Matters: Domestic Reforms and European Integration*. Paris, Vienna, and Geneva: Nomos, 2009.

Popov, Nebojša, ed. *The Road to War in Serbia*. Budapest: Central European University Press, 2000.

Purcell, Darren, and Janet E. Kodras. *Redrawing the Balkan Image of Slovenia*. Tallahassee, FL: Florida State University, 2001.

Pushkala, Prasad. *Crafting Qualitative Research: Working in the Post-positivist Traditions*. Armonk, New York: Sharpe, 2005.

Radaelli, Claudio M. and Theofanis Exadaktylos. *Research Design in European Studies: Establishing Causality in Europeanization*. Basingstoke: Palgrave Macmillan, 2012.

Radeljic, Branislav. *Europe and the Collapse of Yugoslavia: The Role of Non-State Actors and European Diplomacy*. London and New York: Tauris, 2012.

Radovanović, Srđan. *Images of Europe: Research on Representation of Europe and Serbia in Early 2000s*. Belgrade: Institute of Ethnography, 2009.

Ramet, P. S. *Balkan Babel: The Disintegration of Yugoslavia from the Death of Tito to Ethnic War*. Boulder, CO: Westview Press, 1996.

Ramet, Sabrina, and Vjeran Pavlaković, eds. *Serbia since 1989: Politics and Society under Milošević and After*. Seattle: University of Washington Press, 2005.

Reisigl, M. and R. Wodak. *Discourse and Discrimination: Rhetorics of Racism and Anti-semitism*. London: Routledge, 2001.

Ricœur, Paul. *Oneself as Another (Soi-même comme un autre)*. Chicago: University of Chicago Press, 1991, 1992.

Rossi, Michael A. *Resurrecting the Past: Democracy, National Identity and Historical Memory in Modern Serbia*. PhD diss., Rutgers University, 2009.

Rousseau, David L. *Identifying Threats and Threatening Identities: The Social Construction of Realism and Liberalism*. Stanford, CA: Stanford University Press, 2006.

Said, Edward. *Orientalism*. London: Vintage, 1978.

Seidendorf, Stefan. *Europeanisation of National Identity Discourses? Comparing French and German Print Media*. Colchester, UK: European Consortium for Political Research, April 2003.

Shapiro, Michael J. *The Politics of Representation: Writing Practices in Biography, Photography, and Policy Analysis*. Madison, WI: Univerisity of Wisconsin Press, 1988.

Smith, Alan. *The Return to Europe: the Reintegration of Eastern Europe into the European Economy*. Basingstoke: Macmillan Press, 2000.

Smith, A.D. *The Antiquity of Nations*. Oxford: Oxford University Press, 2004.

Smith, A.D. *Ethno-symbolism and Nationalism: A Cultural Approach*. Oxford: Oxford University Press, 2009.

Smith, A.D. *Nationalism and Modernism: A Critical Survey of Recent Theories of Nations and Nationalism*. London and New York: Routledge, 1998.

Spohn, Willfried and Anna Triandafyllidou, eds. *Europeanization, National Identities and Migration: Changes in Boundary Constructions between Western and Eastern Europe*. London: Routledge, 2003.

Sprinker, Michael, ed. *Edward Said: A Critical Reader*. Oxford: Blackwell, 1993.

St. Protić, Milan. *Izneverena Revolucija* (Democratic Revolution Betrayed). Belgrade: Cigoja Štampa, 2006.

Statistical Yearbook of Serbia 2008. Belgrade: Statistical Office of the Republic of Serbia, 2008.

Strath, Bo, ed. *Europe and the Other and Europe as the Other*. Brussels: Peter Lang, 2000.

Subotić, Jelena. *Hijacked Justice: Dealing with the Past in the Balkans*. London: Cornell University Press, 2009.

Taylor, Charles. *Sources of the Self: The Making of the Modern Identity*. Cambridge, MA: Harvard University Press, 1989.

Tekin, Beyza C. *Representations and Othering in the Discourse — The Construction of Turkey In the EU Context*. Amsterdam and Philadelphia: John Benjamins, 2010.

Thomas, Robert. *Serbia under Milošević: The Politics of Serbia in the 1990s*. London: Hurst & Company, 1999.

Todorova, Maria. *Imagining the Balkans*. New York, Oxford: Oxford University Press, 1997.

Todorova, Maria. *Balkan Identities: Nation and Memory*. New York: New York University Press, 2004.

Todorov, Tzvetan. *The Conquest of America: the Question of the Other*. New York: Harper Perennial, 1992.

Tošić, Desimir. *Stvarnost protiv zabluda: srpsko nacionalno pitanje* (Reality Versus Delusion: The Serbian National Question). Belgrade: S. Mašić, 1997.

Šijaković, Bogoljub. *A Critique of Balkanistic Discourse: Contribution to the Phenomenology of Balkan Otherness*. Toronto, Ontario: Serbian Literary Company, 2004.

Uvalić, Milica. *Serbia's Transition: Towards a Better Future*. Basingstoke: Palgrave Macmillan, 2010.

Vajdova, L. and R. Gafrik, eds. *New Imagined Communities: Identity Making in Eastern and South-Eastern Europe*. Bratislava: Kalligram, 2010.

Vasić, Miloš. *Atentat na Zorana Đinđića (The Assasination of Zoran Djindjic)*. Belgrade: Politika, B92, Vreme, Narodna knjiga, 2005.

Vladisavljević, Nebojša. *Serbia's Anti-bureaucratic Revolution: Milošević, the Fall of Communism and Nationalist Mobilization*. Basingstoke and New York: Palgrave Macmillan, 2008.

Vučinić, Marinko. *Druga Srbija: Na Mrtvoj Straži Političke Korektnosti* (Other Serbia: On death watch of political correctness). Belgrade: JP Službeni glasnik, 2012.

Wachtel, Andrew Baruch. *Making a Nation, Breaking a Nation: Literature and Cultural Politics in Yugoslavia*. Stanford: Stanford University Press, 1998.

Weber, Cynthia. *International Relations Theory: A Critical Introduction*. London: Routledge, 2005.

Weedon, Chris. *Feminist Practice and Poststructuralist Theory*. Hoboken: Wiley, 1997.

Weiss, Gilbert and Ruth Wodak, eds. *Critical Discourse Analysis: Theory and Interdisciplinarity*. Basingstoke: Palgrave Macmillan, 2003.

Wendt, Alexander. *Social Theory of International Politics*. Cambridge: Cambridge University Press, 1999.

West, Rebecca. *Black Lamb and Grey Falcon: A Journey Through Yugoslavia*. Harmondsworth, Middlesex: Penguin Books, 1969.

Wetherell, Margaret, Stephanie Taylor, and Simeon Yates. *Discourse Theory and Practice: A Reader*. Buckingham: Open University, 2001.

Wilson, Kevin, and Jan van der Dussen. *The History of the Idea of Europe*. London: Routledge, 1995.

Wodak, Ruth. *Disorders of Discourse*. London: Longman, 1996.

Wodak, Ruth. *The Discourse of Politics in Action: Politics as Usual*. Basingstoke: Palgrave, 2009.

Wodak, Ruth and Michael Meyer. *Methods of Critical Discourse Analysis*. London: Sage, 2001, 2009.

Wodak, Ruth and Teun A. van Dijk. *Racism at the Top: Parliamentary Discourses on Ethnic Issues in Six European States*. Klagenfurt: Drava Verlag, 2000.

Wodak, Ruth, Rudolf De Cillia, Martin Reisigl, and Karin Liebhart. *The Discursive Construction of National Identity*. Edinburgh: Edinburgh University Press, 2009.

Woodward, Susan. *Balkan Tragedy Chaos and Dissolution after the Cold War*. Washington DC: Brookings Institution Press, 1995.

Wolff, Larry. *Inventing Eastern Europe: The Map of Civilization on the Mind of the Enlightenment.* Stanford, CA: Stanford University Press, 1994.

Zapata-Barrero, Ricard and Anna Triandafyllidou, eds. *Addressing Tolerance and Diversity Discourses in Europe: A Comparative Overview of 16 European Countries.* Barcelona: Barcelona Centre for International Affairs, 2012.

Zundhausen, Holm. Istorija Srbije od 19. do 21. veka (The History of Serbia from 19th until 21st Century). Belgrade: Clio, 2008.

Živković, Marko. *"Serbian Stories of Identity and Destiny."* PhD diss., University of Chicago, 2001.

Živković, Marko. *Serbian Dreambook: National Imaginary in the Time of Milošević.* Bloomington, IN: Indiana University Press, 2011.

Index

Alterity
　theories of 38-3
Americanization of culture
　54–55
Antemurale Christianitatis 98
Anti-Enlightenment 96, 142
anti-nationalism 112–119, 176,
　190–192, 203
Anti-Occidentalism 145–146
Antonić, Slobodan 19, 22–24, 45,
　143, 149, 153, 179, 189–194,
　199–202, 211
Arkan, Ražnatović Željko 68
Arsenijević, Vladimir 45, 122–
　123
authoritarianism 59, 61, 77, 114,
　162
auto-chauvinist debate 209–220

B-92 44–45, 61, 102, 121, 181, 205
Balkanism 167–168
Balkans 36, 77–78, 98, 103, 196,
　223, 240, *see also* Western
　Balkans
Bakhtin, Mikhail 18
Bećković, Matija 9, 20, 95, 98–99
Belgrade Circle 22, 71, 108–110,
　116–117
Biserko, Sonja 181–182, 185, 201
Bogdanović, Bogdan 51, 109,
　165
Bosnia 34, 61, 64–69, 96–98, 121,
　180, 190, 228
Brubaker, Rogers 147

Campbell, David 38
causality 32
Centre for Applied Nonviolent
　Action and Strategies
　(CANVAS) 74
Centre for Cultural
　Decontamination 22, 121
Cerović, Stojan 163, 182-183,
　185, 187
Chetniks 49, 51, 66
China 3, 104, 140, 224
Ćirilov, Jovan 45
civilization 21, 98, 106, 131–132,
　155–8, 162–163, 168–169, 191,
　195, 207, 238
civil society 13, 24, 19, 47, 59, 74,
　117, 122–123, 192
Cold War 52, 56, 215, 221, 225
Čolović, Ivan 21, 198–111
communism 60–61, 69, 210,
　212–213
Connolly, William 39–41
Constantine, Roman Emperor
　54, 98
constructivism 19, 30, 33, 86,
　178, *see also* social
　constructivism
Ćosić, Dobrica 20, 70, 92, 95
Critical Discourse Analysis
　(CDA) 17, 29
Cyrillic 144, 153, 199

Dačić, Ivica 11–12, 110, 130, 154
Dayton (peace agreement) 65, 69
debates 6–8, 20, 42–44, 49–50, 107–109, 123–125, 132, 161–169, 177–208, 222, *see also* "Missionary Intelligentsia" and "Point of Departure"
Delanty, Gerard 15, 30, 40, 133, 175 176, 194, 213
Delević, Milica 7-8, 158, 170–171
Democratic Opposition of Serbia (DOS) 73–75, 80–82, 122, 127
Democratic Party (DS) 22, 80–83, 125–127, 129, 156, 213, 232
Democratic Party of Serbia (DSS) 12, 46, 73–75, 83, 87, 89, 103, 132–140, 201
democratization 10, 60, 69, 79
denial 23, 180, 208
diaspora 8, 87, 222
difference 10, 25, 35, 38–42, 155
    and identity 31, 86, 112–115, 134–137
    civilizational 163, 195
Dimitrijević, Vojin 47, 157, 200
discourse 31
development 10, 36, 169, 172–174
discursive practices 98, 107, 228
discourse analysis 17, 30–37
    discursive methodology 29, 32, 226
    and ideology 33, 178
    and language 30–34

diversity 153, 176
Djilas, Milovan 53, 109
Djindjić, Zoran 8, 42, 69, 75–76, 79–80, 123, 181, 201
Djogo, Gojko 92
Drašković, Vuk 24, 70, 87, 150, 235
Dveri 20, 46–47, 106, 132, 142–146

E-novine 45
Eastern Europe 4–10, 16, 52, 55, 60, 78, 140, 149, 174, 209
enemy
    external 39, 71, 107, 129
    within, 16, 188–191, 199, 211
Eurasia 56, 145
Europe 4, 11-15, 132–135
    common legacy and destiny with 8, 158, 172, 227
    historical enmity with 138
    Czech Republic and 13
    Great Britain and 13, 39
    Greece and 13, 221
    Italy and 14, 167
    and Kosovo 10, 81, 105–107, 148–150, 171, 218
    promise of 15
    pro or anti 56, 86, 106
    as a security alliance 223
    as a threat 6, 133, 151, 219
Europeanization 10, 15–16, 36, 126, 135, 156, 217
Europeanness 4, 8, 151, 216
Euroskepticism 47, 203, 230

exclusion 40, 114, 131, 133–134, 152, 176–178, *see also* inclusion

"First" and "Other" Serbia 2, 20, 88, 235
  and Milošević 62–63
  anti-European position 20, 131
"First" Serbia 2, 20, 88, 91–105, 135–155, 193–199, 209
  and civil society 215
First World War 12, 154, 228
Foucault, Michel 17, 30, 31
Fund for Humanitarian Law 121

Gagnon, Valère 85, 89, 95
Germany 39, 41, 94, 138, 140
Gligorov, Vladimir 48
Glišić, Vladan 46, 142–4
Gordy, Eric 60–65, 77, 102, 185
Greater Serbia 47, 119, 190
guilt 91–93, 125, 157, 163, 181–184, 231

Habermas, Jürgen 8, 29
Hansen, Lene 32-36, 164, 168–169, 172, 179
Havel, Vaclav 13, 60
Helsinki Committee for Human Rights 121, 203
history
  differing presentation of 19, 88, 101
  proud 6, 138
homosexuality 47

Hourglass (show) 44–45, 159, 162, 169, 200
human rights 10, 21–22, 36, 48, 90, 109, 120, 131–132, 157

identity 1, 10-11, 31–32, 40–41, 35–36
  contestation 8, 87, 227
  discursive construction of 17, 85–86, 152, 164, 178, 195
  and othering 16, 114, 128, 177
  and religion 135, 142, 194
identity politics 51, 187
illiberalism 5, 14, 90, 188–192
inclusion 15, 66, 133–134, *see also* exclusion
interdisciplinary approaches 29
International Criminal Tribunal of the former Yugoslavia (ICTY) 5, 75, 104, 174, 204
internationalism 70, 106, 122, 151, 171, 222
intertextual analysis 26, 34
Irinej, Patriarch of Serbia 148

Jeremić, Vuk 105, 129, 171–173, 225
Jovanović, Čedomir 22, 127, 160, 232

Kandić, Nataša 47, 124, 185, 201
Karadžić, Radovan 80, 191, 203
Karadjordjević, Prince Petar 54
Kecmanović, Vladimir 45, 209, 211–217
Kolstø, Pål 85, 114

Korać, Žarko 158-161
Kosovo 9–10, 71–72, 81–82, 98–99, 105–106, 147–151, 217–218, 221
   "Kosovo question" 22, 61–62
Koštunica, Vojislav 12, 46, 103, 137–140
   and Church 135–137
   and Kosovo 137–138, 149
   and overthrow of Milošević 73–81
Kovačević, Siniša 45, 213–218
Kusturica, Emir 221

Liberal
   nationalism 197, 226
   pessimism 173
Liberal Democratic Party (LDP) 83, 127, 160, 231
liminality 7
Lompar, Mile 209–210
Lukić, Svetlana 44, 162
Luković, Petar 45, 155, 167–169

Marković, Predrag 46, 209, 212–217
Matić, Veran 186, 205–206
Memorandum, see also SANU Memorandum
methodology 17, 29–37, 43–49
military neutrality 12, 139–142
Milosavljević, Olivera 182, 184
Milošević, Slobodan 51, 71, 88–91
   arrest of 80, 217
   death (11th of March) 235
   political legacy 77

regime 59, 68
misogyny 162
Missionary Intelligentsia 19, 153, 188–193, 195–200, *see also* debates
Mladić, Ratko 80, 160, 231
modernity 13, 240
myth of innocence 230

Naked Island 52
nationalism 24, 47, 50, 62–63, 77, 112–119, 194, 197-198, 205, 224, *see also* nationalists, *see also* anti-nationalism
   discredited by "Other" Serbia 112–119
   vs. internationalism 70, 106, 222
national identity 1, 11, 29, 31–32, 49, 158, *see also* identity contestation
nationalists 196, 198
nationalist ideology 50, 60, 90, 192, 219
NATO (North Atlantic Treaty Organization) 11, 136–8
   1999 NATO intervention in Serbia 71–72, 124–125, 182, 214
Nedić, Milan 110
Neumann, Iver 39
New Serbian Political Thought 44, 209–219
Nikolić, Tomislav 20, 46, 81, 104, 148
NIN 64, 102
Non-Aligned Movement 56, 225

Non-governmental organizations (NGOs) 21–22, 91, 108, 120, 185, 190, 216
nouveau riche 60

Obraz 21, 106, 144–145, 191
"October 5" 75–76, 122–123, 136, 180, 201, 234
"Other" Serbia 2, 20, 88, 107–128, 155–174, 184, 200, 231
   and gender 22, 185–186
   as the enemy within 189–199
   hard and soft liberals 22, 45, 125, 158–162, 184
Othering
   difference and similarity 40
   and the EU 39
   friendly 40, 55, 140
   Otherness 38–41, 86, 167–168, 176, 213
   radical 25, 40, 128
   self-othering 122, 227
Otpor 59, 74–75
Ottoman Empire 50, 62, 139, 221

Pančić, Teofil 48, 201
patriotism 25, 144, 189, 217–218
   as problematic 117, 135, 192, 202, 206
Pavle, Patriarch of Serbia 205
Pavlović, Radoslav 46, 213–217
Perović, Latinka 48, 109, 146, 184
Pešić, Vesna 48, 63, 70, 113–114, 156, 170, 201
Pištalo, Vladimir 201–202

"Point of departure" 43, 163, 179, 181–186 *see also* debates
political symbols 63–64, 94, 136, 228
Politika 44, 64, 95, 102
Popov, Nebojša 48, 119, 200–201, 204–205
Popović, Koča 50-51, 53
Popović, Srdja 47, 161, 184, 207
power 33
Praxis 196
Princip, Gavrilo 228
progress 36, 131, 134, 146, 150, 169–170, 174
Prokić, Nenad 45, 231, 234
protests
   anti-government 69–71, 127
   anti-war 120–121
public sphere 6, 20, 29

Rajić, Ljubiša 48, 109–112, 116
Rakić-Vodinelić, Vesna 48, 204
religion 142-145 *see also* Serbian Orthodox Church
Republika 22, 121, 201, 204–205
Roma 51, 123, 162, 190, 202
RTS (National Serbian Radio and Television) 64, 75, 102
Rumelili, Bahar 38, 237
ruralism 146
Russia 12–13, 55–56, 99–100, 173
   as a historical and cultural friend 102–103, 139–141

sacrifice 12, 97, 143, 149
Samardžić, Slobodan 196–197, 203–205

SANU Memorandum 50, 89, 91–98, 146
Second World War 64, 92, 97, 154, 164, 214
Self and Other 37–41
    analysis of 4, 14-15, 18, 152–153, 167, 178
    'non-self' 40
serbophobia 206
Serbia
    and commemorations 234
    as Europe 158, 170–171, 223–224
    as not Europe 127, 135–145, 155, 166
    and foreign policy 3, 81, 103–104, 171, 225
    and self-image 15, 29, 217

Serbs 50, 85
    barbaric character of the 162, 166, 168
    as perpetrators 91, 102, 107, 125, 163, 184
    as victims 21, 93, 102–104, 129, 163
    anti-Serbs 117
Serbian Academy of Sciences (SANU) 20, 92, 160, 186, 191, 201
Serbian Kingdom of the Middle Ages 50
Serbian Orthodox Church (SOC) 67, 99–100, 136–145, 156, 186–187, 205–206, 222
Serbian Progressive Party (SNS) 83, 104, 129, 221

Serbian Radical Party (SRS) 20, 68, 81–83, 88–89, 132, 180
Serbian Renewal Movement (SPO) 63, 66, 73
Šešelj, Vojislav 20, 82, 88
shame 45, 101–102
Socialist Party of Serbia (SPS) 65, 70, 76, 82–83, 89
sovietization of culture 54-55
social constructivism 37–38, *see also* constructivism
sovereignty 6, 226
    Europe as a threat to 149
special relationship 40, 96, 229
Srebrenica massacre 45, 52, 157, 160–161, 166, 184, 222, 231
St. Savism 47, 144
St. Vitus' Day (Vidovdan) 76
Stalin, Josef 53
Stojanović, Dubravka 48
Stojanović, Lazar 48, 173, 185
Subotić, Jelena 80, 89, 103, 105, 127, 147, 172

Tadić, Boris 22, 80–83, 127, 232
    and national identity 125, 147, 156
textual sources 43
"the past" 36, 57, 197, 160–164, 180, 220
"Third" Serbia 49, 239
Thomas, Robert 60, 63, 70, 94
Todorov, Tzvetan 36, 38
traitors 67, 93, 117–120, 165, 195

uncivil society 24, 192
United Kingdom 13, 39–40, 140, 221
United States 40, 94, 126, 171, 214, 216, 221

Velimirović, Bishop Nikolaj 99, 146
victimization 88–98, 116, 228
Vreme 10, 44, 82, 121, 126, 130, 179–188
Vučić, Aleksandar 3, 8–9, 20, 221–224, 228
Vukadinović, Djordje 45, 141, 151, 216
Vuković, Svetlana 44

Wachtel, Andrew 51, 53
wars of the Yugoslav succession (of 1990s) 61–72
  anti-war activism 107–116
  political legacy of 77, 180
war-crimes 6, 82, 103, 111, 120–121, 161–166, 179–185, 190, 203–205
  trials 20, 124, 181
Wæver, Ole 1, 34, 36–37, 164
Wendt, Alexander 39
West 10–11, 14, 41, 78, 103, 137, 157, 179, 188–189, 214, 230
  spiritual corruption of the 99–100, 196, 145–147
Western Balkans 14, 59, 63, 65
  see also Balkans
Women in Black 121, 120

Yugoslavia 46, 49–58, 162
  control of travel 58
  dissolution of 61, 64–65, 80, 109, 180, 184
  as mediator between East and West 53
  women's employment in 56
Yugoslavism 66, 106

Zajedno ("Together" political coalition) 69–71, 122

ibidem-Verlag

Melchiorstr. 15

D-70439 Stuttgart

info@ibidem-verlag.de

www.ibidem-verlag.de
www.ibidem.eu
www.edition-noema.de
www.autorenbetreuung.de